Ritual Soundings

NEW PERSPECTIVES ON GENDER IN MUSIC

Editorial Advisors
Susan C. Cook
Beverley Diamond

A list of books in the series appears at the end of this book.

Ritual Soundings

Women Performers and World Religions

SARAH WEISS

UNIVERSITY OF
ILLINOIS PRESS
Urbana, Chicago, and Springfield

Publication of this book is supported by the Lloyd Hibberd Endowment of the American Musicological Society, funded in part by the National Endowment for the Humanities and the Andrew W. Mellon Foundation.

1 2 3 4 5 C P 5 4 3 2 1
♾ This book is printed on acid-free paper.

Library of Congress Cataloging-in-Publication Data
Names: Weiss, Sarah, author.
Title: Ritual soundings : women performers and world religions / Sarah Weiss.
Description: Urbana : University of Illinois Press, [2019] | Series: New perspectives on gender in music | Includes bibliographical references and index.
Identifiers: LCCN 2018033007| ISBN 9780252042294 (cloth : alk. paper) | ISBN 9780252084089 (pbk. : alk. paper)
Subjects: LCSH: Women musicians. | Gender identity in music. | Music—Religious aspects. | Marriage customs and rites. | Women—Social conditions.
Classification: LCC ML82 .W53 2019 | DDC 781.70082—dc23 LC record available at https://lccn.loc.gov/2018033007

Ebook ISBN: 978-0-252-05113-5

For Tony

Contents

Acknowledgments

I wish to thank the readers for University of Illinois Press for their careful reading, the time they spent to understand the goals of my project, and the sage advice they provided.

I give my heartfelt thanks to the following research assistants for their help at different stages in the process of the development of this project: Micah Hendler, Estelí Gomez, Lynda Paul, Lauren Holmes Frankel, Danielle Ward-Griffin, Rex Isenberg, Sarah Larsson, Ryan Harper, and Santana Haight. I thank the members of the Women, Religion, and Globalization Faculty Colloquium 2007–2009 at Yale University, most especially Melanie Boyd, Alicia Schmidt Camacho, Fatima Azzahrae Chaabani, Geetanjali Singh Chanda, Harlon Dalton, Paula Hyman, Marcia Inhorn, Alyssa Mt. Pleasant, Sally Promey, Harry Stout, Emilie Townes, and Laura Wexler. Thank you all for invaluable insight and critique at various moments during the years I have been working on this book. This project was generously supported with leave of one semester while I was teaching at Yale University and with six weeks leave while I was teaching at Yale-NUS College. The publication of this work has been generously supported by a subvention grant from the Lloyd Hibberd Endowment of the American Musicological Society, funded in part by the National Endowment for the Humanities and the Andrew W. Mellon Foundation.

I would like to thank the many scholars in different fields who provided their thoughts, comments, and critique, whether friendly or not, helpful or not. You all have had significant impact on the ways in which I have thought about various parts of this diverse project. I would especially like to recognize Inna Naroditskya,

Kay Shelemay, Zoe Sherinian, Anne Rasmussen, Ellen Koskoff, Jeff Summit, Barney Bate, Katherine Hoffman, Loring Danforth, Tony Day, Gavin Flood, Henry "Sam" Chauncey Jr., Rona Johnston-Gordon, Martin Jean, Rainer Weiss, James Hepokoski, Milette Gaifman, Anne MacNeil, Gary Tomlinson, Michael Veal, Gail Holst-Warhaft, Margot Fassler, Michael Carroll, Gabriella Ilinitchi Currie, Lisa Knight, and Adrian Vickers, as well as Julianne Laut and Julie Gay at University of Illinois Press. I am grateful to all of you for your thoughts and guidance. I apologize in advance if I have not used your suggestions in the ways in which you had hoped. To Sam and Tony and Ben, thank you for moving around the world and supporting me unconditionally. I could never have finished this work without you. Finally, there is no way to thank Laurie Matheson, editor-in-chief of University of Illinois Press for her enormous wisdom and great patience. Any faults in this book remain entirely my own.

Ritual Soundings

Introduction

The ostensible richness of tradition is not a fixed set of gems, but a shifting and open-ended source of possibilities.

—Mary McClintock Fulkerson, *Changing the Subject: Women's Discourses and Feminist Theology*

If we listened to the voices of Indian women, we would find alternative conceptions of Indian civilization that are often startlingly different from what we find in our classics.

—K. Ramanujan, "Talking to God in the Mother Tongue"

No religion exists in a vacuum. On the contrary, every faith is rooted in the soil in which it is planted. It is a fallacy to believe that people of faith derive their values primarily from their Scriptures. The opposite is true. People of faith insert their values into their Scriptures, reading them through the lens of their own cultural, ethnic, nationalistic and even political perspectives.

—Reza Aslan, "Bill Maher Isn't the Only One Who Misunderstands Religion"

The question is not what you look at, but what you see. It is only necessary to behold the least fact or phenomenon, however familiar, from a point a hair's breadth aside from our habitual path or routine, to be overcome, enchanted by its beauty and significance.

Henry David Thoreau, *Unpublished journal entry—August 5, 1851*

World religions and the communities that practice them mutually constitute one another. Individuals and groups in local circumstances interpret the "universal" aspects of their religions idiosyncratically, making them their own. These local forces often take the shape of communal activities involving song, synchronized movement or dance, and other aspects that some might identify as performance. Aspects of performativity have been long acknowledged and frequently theorized in accounts of religious ritual, where religious cultures have been read as constructing the experience of listening to or performing music as a primary route for accessing the holy, the transcendent, or religious experience itself.[1] Scholarly focus on women's ways of worship, as well as gendered studies of religious scripture and practice, has been burgeoning since the last quarter of the twentieth century. These studies interrogate and reconfigure the long history of primarily male scholarship on male-dominated religious ritual and textual worlds.[2] Ethnomusicologists and anthropologists have produced deep ethnographies of women musicians and their performances in specific religious communities, examining the ways in which performance creates and organizes activities at life-cycle and other events in which religion is integral.[3]

My study draws on the rich resources developed in all three of these disciplines—ethnomusicology, gendered studies of religion and religious practice, and religious music studies. As such, it is a meta-ethnography, a form of comparison generated by the synthesis and reanalysis of interpretive ethnographic work.[4] Not simply an act of gathering sets of materials and juxtaposing them in order to observe their similarities and differences, comparison involves rereading original material in new analytical contexts.[5] As Kimberly Patton notes, "scholars can risk positing a comparative framework, not to reach closure in the service of a particular theory, nor to achieve moral judgment or gain intellectual control over the 'other,' but to empower mutual dialogue and the quest for understanding."[6] Comparison is a hermeneutic that reveals alternative narratives and generates new ways of understanding the data at hand. But comparison also involves risks. While I have read deeply into studies of Christianity, Islam, Hinduism, Judaism, Buddhism, gender studies in religion, ethnomusicological studies of religious contexts, and religious studies, I am certain that large gaps in my knowledge still remain. I am also certain that some individual scholars reading this book will find fault with the ways I have represented materials from their particular research worlds.

I am an ethnographer who has studied and become expert in several music cultures in Indonesia, part of the world where multiple world religions have taken root and maintained influence over cultural expression for centuries. Java and Bali are places where Hinduism, Buddhism, Islam, and Christianity have settled in various waves since the second century CE. These world religions have been localized over the centuries but still retain connections of varying sorts with the practice of the religions elsewhere around the world. In and out of the field I have always wondered about the role of these large world religions in shaping the ways in which Indonesians engage and understand their performance traditions. Musing about this question led to my imagining this project. Our training as ethnographers specialized in the culture and practices of people in particular locations does not ask us to think comparatively. Yet the religious-cultural contexts we study are not simply local, even as it is always individuals in particular locations who engage the ritual practices we observe and analyze.

This comparative study of women's performance practices in world religions begins from Catherine Bell's idea that individuals are empowered when they become ritualized agents. Every given religious event has multiple stages, each of which generally requires the engagement of more than one agent and only some of which fall under the auspices of an official from the associated religious institution. Each of the possible ritual actors is empowered through influencing and determining the context in which the event is celebrated. Groups of empowered agents appropriate and condition experience, their own and that of others, deploying and manipulating basic schemes in ways that construct and articulate their communities as distinct yet connected to the world religion they practice. I analyze women's performances at religious events in cultural settings spread across the world as a way of demonstrating the pivotal roles women can have in localizing the practice of world religions, exploring moments in which performance allows women the agency to move (however momentarily) beyond culturally determined limits while revealing patterns that suggest unsuspected similarities in widely divergent religious contexts.[7]

I want to end this brief introduction with a short explanation of my use of footnotes in this volume. For some who read this book, everything in the footnotes might better be incorporated into the text. For others, there might already be too much cultural and historical detail in the main body of the work, let alone in the footnotes. As I contemplated how to deal with this problem, I realized that everyone who opens the covers of this book will be simultaneously an expert in some of the topics addressed here and perhaps somewhat new to some of the others. It has been particularly challenging to write for both of those groups in each chapter, providing not only analytical ideas for scholars with deep knowledge of particular cultural contexts (and strong opinions as to which trends and research in the subfield are most important) but also enough basic detail for people who have never even heard of a particular performance culture. Nevertheless, from the responses of readers, anonymous and otherwise, it is precisely the depth of my footnote referencing that allows both experts and non-experts from each of the fields into which I wade to "believe" the comparisons. One reader stated that she didn't know all of the fields or culture areas she encountered in the manuscript well, but because I had referenced, and used sensibly, the most important studies in those that she did know well, she was also inclined to "trust" the text in areas where she was not an expert. Because of this, I have decided to maintain a richness of citation of other works (even detailing scholarly debate) throughout, but to put the majority of this in the footnotes.

CHAPTER 1

Women Performers and World Religions

On Ritual, Local Practice, Universals, and Comparison

This book is composed of interpretive chapters meant to provide the spark for conversation and debate both about the ways in which women's performance practices engage and localize world religions and the ways in which those performances create opportunities for women's agency. That most of the world's major organized religions are patriarchal has already been argued and demonstrated by many, albeit from varying perspectives—feminist or not—and with more or less nuanced approaches.[1] Women are not customarily the religious officials who perform the acts that confer religious authority on an event, be it a regular gathering for communal worship or an episodic life-cycle ritual. It is men, most often, who have the role of scripting and officiating at the major ceremonies in religious contexts. If what happens in the context of mosque, church, temple, or shrine worship fully defined the boundaries of a religion, then we could be justified in observing that these religions are rigid patriarchies in which women are devalued in relation to men. But much of religious life and activity happens outside communal moments officiated by male religious officials and is organized and enacted by women. Both kinds of activities are part of a larger system, a continuum of religious practice. In that larger system, women's roles and rituals, while undertheorized, are not subsidiary.[2] Women's performative activities are central to the celebration of life-cycle events such as marriage and death in all major organized religions. Their practices surrounding these events involve women making decisions, artistic and structural. In a compelling way, these activities embody women's agency within their religious contexts. Women's performances engage with their respective world religion as a lived local reality. Among a community of believers who identify with a particular religion, the multiple, male and female, scriptural and contextual expressions of religious engagement in any one place constitute the practice of the religion in that specific location. None of the practices described in the following chapters is found in scripture; indeed, the actions might even be prohibited by scripture, according to some interpretations. The people participating in these performance contexts are, for the most part, non-ordained women, yet their activities are often iconic with aspects of the most important ritual practices in their communities. Following Thoreau above in the introduction, it is possible to "see" striking similarities between these women's practices, despite their having been imagined and developed in different religious contexts, periods, and locations.

This book revolves around three different, related themes: women's agency in religious performance contexts; the productive tension between similarity and difference in the comparative process; and the embeddedness of the universal in the local and the local in the universal. Women are often observed to use performance in religious contexts to express their opinions and occasionally to protest in some way. There is infinite variety in the ways in which they do this, but the phenomenon is still abundantly evident, present in cultural contexts from the most open and liberal to the most restrictive and closed.

To explore these themes in as comprehensive a manner as possible, this book comprises of two different kinds of chapters: comparative chapters that reach across religions and geographic areas to examine a particular expressive practice and chapters that provide a deep dive into one particular performance practice. The four chapters are united in their exploration of two things: the ways in which women's performance practices in religious contexts provide possibilities for agency within, and occasional protest against, close-fitting societal restrictions; and the ways in which the public nature of those performances might actually provide protection from, or mediation of, the ambiguity with which women who move beyond their usual boundaries in public might otherwise be regarded.

It turns out that in addition to the expectant and celebratory affect that marks the joining of families and fates in marriage, lamentation and mockery are two genres commonly performed by women at weddings in contexts around the world. The performance of lamentation focuses on the daughters and sons lost "forever" from their protective natal family circles and on generational iterations of lost youth and innocence. Performances of mockery feature lewd caricatures of sexuality and representations of the "horrific" or "miserly" features of those "foreign" others who will soon be related. Fear of change, loss, and the unknown are expressed in both kinds of performance. The ambiguity that is an essential element in the liminal positions of the bride and groom are mediated and normalized to some degree through these performances. Whether lamenting or mocking, the women performers can be understood to generate agency for themselves, either temporarily or more permanently, by the articulation and mastery of their emotions in and through their performance.

Even while they soothe and smooth the transitions inherent in wedding processes, performers of wedding lamentation and mockery occupy ambiguous positionality themselves given that their sung texts and actions—emotive, scurrilous, hypersensualized, insulting, or otherwise—fall outside normative behavior in their various communities. I suggest that expressing these kinds of transgressive sentiments in an ephemeral moment through the performance of music and dance ameliorates the disturbances that might otherwise be caused by the articulation of such words and actions. Different from performances for entertainment in these same cultures, the music and dance in these ritually sanctioned contexts shield women from the opprobrium that might normally be heaped on them for expressing themselves in public, visible not only to women but also to men. The protection occurs precisely because the performative moments are temporary and contained by the liminality of the cultural moment. Ironically, in these contexts the limited nature of the performative moment actually provides additional freedom for the performers to communicate much more than they would normally be allowed to do in daily life. Any ambiguities about their character or propriety that might otherwise be generated by women performing music and dance on stage or in public, without the shepherding presence of their male family members, are ameliorated by the performance itself.

The performativity of the moment mitigates and mediates, makes ephemeral, both the inappropriateness of the interaction and any possible ambiguousness that might sully the reputation of the women (and their families) who have, however temporarily, occupied transgressive positionalities—here defined as public actions that would, in most other contexts in their lived experiences, be regarded as inappropriate. It is this idea that grounds the comparative elements of my study of women's performance practices in ritual contexts in world religions.

In the spirit of a gentle call for increased academic enquiry across religious cultures and practices, I think that the identification of similarities in themes and expressive methods signals similitude in women's experiences across religions and cultures. Note that I am neither claiming universal experience for women nor suggesting that the cultures described are somehow related through contiguity or any kind of evolutionary development. Rather, in identifying intersections such as these in women's ritual practices across cultures, religions, and historical periods, I am suggesting that it is likely other connections are present and awaiting description. If these independently generated similarities are compellingly present across various cultures, it might be possible to use comparative work to suggest that religious communities have more in common than some practitioners might choose to recognize.

Focusing on the ground-up, performative aspects of religious practice—instead of top-down approaches featuring scriptural traditions—and comparing them is not a new idea.[3] But preserving the discourse on differences between religions is still more common in ethnomusicology and other fields exploring religion and religious practice. In ethnomusicology as well as anthropology this habit springs naturally from important and necessary requirements to describe what is present and culturally specific in any given ethnographic context before one can say anything holistic about a culture. Despite my best intentions with respect to the relativism that has characterized my ethnographic disciplines for the last thirty years, elaborating the differences between these instances of women's expressive agency in their performance contexts has not relieved them of compelling comparative similarities that reaches across time, culture, and religious contexts. Because of these observations, I suggest that while examining the minutia of cultural practice, it can be politically instructive to step back and see larger-scale patterns across cultures. As the chapters in this book demonstrate, ethnomusicology can help to counter the corrosive rhetoric of religious exceptionalism and stark difference by revealing patterns in widely divergent contexts, simultaneously describing localizations in, and intersections across, religious practice.

On the Term "World Religion"

The idea of "world religion" has its roots in the development of the modern science of religion in the 1870s in Holland, France, Germany, and Britain.[4] Springing from a European quest to find the origin of human religion that, it was theorized, could still be found in the least developed forms of spiritual practice among the "primitives" Europeans encountered on their global expeditions, the science of religion engaged the social evolutionary ideas emerging at the time. Whether the history of religion was understood to be linear—from simple to complex—or lapsarian—from primordial innocence through corruption and degeneration to redemption—the story ended in the evolutionarily advanced West and most particularly with Christianity.

In her book *The Invention of World Religions*, Tomoko Masuzawa explores the history of the geospatial mapping of the world in religions. She notes that while they were enlightening themselves with respect to the spiritual practices of the different peoples of the world, European scholars encountered with horror and fascination myriad variations of "superstitions . . . and umbrageous priestcraft."[5] Their search for the origins of religion generated comparisons of spiritual practices from around the world, both to one another and to the European religions in a process that simultaneously "orientalized" those practices in a "discourse of Othering."[6] The concept of world religion provided a means for "consolidating and totalizing a large portion of the social, cultural, and political practices observable among the inhabitants of regions elsewhere in the world."[7] One of the most significant effects of this process is that it spiritualized the material practices of much of the world, "turn[ing] them into expressions of something timeless and suprahistorical."[8] In this process, living cultural practices are essentialized, snapshots of contemporary lives turned into ancient and perpetual history, neither as malleable nor as "advanced" as those religions spread widely across the world's populations, that were imagined to be somehow more separable and moderately deracinated from their founding cultures. It is important to note that a distinction exists between the "religions of the world," a term that includes all of those "spiritualized" cultural practices, and "world religions," faiths that have transcended the boundaries of an original culture and spread across the world.[9] The focus on religions of the world is simultaneously a decentering of Eurocentric and Eurohegemonic conceptions of the spiritual practices found in the world and a positioning of world religions, in particular Christianity, at the more developed end of a continuum of religious practice in the world.[10]

Lists of the major world religions are not always in agreement with one another. Most often they include the following, noting that most religions listed generally have at least several sects: Baha'i, Buddhism, Christianity, Confucianism, Hinduism, Islam, Jainism, Judaism, Shintoism, Sikhism, Taoism, and Zoroastrianism. World religions are often classified into two broad categories, ethnoreligions and universalizing religions, in which the former are integrally tied to cultural practices such as diet, dress, and customs—marriage and death practices, and the like—specifically associated with particular regions, while the latter are understood as universally applicable and able to be modified, to varying extents, to be practiced in any cultural context as long as the core beliefs are maintained.[11] This binary is primarily useful in terms of determining whether a religion is open to and actively seeks new believers or not. While most of the religions listed above do accept converts into their ranks at some level, those that actively seek new converts, and so would normally be understood as "universalizing," are primarily forms of Christianity, Islam, and Buddhism and, to varying extents, Hinduism and Judaism (depending on denomination, movement, or sect.) It is important to note that the very idea that the practitioners of these "universal" religions around the world do not imagine their religion as part and parcel of the everyday aspects of their lives—inclusive of their diet, dress, and marriage practices, among other things—is plausible only from an outsider's theoretical and theorizing perspective. All of this suggests that one of the prime distinctions between the "ethno" and the "universal" religion categories is weak at best, and perhaps the distinction is less useful than might originally have been thought. In addition, the terms "universal" and "universalizing" religion are problematic in general because of the assumptions about similarities in human experience that are enlisted as soon as the term universal is employed. As ethnomusicologists, we are trained to resist the word for precisely this reason. Given the abundance of local manifestations around the world, it is clear that as a group, universal religions are malleable to a significant degree, or at least they have been in their various pasts. The possibility for local cultural practices to be maintained in various ways is, of course, essential to the success of a "universalizing" religion even as the idea of universality is resistant to it. The ways in which universal elements underlie local practice are based on the ways in which practitioners in that location have cultivated their relationship to their "world religion."

Instead of struggling with the intellectual dissonances of the term universal,[12] in this book I have chosen to use the term "world religion" to describe those religions that have traveled across the globe and been absorbed by people living in many different cultures. Using the term "world religion" avoids the problematic associations of the word universal; it provides a single expressive term that generously encompasses the complex of practices and beliefs of any one of these complicated, multicultural formations; and it helps outline a framework that can structure comparisons both between and within faith traditions. In addition, the term "world religion" references a meaning of the word "world" that is already familiar to ethnomusicologists in the idea of "world music," a contested term in and of itself, but now one generally accepted (with slightly varied definitions) by music specialists from ethnomusicologists to marketers of recorded musics.[13] Arguably, the "world" in world religion is more restricted than the way in which the word is understood in the term "world music." The term "universal" will appear occasionally in this text but only when the concept, with all its attendant baggage, is practical and important for an argument.

Most of the case studies referenced in this book come from communities that identify as Christian, Muslim, or Hindu, although Jewish communities are referenced in several contexts. These choices were, in the end, somewhat arbitrary. My selection of the particular case studies analyzed here emerged gradually over the course of my research, a process which involved reading deeply into the literature—musical, anthropological, historical, scriptural, theoretical, and the like—on these three religions, as well as Judaism, Buddhism, Sikhism, and several others. Because this book engages meta-ethnography as a primary analytical method, one important limitation was that I had to follow the ethnographic explorations of others.[14] As I was building the argument in this book, my primary goal was to find performance phenomena that occur in cultures practicing different world religions ranging across broad swaths of human culture. My ulterior motive here is to suggest that if women's practices found nested deep inside local contexts and performed primarily for their own communities can be productively compared across regions and religions, then perhaps other opportunities for communicating through those now rarely crossed boundaries can also be cultivated. I view my work here as a form of leading by example. If we in ethnomusicology aim to cultivate and curate opportunities for inclusion and respect around the world, communication across cultures and religions is a primary location for our development and focus. I believe it is essential to model and embody the process we hope to cultivate, and comparative studies are an obvious way forward.

On Diversity in Christianity, Hinduism, and Islam

Although the words Christianity, Hinduism, and Islam seem to suggest unity among their practitioners, nothing could be further from the truth. Christianity and Islam have each withstood multiple sectarian divisions generated by internal conflict, and the word Hinduism has only relatively recently been used to identify a religion, derived principally from the word Hindu, which had long been used to identify the people who populate India more generally.[15] Yet, whatever their internal differences, the terms Christian, Muslim, and Hindu—often without identification of a specific sect or denomination—are regularly used in the media and in scholarly literature, not to mention in statements from religious authorities and practitioners of all three religions.[16] This usage suggests that local manifestations of world religions or, at least, practitioners within the larger denominations are understood to share certain beliefs and habits wherever they are practiced—a Sunni Muslim from Jakarta would mostly know what to do and how to interpret the beliefs demonstrated at a Friday service in a Sunni mosque in Saudi Arabia, likewise a Hindu who worships Durga from Mumbai at a Durga Puja in London, or a Catholic from Cleveland at a Sunday Mass in Lisbon. However, a Greek Orthodox from Athens who would have a reasonable understanding of the actions and symbolism at the Orthodox Cathedral of Saint Luke in Hong Kong might feel less knowledgeable attending the Episcopal service of Emmanuel Church in the same city, despite sharing a broadly construed Christian background with the members of that Church. Aspects that define a particular denomination within a world religion are shared to some extent by other groups within that denomination, but local practice will usually have an effect on how a group interprets the elements specific to their denomination. Certainly, some people reading these last sentences would disagree based on their knowledge of one or many religious groups and practices—all of which suggests that it is only the most elemental, least location-specific aspects of a world religion, those that can be acknowledged and experienced as shared across denominations, that can be described as universal aspects of any particular world religion.

In light of the previous paragraph, one would be forgiven for thinking that the universal elements of a particular world religion may be nothing more than tepid articulations of belonging, able to do no more than hint at what it means to be a Muslim, Christian, or Hindu. That which falls within the main rubric of any category such as Christianity, Hinduism, or Islam has never been completely unified or singular, even early on in the history of the religions. World religions are actually multiple series of hard-won historical fissures and disputes, all of which have generated distinctive local sects of varying sizes. Yet each of these localized versions of any religion pays homage to an originary center and its sacred texts in some way, sometimes by proclaiming that the other related factions or groups have overlooked the center or fallen away from it. The relationship of universal elements and local practices is often hotly contested, both between and among groups. Fundamentalist or "back to the book" movements emerge at moments when there is interest in stripping away local interpretations and elaborations and a reinvigorated engagement with the practices at the (sometimes imagined) originary center of a world religion, however these may be constructed at that moment by those seeking certain kinds of authenticity. The rise of the Wahhabi movement in eighteenth-century Saudi Arabia,[17] the slow development of Hinduism as a national religion, beginning in the nineteenth century and continuing through the twentieth century, in India,[18] and the rise of fundamentalist Protestant Christianity in twentieth-century America[19] are all modern examples of what can be seen as a struggle between universal and local or as monolithic and pluralistic interpretations of world religion.[20] Ironically, despite claims to the contrary, in these situations an essentially "local" form of religious practice and belief lays claim to the authenticity of origins in order to portray its cause in the language of the universal. Yet, even if the reality is constructed, the language about that reality and the desire to claim it empower the concept of the universal. Far from insignificant or tepid, the idea of universal elements shared by members of communities practicing a particular religion in different places is a powerful bond, a source of authenticity even as those elements are reinterpreted by each denomination.

World religions necessarily intersect with existing ceremonial and religious practices in the cultures to which they spread—for instance, the Christian celebration of the birth of Jesus on December 25 adjacent to the Roman pagan festival of Saturnalia rather than on the (likely unknown) birth date itself.[21] Local social hierarchies also change to accommodate the new religious culture, usually gradually, but they can also be sustained, perhaps partially, even when they are not in accord with hierarchies formulated by the new religion. In some cases, local gender constructions have persisted even when they are quite different from those of the world religion. For instance, over the course of its first millennium of its existence in many places in the Arab world and throughout Southeast Asia, Islam was adopted into societies that were predominantly matriarchal, contexts in which there were inheritance, marriage, and ownership patterns that did not fit into the gender structures of Islam as it was developing.[22] It should be noted that the persistence of competing constructions of gender roles in a society implies neither quiet comfortable acceptance nor constantly engaged battle but rather adjustment and negotiation over time. In some cases, those original patterns and daily spiritual practices were maintained or adapted and have persisted into the present. Female-headed households and female ritual practitioners in Muslim communities in Sri Lanka provide gendered traces of pre-Islamic cultural and religious practices. Similar evidence can be found in many Yoruba-based women's rituals in New World Catholic practices.[23]

Theorizing Ritual—A Comparative Process

The act of theorizing ritual is a comparative one that, at least in the work of the scholars who initially described the theory, generally assumes that both men and women engage in ritual; but the theorizing process itself is not practically concerned with the gender of the participants. That said, the case studies employed as data for the theorizing process usually pertain to small, settled societies with yearly agricultural or other season-based patterns in which male and female activities are separated and so the rituals described do refer to either male or female practices, or to young, uninitiated people, who are, ritually speaking, not yet men or women. In his book *Les rites de passage*, French ethnographer and folklorist Arnold van Gennep compares cultural practices from around the world and discerns a common underlying tripartite process and structure for rites of passage in which individuals move from an original state, through a liminal state, to a final altered state.[24] To transition between the first and second stages, rites of separation are enacted; to transition between the second and third stages, rites of incorporation are performed. In any given cultural context, the ritual actions are designed to protect and transition the person through the liminal spaces between the old "normal" and the new states. The movement and pacing through these stages are culturally determined—some rites of passage are completed in a day, others over the course of years.[25] Although they are not his primary focus, van Gennep notes the use of music, dance, and song in many of the case studies he touches on briefly as he prepares his analysis.

Van Gennep did not develop his ideas about ritual process in a void. In his conclusion, he acknowledges several other scholars who were thinking along the same lines.[26] Yet fellow French scholars working on similar topics in the early twentieth century largely ignored van Gennep's work over the ensuing fifty years. His theory was taken up again, however, in the 1960s, when British anthropologist Victor Turner engaged the ideas, in particular liminality, in his analysis of Ndembu ritual performance.[27] Turner and performance theorist Richard Schechner subsequently brought the ideas into performance studies and back to the study of ritual over the course of the second half of the twentieth century, making van Gennep's work a major and continuing contribution to interpretations of the relationship between performance and ritual at the beginning of the twenty-first century.[28]

Broad scholarly interest in ritual studies burgeoned in the middle of the twentieth century, so much so that it seemed that just about any observable pattern or process could be interpreted as ritual. In response to the overuse of the concept of ritual, British social anthropologist Jack Goody questioned whether ritual as an idea or a process still had analytical value.[29] If every moderately repetitive cultural act could be constructed as a ritual, what did this do for our understanding of the concept of ritual? This question was especially pertinent if, as Goody believed, there was need to differentiate between everyday "ritual" and ritual that was performed with an intent that lay beyond rational interpretation. Ultimately, Goody decided the term was too loosely defined to be useful, primarily because the implied oppositional pairs such as religious/secular or ritual/nonritual no longer defined separate categories. In his opinion, the very success of ritual theory had rendered the term "ritual" useless.

Fifteen years later Catherine Bell responded to Goody's criticism, setting out to rescue ritual by reducing its universality as an analytical concept. She aimed to restore ritual to its status as social activity rather than a paradigmatic act. Inspired by Bourdieu's theory of practice while contesting some of his ideas, Bell argued that actors who engage in ritualization probably do so for a rational reason—not because they could imagine nothing else or because they were necessarily forced to. She proposed that acting ritually is a particular cultural strategy of differentiation linked to specific, locally defined social effects and rooted in a distinctive interplay of a socialized body and the environment it structures.[30] She contested the interpretation that sees ritual primarily as a form of social control and argued that ritualization is a strategy in the negotiation of power relationships that are not necessarily economic. Self, society, and authority are, for Bell, all in play in ritualized contexts through the possibilities of consent and resistance, misunderstanding and appropriation. In her conclusion, she writes:

> The ultimate purpose of ritualization is neither the immediate goals avowed by the community or the officiant nor the more abstract functions of social solidarity and conflict resolution: it is nothing other than the production of ritualized agents, persons who have an instinctive knowledge of these schemes embedded in their bodies, in their sense of reality, and in their understanding of how to act in ways that both maintain and qualify the complex microrelations of power. . . . [I]t is the ability to deploy, play, and manipulate basic schemes in ways that appropriate and condition experience effectively. It is a mastery that experiences itself as relatively empowered, not as conditioned or molded.[31]

As Bell demonstrates through her multiple case studies, a focus on the agency of individual actors and strategies for negotiating power in society through ritual allows for the development of a comparative framework in which the rich specificity of the local is engaged rather than spurned in the effort to theorize across cultures and periods.

During the same period as the demise of ritual studies in the middle of the twentieth century, religious studies—an inherently comparative discipline—was suffering a similar fate for ostensibly different reasons. As a discipline, religious studies developed originally as an investigative social science with the goal of positioning the belief systems of the people of the world—those previously identified as "pagan"—on equal footing with those of the Abrahamic religions (Judaism, Christianity, and Islam)—through the process of comparison. Field-defining works such as Friedrich Max Müller's *Introduction to the Science of Religion* (1882) and Mircea Eliade's *Patterns in Comparative Religion* (1959) came to be viewed negatively from two different angles during this period. On one side they were criticized for suggesting that ritual and spirituality were human universals, thereby positioning "pagan" religions as similar to the major world religions, in particular Christianity.[32] On the other side, emerging from the discourse of cultural relativism in anthropology,[33] comparative religion was criticized for "conjur[ing] and impos[ing] abstracted categories that too often erase[d] culturally embedded distinctions and realities."[34] In the second half of the twentieth century, this line of criticism was adapted and enhanced by postmodern and postcolonial theorists who have argued that comparative endeavors strip the important detail of religious cultures and impose categories that may be irrelevant to the people of the culture, effectively recreating forms of colonial-style, intellectual imperialism. From this perspective, comparison is understood as a political act, directly connected to the pernicious ideas of long-ago-debunked Social Darwinism and the evolutionary development ideas that put all religious cultures in the world on the same continuum leading to Euro-American expressions of Protestant Christianity.

Since the early 2000s, however, a movement to rehabilitate comparative religious studies has been developing.[35] Wendy Doniger warns against "jumping from the frying pan of imperialist universalism into the fire of an academic essentialism." She notes that "[s]imilarity and difference are not equal, not comparable; they have different uses. We look to similarity for stability to build political bridges, to anchor our own society, while we spin narratives to deal with our uneasiness at the threat of difference." She asserts that an unwavering focus on either similarity or difference "may lead to a form of paralyzing reductionism and demeaning essentialism. . . . [E]xtreme universalism means that the other is exactly like you, [but] extreme nominalism means that the other may not be human at all."[36] New arguments for comparative studies note that comparison is a persistent part of human life. Rather than eschewing it for political reasons, the goal should be to find comparative processes that are transparent and responsible. Corinne Dempsey points out that, "religious categories applied cross-culturally can become, when properly contextualized, a means for understanding a tradition more profoundly, and paradoxically more on its own terms."[37] "Not to reach closure in the service of a particular theory, nor to achieve moral judgment or to gain intellectual control over the other," scholars working anew in the field of comparative religion argue that it is worth risking the postcolonial, postmodern perils of comparison "to empower mutual dialogue and the quest for understanding."[38] Comparison is a kind of translation. It is usually not possible to express an idea from one language precisely in another. There is always a gap between the two expressions. Similarities may be revealed but unexpected differences may also surface. It is within those intersections and dissonances that comparison offers deep understanding of both the familiar and the unfamiliar, and it is through these kinds of comparison that this study develops interpretations of women's performance.

Comparative Studies and Ethnomusicology

Vergleichende musikwissenschaft, or comparative musicology—a term most likely first used in print by Guido Adler in 1885—is considered one of the disciplinary ancestors of ethnomusicology.[39] In addition to colonial engagements earlier in the century, the burgeoning availability of recordings and travel at the end of the nineteenth century brought the experience of musics from around the world to the ears of curious music scholars who worked to understand and organize, in their own ways, what they were hearing. The intellectual context in which they heard these musics was informed by the anthropological ideas of the time, shaped by "evolution and sociocultural theories as put forward by [Lewis] Morgan, [Walter] Spencer, [Edward] Tylor, and others."[40] Albrecht Schneider has written a substantial history of the development of comparative musicology and its sister discipline, systematic musicology, in Germany in the context of the gradual separation between scientific and interpretive methods in the study of human cultures. Schneider outlines the primary research traditions focusing on: the documentation of details of musical scales and instruments; exploration of the psychology, anatomy, and physics of music perception; and the construction of taxonomies modeling scientific methods of experimentation and documentation. Writing on comparative musicology in 1924, Robert Lach predicted that research in the field "would have to proceed from descriptive and analytical studies [of the sort mentioned above, before it could conduct] truly comparative synopses, [moving] from morphological evidence to coherent historic-genetic relationships."[41] But the widening gap between the study and documentation of observable aspects of nature and the interpretation of human behavior and culture could seemingly not be narrowed, as there are few studies which bring the two methodologies together. Comparative musicological studies, then and now, tend to focus primarily on the analysis of musical structures with the intent to show some kind of intrinsic order.[42]

Bruno Nettl observes that there is the "implication that comparative musicology requires a rather rigorous comparative method, somewhat like that of comparative linguistics . . . or comparative literature." Each of these fields, he asserts, uses "intercultural or interlingual comparison leading to a class of conclusions."[43] But this kind of rigorous methodology was never widely cultivated in the American community of ethnomusicologists. In fact, the term comparative musicology persisted only through the mid-1950s, when it was suddenly dropped due to a preference for the new term *ethnomusicology*. Nevertheless, Nettl observes three kinds of musicological work, common in American ethnomusicology, in which comparative techniques are fundamental: the description of musical styles, instruments, and sonic elements that facilitates comparison of styles through documentation and measurement; the reconstruction of geographic distribution and diffusion of style traits and instruments; and the reconstruction of musical history through the geographic distribution of particular pieces, melodic fragments, and modes.[44] From Nettl's overview it is possible to surmise that ethnomusicologists in the middle decades of the twentieth century were still doing the kinds of research that had previously been identified as comparative musicology but they were embedded in the field of ethnomusicology. The gradual turn toward cultural relativism and interpretive ethnography from the 1960s on encouraged American ethnomusicologists to spurn comparative musicology, at least in their rhetoric. Significantly, Nettl notes that "the studies of non-Western and folk music before 1950 were not [. . .] "especially" comparative and that after 1950, comparative study continued to play an important role (2010, 85). The change in terminology was, ultimately, more political than methodological, having to do with international relations, postcoloniality, and changing perspectives on the ethics of representation and authority.

One important problem presented by comparative work in the study of the practice of performance is the interpretation and meaning of any similarity discovered. On the one hand, one might simply observe that two or more groups of people in different places and cultural contexts came up with the same performative idea. On the other hand, one might present a more controversial interpretation invoking the existence of universals beyond those of basic physiological experience and involving human decision making. The former generates the question "So what?" and the latter is politically problematic in that it suggests forms of intellectual and cultural imperialism. For many compelling reasons, cultural relativism, the dominant paradigm of the intellectual world of ethnomusicology, generally eschews universals. Universals can erase the particularity of specific groups and cultural contexts; they can also allow for the perspective of the comparing observer to represent the similarities between the practices rather than relying on the observations and experiences of the practitioners themselves. The shadow of colonial power structures and the experiences of inequality around the world demand that the issues of power and hegemony lurking behind the identification of universals be acknowledged before any analysis might move forward. I agree that comparison for comparison's sake often produces an empty conclusion or even false histories of cultural interaction and influence. But I suggest that there is something important to be found between the bland observation of similarity and difference and the complete evisceration of individual agency and cultural particularity suggested by the search for "human universals."

Women in different religions and cultural contexts around the world perform elaborate lamentation rituals at the weddings of their children. They sing bawdy songs and dance suggestively with their daughters who are soon to be married. They perform ritualized, musical mockery of their intended in-laws. It is not surprising that many of these ritual performances occur as part of local wedding rituals, since marriage and death are two major life-cycle events in which women nearly always play an important role in religious contexts around the world. What is gained in documenting and interpreting these kinds of similarities? Viewed variously as sensualized object of the male gaze—a mute, protected property of an extended family—but also as dangerous temptress and destroyer of community and family worlds, women in religions and cultures around the world have found that the liminality of performance allows them to negotiate the ambiguity of their socially constructed positions in their communities, garnering agency to effect change, whether temporarily or more permanently. A comparative approach is productive in understanding these kinds of performances, for in noting and then examining these kinds of similarities the conclusions may serve to nuance interpretations of gender constructions inside religions and illuminate understandings of the same across religions.

At a time of rampant cultural and religious conflict across the world, it is useful to penetrate the tropes of separatism and exceptionalism that drive such movements forward. Demonstrating the presence of similarity through comparative work is one way of inserting seeds of doubt about the exceptionalism claimed and the exclusionary nature of difference rhetoric in any context. As scholars, we have a responsibility to model openness rather than a lockdown mentality. The comparative case studies presented here reveal surprising similarities between rituals of women practitioners of world religions with factions that have sworn enmity against one another and threatened one another with annihilation. Through slippages of familiarity, comparison renders the distant and foreign interpretable and perceivable. Comparison has the potential to allow one to look beyond or beneath prejudice. Comparison between women's ritual performances in different religions may provide a sliver of similarity to serve as the smallest wedge in the door opening beyond religious separatism and conflict. It is one of the few, potentially effective tools ethnomusicologists may wield in a world filled with conflict.

Women's Agency and Local Practice: Two Meta-Ethnographic Case Studies

To focus on women's practices within local expressions of world religions reveals alternative workings of lived faith that are, following Ramanujan, "startlingly different" from more dominant conceptions of how that religion should be experienced. Although women's practices are usually not institutionalized under the auspices of their religion, they are often expected, viewed as essential to the process of an event, by their community. Far from peripheral to the practice of religion in a particular place, women's activities are instrumental in focusing and shaping local variants of the practice of world religions around the globe. In what follows here, I present two short case studies, one musical and the other not, both from Christian communities—one examining the Dormition Pilgrimage of the Greek Orthodox community in Jerusalem, and the other, perhaps more unexpected, examining of the development of Christian feminist theology in the English-speaking world—in order to introduce some of the possibilities of meta-ethnography and to demonstrate the ways in which focusing on women's activities provides alternative perspectives, revealing both women's agency and their roles in the development of local practices.

UNRULINESS AND THE GREEK ORTHODOX FEAST OF MARY'S DORMITION IN OLD CITY JERUSALEM

The Dormition Feast of the Greek Orthodox Church is a two-week festival celebrated in mid-August throughout the Greek Orthodox diaspora. In Jerusalem this important yearly celebration of the Greek Orthodox community involves the progressing of a delicately painted wooden icon of the "sleeping" Mary from the Church of the Holy Sepulcher in the Old City of Jerusalem to a grotto in the Valley of Kidron known as Gethsemane Church or the Tomb of Mary.[45] For the members of the Greek Orthodox Church, the Feast of Mary's Dormition commemorates Mary's death and her ascent to Heaven.[46] In the narrative associated with the Greek Orthodox Dormition celebration, Mary is made aware of her impending death predicted to occur three days hence. With the exception of Thomas, all the apostles miraculously arrive to attend to her. At her request, Mary is buried in the grotto at Gethsemane. When Thomas finally arrives, three days after Mary has died, he asks to see her body, but it is discovered no longer to be in her grave. Paralleling the fate of her son's corpse, Mary has been taken directly to heaven, apparently accompanied by Jesus, who has invited his mother to join him.

The most significant aspect of the Jerusalem pilgrimage is that, unlike other Marian pilgrimage routes associated with Christian traditions around the world, the route of the Jerusalem Dormition Feast traverses roads and sites directly associated with Mary's own path both before and after her death. Many of the sites on the pilgrimage are documented in liturgical accounts, and archeological work has confirmed the existence of Marian ceremonies in the area as early as the fifth century.[47] The myriad details of the pilgrimage in Jerusalem have been carefully preserved, with great attention from church leaders devoted to correct procedure of the pilgrimage, including the specific utterances to be made at appointed places along the route. Given regular public and international interest in the pilgrimage, the Patriarch and his fellow leaders at the Greek Orthodox Church in Jerusalem have much invested in ensuring correct procedure and decorum among the participants on the pilgrimage and in the grotto once the icon finally arrives.

It is important to note that Mary is understood to have the ability to intercede with God on behalf of her faithful followers. As she is the most important mother in the Christian pantheon, Mary is a key saint for women in the Greek Orthodox Church, and they identify directly with her, for they are the central performers of the maternal ritual actions designed to secure their families' health and life. Orthodox women from around the world embark on the Jerusalem Dormition feast pilgrimage as a way of honoring Mary in order to ensure her intercession for their specific causes and needs. The actions of the women as they seek to demonstrate their convictions without restraint generally do not accord with the decorum and orderliness demanded by the priests of the church hosting the pilgrimage. Tensions often arise during the Marian festival between the leadership of the church and the predominantly female pilgrims, for both groups are intent on ensuring the efficacy of their engagement in the celebration, but their methods are not the same.

People from around the world convene in the Old City of Jerusalem for the Dormition feast pilgrimage each year. Different groups of women—Armenian, Greek, Palestinian, Russian, Serbian Cypriot, French—behave in different ways in the procession, along the procession route, and then in the grotto. The priests prefer that pilgrims dress in dark, modest mourning clothes in order to honor and respect the passing of the Virgin and the solemnity of the moment that is commemorated. They also instruct pilgrims that they must wear shoes.[48] The Orthodox sisters associated with the church are always the first in line to follow the icon of Mary in the progression. They are dressed in funeral black and walk sedately behind the male church leaders. Other women, modestly dressed but garbed in colors from their homelands, also walk the pilgrimage route behind. Many of them are in bare feet—bare to recall, they say, Mary's own trek on the pathway. These pilgrims walk barefoot to ground themselves in the earth where she walked. Crowds of young Palestinian families and teenagers—some Christian and some not, most clothed in jeans and informal dress—chat and laugh gathered along the route watching the events, adding to the festive feeling among the communities along the route. Although the Greek Orthodox priests are adamant that everyone should sing in ecclesiastical Greek, as well as intone the assigned prayers and correct songs, the women pilgrims from around the world sing in their own languages. They are on their own pilgrimage and they must communicate with Mary in the languages in which they can make their vows and declarations to Mary best understood. Christian Arab women making the pilgrimage often hand out sheet music for some of the approved songs with alternative texts in Arabic. These Arabic versions ring out above the singing of the other ethnic groups,[49] often drowning out the official versions of the songs because observers watching along the edges of the procession also join in singing.[50] The cacophonous, energized atmosphere and the crush of the disorderly crowds eschewing any aura of funereal gloom disrupt the possibility and expectation of an enactment of the pilgrimage in the way said to be preferred by the Patriarchy of the church. According to Stadler, the Orthodox priests are regularly irritated as their plans for a somber atmosphere are disrupted by revelers and pilgrims alike. Police are always required in order to control the crowds in the narrow Old City streets. This is particularly true once the procession reaches the area around the grotto.[51]

The procession moves slowly as the icon is progressed along the pilgrimage route. Once the grotto comes into view, the singing in all languages increases in volume and intensity. The crowd crushes toward the other smaller shrines outside of the grotto, which people are desperate to kiss and touch. The priests have a difficult time maintaining their own safety, let alone the required/desired ritual order. The sounds of the gathered crowds mingle with the already multilingual singing of the pilgrims as well as the languages of many other visitors. Thousands of feet scuffing slowly through the dusty street and dirt plaza near the grotto, babies crying, the myriad murmurs and shouts of thousands of human beings permeate the soundscape of the pilgrimage, penetrating both participants and observers. The scene inside the grotto is even more frenzied, with women singing and making multiple passes by the icon of the sleeping Mary. Because they are requesting intercession by Mary, the pilgrims wish to demonstrate their commitment to her in as ardent a manner as possible. Many approach the icon scrabbling forward on their knees or crawling on their stomachs, craning their lips up to kiss the icon. Such approaches to the icon are decidedly against the rules for orderly behavior of the crowd as outlined by the Patriarchate. The women pilgrims insist on their right to access the icon in their own way. It is clear that the supplication they embody is a form of worship they view as essential to the pilgrimage experience in order to ensure that their participation in the pilgrimage is personally fruitful.[52]

While the Dormition itself is contested among the various branches of Christianity, within the Greek Orthodox tradition it is universally accepted (although not considered dogma), with procedures, practices, local interpretations, and institutional traditions reaching back to the fifth century CE. Yet each year the struggle between monolithic and pluralistic interpretations of the ritual is reenacted not only in Jerusalem but throughout the diaspora as well.[53] The Jerusalem Dormition feast pilgrimage is an example in which female personalized and pluralist ritual traditions and practices defy male scriptural and institutional preferences. It is predominantly women who make the pilgrimage and who generate the resistance.

Women on the Dormition pilgrimage, traditionally denied access to the power structures of the Greek Orthodox Church, contest the orderliness desired by the Patriarchy not with words or violence but with expressions of ardent love and song. Their actions are not designed to alter in any significant way the official plans and requirements for the Dormition pilgrimage, nor are they intended to overthrow the structures of religious hierarchy. In some perspectives, the women may not even resist the Patriarchy intentionally. Instead, their certainty about what they must do to fulfill their personal goals and ensure the efficacy of their pilgrimage drive them forward. There is also confirmation of their own actions in those of other women. Pilgrims make the pilgrimage with many other women, all of whom are similarly moved to offer themselves to Mary. From their various perspectives, the rules and orderliness desired by the priests must necessarily be understood as secondary to the outcome of the pilgrimage given the goals of the women. The women are not seeking to have these rules rewritten. Rather, the difficulties they confront and the chaos they collectively create as they strive to complete their pilgrimage with so many other supplicants can be understood as enhancing their efforts to demonstrate to Mary the strength of their commitment to the pilgrimage and their hopes for her intercession. In addition, the sonic resistance of Arab Christians has two aims. First, they participate full-throatedly in the pilgrimage like all the others and do so in their own language. Second, they engage the ongoing, everyday efforts made by Arabs of every creed in Jerusalem to assert control over a city they feel is their own but which many others claim, while simultaneously warding off the perception that they have somehow sided with the Israelis because of their connections to a religion understood to be primarily European, irrespective of its origins in the local region.[54] Despite its official position, the Patriarchy, too, may not mind the chaos. The crowds may be unruly, but they are full of women from around the world, demonstrating the international importance of an event orchestrated by the Patriarchy and so well attended that extra help, in the form of police and other security, is required to control the masses. The crowds that arrive each year and their perennial unruliness confirm the need for the Patriarchy to continue its efforts to "tame" the ardent women and maintain the orderly process of the important pilgrimage. This reading of Stadler's rich ethnographic material further reveals the multiple beneficiaries of the resistance performed at the Jerusalem Dormition pilgrimage and suggests that any gendered analysis of religious contexts must be nuanced so as to reflect the power negotiations and dependencies evident in the interstices between religious doctrine, local gender hierarchies, and lived culture. To read without attention to those resistances, perhaps from a top-down perspective focusing on the breaking of the rules outlined by the Patriarch, would yield an impoverished interpretation. Indeed, far from peripheral, women's actions at the Dormition Pilgrimage in Old City Jerusalem are instrumental to a multisided success of the event and also reflect local variants of the practice around the globe.

INTERPRETING THE RISE OF CHRISTIAN FEMINIST THEOLOGY AS LOCAL TRADITION

Whether the Greek Orthodox women or their compatriot celebrants on the Dormition pilgrimage in Jerusalem think of themselves as feminists is not recorded by Nurit Stadler's 2011 study. Whatever these women's perspectives may be, their actions resonate with those of feminist theologians working in America and Europe throughout the twentieth century. Although it has some roots in the fourteenth century, feminism is a phenomenon that began with a brief florescence in the late-eighteenth century in Europe and America and subsequently revived in the late-nineteenth and twentieth centuries.[55] Over the last one hundred years, feminism has actively become a worldwide phenomenon, springing up in different places and in different guises and with particular cultural and political agendas but always having at its core a concern about gendered inequality and a drive to identify and remedy the causes. Forms of feminist critique have arisen inside every world religion, but in unique ways, and sometimes in opposition to the liberal feminism of the West. Indeed, critique of Western liberal Christian feminism parallels the critique of secular feminist theory and practice by women of color and women in/from the Global South. A rights-focused, liberal feminist perspective emerging from the West has always been privileged within a white, higher-socioeconomic women's movement, one that often flattened the category of "women," ignoring local differences and acting (often unwittingly) as a tool of colonial power. Scholars such as Sylvanna Falcón and Jennifer Nash, Chandra Talpade Mohanty, and many others have written strong theoretical challenges to liberal Western feminism. As a result, the theoretical underpinnings of feminism have evolved toward the acknowledgment of intersectionality.

The roots of contemporary feminist Christian theologies can be found in the social and political movements of the late nineteenth and twentieth centuries, in particular in liberation theology, the Christian movement and political theology that interprets the teachings of Jesus of Nazareth as representing everyone equally and therefore demands liberation for all from economic, political, or social conditions in which inequality predominates. Emerging from local, practical experience—like the women's rituals that are the focus of this study—liberation theology has had a potent influence, both positive and negative, on the development of Christian practice around the world. It began in the 1950s and 1960s within Roman Catholicism in Latin America, amid the leftist movements of the time. Peruvian priest Gustavo Gutierrez, author of one of the foundational works of the movement—*A Theology of Liberation: History, Politics and Salvation*—created the term "liberation theology."[56] Focusing on the experience of the oppressed both as religious practitioners and individuals caught in power structures beyond their control, liberation theology served as the background from which mid-twentieth-century feminist theologians and religious activists imagined, theorized, and "wrote back" to[57] Christian theology.[58] Feminist Christian theology focused on women and women's experiences from ancient to present times as a primary method of introducing multiple female voices into religious and theological discourse, adopting a strategy of inserting women into the frame of an already-standing paradigm[59] and creating scholarly and interpretive discourses in which the distance between institution and practitioner was greatly reduced. This compression of separation was effected through a shift in focus toward the experience of individuals, an identification and articulation of the male-centrism of most Christian theology, an insistence on increasing the attention paid to female perspectives on scripture and daily practice, and a focus on increasing opportunities for women to rise into leadership positions within existing ecclesiastical structures. Authors such as Mary Daly, Sallie McFague, Rosemary Radford Ruether, Elisabeth Schüssler Fiorenza, Teresa Berger, and Mary McClintock Fulkerson wrote, and continue to write, about Christianity from feminist perspectives. While some of them may reject all preexisting interpretations of the Bible and institutionalized power structures of Christianity, right down to questioning the gender of God, these scholars did not choose to move away from the Church and begin anew by creating another, more women-centered religion. They claim Christianity as their own even as they resist its male-oriented hierarchies and commitment to gender inequality.

It should be noted immediately that Christian feminist theologies and goals have not been sought or accepted by all Christian women. This is as true for some European-American Christian women as for Christian women outside of that cultural area. For instance, feminist theological perspectives do not resonate with the experiences of an American Pentecostal sister who "obeys God's call to ministry to speak out about her worry about women's liberation" and its "seductive call" to women to desert home and family,[60] let alone with the Christian women of the Church of Central Africa Presbyterian in Malawi,[61] a state of affairs we could expand to women of many other races, ethnicities, and cultural and geographic locations.[62] Christian feminist theology now faces the problem that a generalized theology of any sort has when it seeks to understand women as a category. Every woman, every writer, is located in her culture and race, in her economic, political, and educational milieu. Most of the Christian-feminist writers listed above sit at the intersection of several specific cultural locations—they are white; American or European; Catholic or main-line Protestant; now middle-class or higher; and acculturated to the idea of the equal importance of every individual and the right of individuals to construct their worldviews and contest authority. That much "canonical" Christian feminist theology has emerged from people located in this particular demographic[63] suggests that this Christian feminist position is no more "universal" than those of the many generations of men who have written and interpreted the Bible and generated the ideologies of the various Christianities through history. Instead, these Christian feminist theorists represent a specific localization or interpretation of Christianity, one that has been developed based on their group's personal practices and cultural preferences. Their cultural position is at an intersection of some of the most privileged positions in the world, yet, within the relativism of intersectionality, it is, like all other positions, rendered incapable of accurately representing any other group. Following the line of this argument, intersectionality must necessarily encourage essentializing, such that no person could write about or even understand the experiences and thoughts of any other person or group in the world unless their intersections are perfectly matched.

As an intellectual position, relying solely on a strict adherence to the principles of intersectionality is unsustainable and, ultimately, unproductive. As powerful and empowering as the concept of intersectionality is, if taken to its logical endpoint, it must inevitably foment the splintering of human knowledge. Someone located at a particular intersection of race, class, ethnicity, religion, and so on is denied, absolutely, the possibility of understanding the perspectives of anyone located at a different intersection of identities. Sylvia Walby identifies this denial of possible engagement across intersectionalities as a form of intellectual defeatism. Writing about gender inequality in different places in the world, Walby argues that,

> [t]he politics of location, with its focus on difference, can inappropriately exaggerate and reify the boundaries between such social groupings. . . . [B]oundaries are permeable, communities overlap and communities have relationships with each other in a global context. Differences may be implicated in varied, but actually comparable, not incommensurable, forms of gender inequality. There may be sufficient com-

> mon ground among women in different locations to make it possible to compare diverse forms of gender relations. In this way we are not inevitably confined merely to particular local knowledge, even if that is the starting point.[64]

Walby articulates a compelling rationale for comparison across intersectional positions, and her argument is one I take up and develop throughout this book.

Christian feminist discourse has had an enormous impact from the second half of the twentieth century to the present, generating both progressive and reactionary responses in Christian communities around the world, and indeed in communities of practitioners of other religions around the world. Thinking of Christian feminist theology as a local practice requires both acknowledgment of the circumscribed nature of the group that has generated that theology—like so many of the other women's practices found around the world—and acceptance of the idea that local practices can have real impact, whether geographically confined or reaching across the world.[65] Recognizing the roots and positionality of Christian feminist writing allows us to draw striking parallels with other local women's traditions discussed throughout this work, despite their intersectional differences. Women's local traditions can become central to the practice of a religion at a particular place and time. Like the tradition-sustaining, bodily, and sonic resistance to the rules of the Patriarchy at the Greek Orthodox church in Jerusalem,[66] the feminist critique and reinterpretation of scripture and practice demands attention. Both traditions challenge and resist the male orientation of practice and/or scripture, creating a persuasive discourse that questions authority without abandoning the possibility of change from within.

But is all religious practice necessarily local practice? Is there such a thing as universal practice? Certainly, all practice is local to a degree—even at the Vatican, in Mecca, in Canterbury, or on "top" of Mount Meru[67]—but the idea of universal practice is particularly useful and powerful in its many locally interpreted yet related imagined realities, as the worldwide recognition of the four religiously important sites above suggests. The relatively fixed interpretations and patterns of universal institutional and textual traditions have helped to sustain world religions through major political and social ruptures. The ongoing negotiation between local practice and the local interpretation of the universal elements of a world religion simultaneously confirms communities as part of that world religion and articulates their specificity within it. There is no fixed opposition between local and universal practices because, like other binary pairs, they are mutually constituting, in a relationship that is malleable through time and place.

CHAPTER 2

Wedding Lamentation

Singing Sorrow, Embodying the Future

If one has given a daughter, what has one kept back?

One has somehow to endure a daughter's birth:
there's crying when she's born and crying when she goes away.
—Proverbs from Pahansu Village, Uttar Pradesh

Lamentation at a wedding might seem contradictory to the positive, family-sustaining expectations with which wedding nuptials are often greeted. But weddings also signal departure and radical change. Those whose lives will be most drastically affected may harbor fears about the process and feel the loss of their loved ones in an anticipatory way, especially in contexts when the choice to marry is made by people other than those being wed. It is even possible to make an emotional connection between the departure of a loved one caused by marriage and the more permanent departure generated by the death of a loved one. People in some cultures have cultivated a sonic link between these two forms of mourning, borrowing lamentation from death rituals for performance at prenuptial events or inventing lamentation traditions specific to weddings. This chapter explores examples of wedding lamentation in seven different contexts. The case studies from United Kingdom, Greece, Russia, and Northern India rely on data drawn from ethnographic studies; the case studies from Finland, India, and Italy are historical and rely on data drawn from documentary film, literature, and song. The point of examining similar phenomena occurring in different cultures, religions, and historical periods at the same kind of event is to demonstrate both the ways in which women's performance at ritual events plays an important role in localizing the religion as it is practiced in by people in that particular culture and to show that women's practices across religions can be compared productively in a way that may enlighten more general understandings between religions. This chapter begins with an ethnographic account of wedding lamentation performed in a Muslim Pakistani family preparing for a wedding in an urban, British context from the 1980s.

Preparing for Marriage in a British Pakistani Community

The bride's close friends and female family members prepare and then perform the ablutions of the *thel* prenuptial ceremony.[1] The bride's body is shaved, massaged with oil, and anointed with *batna*—a mixture of grain, oil, turmeric, and scents presented by the groom's family for this occasion. Seven days later a larger all-female group gathers for the *mehendi* ritual. While a similar event takes place at the groom's house, the bride is once again massaged and fed sweets and dried coconut. She and her guests spend time tracing intricate patterns on their hands and feet with a henna mixture called *dulham*, a word that also means bridal couple.[2] While these decorations are applied, the older women in the group sing songs of lamentation, drooping melodies filled with pessimism about the future and marriage in general. The bride weeps as she contemplates her departure from her natal home and the friends and family who surround her. As the henna application nears its end, the younger girls take over the floor, performing erotic dances and love songs, teasing the bride, and giving her suggestive gifts. When the henna application is finished, the bride is bathed. The thick henna gel is washed off, leaving delicate patterns of intertwining leaves, buds, and blooms. After the bride has been massaged with oil once again, she and the other girls hold their hands over a hot flame to cure the henna. A clowning figure, a young woman dressed as an old man, enters and makes suggestive comments to the women. "He" then demands that one of the girls be given to "him" in marriage. The mother of the bride banters with the clown. They exchange lewd insults, causing raucous laughter among the group, both young and old. The girls admire the sexually explicit gifts they have given to the bride, such as panties adorned with the English words "Screw Hole" and sexy, lacy bras, as well as baby dolls and many other objects suggestive of sensuality and fertility that are later hung from the ceiling. Even the formerly pessimistic older women participate in the dancing, singing, and laughing at this stage in the event. These activities continue until the early hours of the morning.

The flow of musical performances in this scene captures the tensions and emotions generated by the long process that culminates in marriage. The daughter will leave her home with its comforts, familiar patterns, sisters, and friends. The mother will lose her child, who will never again belong solely to her natal family. The impending departure into unknown territory generates fear and a worried, excited tension in the bride and her friends as they anticipate the separation and resulting changes to their relationships. All these conflicting emotions are imagined or relived by the rest of the women present when they hear the sound of the lamentations sung by the older members of the gathering. The pleasures of marriage imagined by the younger girls are damped down, at first, by the pessimistic commentary of the married women, who have already weathered the fluctuating moods of their in-laws and husbands and have borne and raised children. Ultimately, the transition to sensual excitement overcomes the preliminary gloomy pessimism.

Pnina Werbner interprets these ritual activities among Muslim migrants in a British city as preparation for the rupture in morality that marriage represents. A girl who has been protected from outsiders, lovingly cared for solely by her family, and prevented from interacting with men who are not in her immediate family will—in a single act on the day of her marriage—cross every cultural boundary set for her during her girlhood. In this liminal, transitional state she could become dangerous to herself and others, sexually voracious, and in need of ritual tempering.[3] The old-man clown, who is neither old nor male, is overtly lewd and lecherous in public; by his very presence at the women's event "he" represents an overturning, however temporary, of societal norms. Rules will necessarily be set by the married bride's new family, where her potential for wild, sexual enthusiasms and possibilities will be tamed and transformed into productive, fertile potency.[4] The presence of women at many different life stages at the mehendi ceremony ensures a broad representation of female lived experiences and an inhabited representation of the arc of female positionality in the community. The pessimistic older women lamenting the woes of marriage were once themselves eager girls preparing to marry. These mixed perspectives help prepare and mediate the multiple transitions of the bride, simultaneously increasing and managing expectations for the marriage. The songs—first of lamentation and then of anticipatory, sensual joy—and the experience of communal physicality—weeping, rhythmic clapping, singing, and eroticized dancing—together articulate the range of emotional experience generated by the marriage act in this British Pakistani community. Externalizing the emotions eases the sorrow and both stimulates and corrals the sensual heat of the bride, however momentarily. The songs articulate concerns about and expectations for the event and the future, making it possible for the gathered bodies and minds to share feelings simultaneously through their common vocalizations and movements. The emotional arc of the marriage process is experienced through these performances, borrowed by those who have not yet married and relived by those who have.

Marriage is most often not the simple binding together of two individuals who love one another. Those two individuals embody complex social, political, and financial negotiations. And ultimately, marriage causes a breach, albeit a fracturing that is expected to be beneficial and generative. The position of the bride and groom in their families and communities will be altered forever, but so too will their communities be changed, for marriage can encompass legal acts, social and political connections, family alliances, monetary exchange, and religious and cultural obligations, all the while holding out hopes for the future, including progeny. Perhaps to mitigate the potentially destabilizing effects of marriage, in addition to the rite performed by their religious officials, communities around the world have developed practices and ceremonial activities to articulate and assuage expectations and concerns raised by the new relationships. Rituals like thel and mehendi ceremonies can be as important to community members as official, religious sanctification or legal affirmation of the union.

Lamentation as the Sonic Expression of Sorrow

The scenes from the British Pakistani mehendi context outlined above contain one significant element from Greg Urban's generalized description of lamentation: that is, a mournful, downward-arcing musical line (sung by the older women at the event) imbued with the capacity to make others weep (the bride breaks down in tears during the first part of the event). Urban's general description of lament includes the following attributes: the existence of a musical line marked by a characteristic intonational contour and rhythmical structure; the use of various icons of crying; and the absence of an actual addressee, which renders wailing an overtly monologic or expressive device, although as a public performance it will be overheard.[5] The cry break, the voiced inhalation, the creaky voice, and the falsetto vowel have been described as an "icon of crying." These phenomena refer to timbre rather than pitch or rhythm, and they are all found within the sonic domain of human crying. Although Greg Urban derives these attributes from the lamentation of Amerindian groups in Brazil,[6] they also aptly describe the sonic aspects of lament in northern Greece, Bihar Northern India, Russia, and Finland.

The process of lamentation produces a persistent state of tension in relation to the audience. The lamenter speaks to one who is absent, but the lament is not a confidential outpouring intended only for ears no longer present; it is designed to be heard and observed by those who are present but not addressed. Because laments are addressed to someone, they incorporate speech. And, because they are performances meant to be observed, they make use of musical features found in the local culture mixed with some of the sonic markers for lamentation as described above. But the sound of lament is an uneasy combination of crying, speaking, and singing.[7] There is an unresolved opposition between personal dedication and aesthetic performance that parallels the tension between expressive abandonment and demonstrative control.

Lamentation in Greek Communities: The Resonances of Death in Marriage

Greek Orthodox communities have a longstanding tradition of death lamentation, a tradition with roots in the pagan rituals of war and recovery of early Greece long before Christianity arrived and documented in many classical texts in which women's lamentation articulates the emotions men cannot utter themselves.[8] In rural Greek Orthodox Potomia, lamentation is used for collective mourning, to articulate the despair of individuals by allowing others to share the burden, and to draw out the emotions of those who are suffering loss. Grievers must somehow accommodate themselves to the disappearance of a loved one and try to prepare themselves for a new state of being that does not include the presence of the person for whom the laments are sung. The burden of disempowerment and rage caused by an inability to alter the circumstances is soothed and controlled through collective lamentation. Laments are also understood to aid the dead by accompanying the departed soul on the way to its next destination.[9]

In a performance of funeral laments from Potomia, a rural village in northern Greece, recorded by Loring Danforth in the early 1980s, a group of women is gathered in the local cemetery.[10] With the sound of the priest chanting the service for the dead audible in the background, the women take turns reminding themselves of the person who has died. One woman utters a sigh with the sound "ach" and then sings the first few words of a lament in a trembling voice. As her voice leaps up a fourth, the rest of the group joins her on the descent down a whole step and then a minor third to their beginning/resting tone. Together they delicately ornament the middle note with mordent and turning gestures, repeating the descent pattern and interpolating repetitions of the ornamental motives until they finish their text. They occasionally fall below the home tone on the way down or rise above the fourth for emphasis in the middle of their verses. When they reach a momentary cessation of singing, another sigh and a few words begin the pattern again with new text. Topics articulated reference the specifics of the death concerned, praiseworthy attributes of the deceased, the suffering and bravery of the survivors, anger at the deceased, and calls for all who hear to sympathize. Occasionally, a lamenter begins lyrics that are perhaps not as familiar to her fellow mourners, who then trail further behind her melodically but persist in following her lead through the new text. The mournful sound is enhanced by the heterophonic variance in the melodic lines. Individual women are credited with composing the texts for specific deceased individuals, but although composed originally for particular people, lament texts and melody are then used and reused as necessary. The most moving and most powerful texted melodies maintain their connections to their composers for many years.[11]

In Potomia, contextual differences are encoded in the performed melody through declamation, vocal timbre, and ornamentation style. On the first day of ritual mourning, the lead lamenter's voice quavers and trembles. She employs a small, quick vibrato, and the sound of the rest of the voices is collectively breathy and weak. Progressively stronger voices are used for lamentations performed at commemorations marking moments that are increasingly further from the day of the death.

The lyrics and the basic melody of each lament will be relatively similar wherever it is performed, but there is clearly some elemental improvisation in the performance of these laments. Word order can be changed; phrases can be repeated and interrupted in places for sighs and envoiced breaths. Gail Holst-Warhaft has noted that when the same songs are sung at weddings, the style is more forceful, vigorous, and even joyful; the melody is more elaborate, with trills and light melismatic phrases. At death rites, the style is more somber and restrained, the melody more conjunct and less elaborated.[12] In addition, the funeral lament may be punctuated with sharp cries, sobs, sighs, murmurings, and sudden intakes of breath—sounds of deep grief that are not included when the laments are sung for the onset of a new married life.

> "My little partridge, beautiful and proud,
> how can you sleep alone out on the mountainsides, out in the fields?
> Aren't you afraid of the hawks and the vultures?"
> "The hawks are my brothers; the vulture is my father."

This text is from a rural Greek wedding lament that is sung as a Potomian bride leaves her family home. In it, the bride "speaks" to an imagined partridge, a defenseless, exposed, ground-dwelling bird without cover in the world. The bride tells the partridge about the hawks and vultures, leaving analogies to her new male in-laws unspoken but present and perhaps implicating her own father at the same time. The multiple talons and sharp beaks of these birds of prey contrast with the benignity and helplessness of the partridge, who is alone on the mountainside as the bride will be alone in her new home. Sung as the bride departs from her mother and family to be delivered into the realm of her in-laws, she is depicted simultaneously as live prey and dead carrion to be ravaged according to the individual tastes by her new family members, both male and female.[13] Like the soul of one who has died, the bride leaves the sphere of the familiar to enter into that of the strange and new, where the familiar is no longer accessible; both the deceased and wedded are aided in their transition by the sound and words of lamentation. This image contrasts starkly with the joy and happy anticipation common to many other marriage traditions around the world and, indeed, different moments in those same Greek Orthodox weddings. Joyful anticipation and mournful lamentation articulate two perspectives on the same experience, for they suggest the unpredictability of the outcome of the movement of two, usually young, people from the status of children to adults. Both responses express awareness of the possibility of failure and unhappiness amid a desire for success on the part of families who are marrying off children who are themselves products of unions that would likely have begun with similar anticipatory anxiety and confrontation of the unknown.

In Potomia, as mothers and daughters work through the various elements of preparation for the wedding ritual, they sing laments at every stage of the procedure. Laments are also sung by the groom's female relatives as they mourn the passing of his youthful existence and decry the emotional distance his new adulthood, and his new wife, will place between him and his female relatives. Some laments suggest that the groom's experience with the foreignness of his bride's family, not to mention the foreignness of the bride herself, is similar to journeying to a foreign (*xena*) place that is unknowable to the untraveled or those who remain, a place that is identified with the unknowingness associated with death.[14]

The following wedding lament, once again also used at funerals, was recorded by anthropologist Loring Danforth in Potomia in the 1970s.

"DOWN BY THE RIVER"

Down by the river Dhafnos,
by the dense rose bushes,
there, three partridges are singing.
But one partridge isn't singing.
"My little partridge, why aren't you singing?"
"Why should I sing? What should I say?
I abandoned my mother
without any solace.
Don't cry, my sweet mother
Don't have a heavy heart.
Our fate has written
that we must be parted.
Go home, mother.
Farewell.[15]

Danforth notes that when sung at a funeral, this lament "emphasizes the unavoidable nature of the separation that takes place at death. It also suggests the complete break in communication which occurs when the deceased crosses the boundary (represented perhaps by the river) separating the living from the dead."[16] Note also that just as the flow of water in a river cannot be halted, so too the inexorable progression toward one's fate is inevitable. When used for marriage rituals, "this lament is sung while the bride, the silent partridge, stands, surrounded by her female relatives and friends, awaiting the arrival of the groom [and his entourage] to take her away."[17] The departure of the daughter from her mother, a long-imagined and (even) desired event, literally since birth, is about to be realized. While the arrival of the groom's party is awaited, normal daily activity and even the flurry of wedding preparations come to a momentary standstill. Anticipation of the impending departure is over, and distraction from the feelings of loss is no longer possible. Lamentation is the only activity left with which to articulate and perform the grief generated by the recognition of the situation that is now real. The bride and the deceased are depicted as subject to the inevitable nature of fate, which perhaps serves as some small comfort to those who are "left behind," even while they voice their sorrow. Embedded as it is in the life-cycle process of the communities, lamentation provides and demonstrates both affirmation and continuance even as it articulates discontinuity. This dual function mitigates to different extents the permanence of the separation from both the dead and the wed.

Public lamentation—both the singing of the sound and the hearing it articulated by others—separates the grief from the singers and listeners as well as the other mourners. Sung out into the world, grief is externalized. It is moved beyond those who suffer; the emotional burden is shifted, however momentarily, to the shoulders of the community members who can hear the lament. When laments are sung for someone who has died, the performers may be professional mourners. In the lamentation sung in the context of weddings, the women involved often perform for themselves. The departing bride herself participates in the lamenting. She who is being mourned, also mourns—something that is not possible during a funeral. The dialogic experience of wedding laments reflects the embodied continuation of all those engaged in the wedding and profoundly changes the emotional experience of performing and hearing the lament when compared to lamentation sung for someone who has died.

Karelian Wedding Laments and the Folkloric Legacy

Karelian lamentation, or *itkuvirsi*, is found in eastern Finland and has roots in the ancestor worship of the ancient Karelian folk religion and Eurasian shamanism, as is evident in the ecstatic and trance-like manner of its performances.[18] As in the Greek communities above, lamentation in this region is also found predominantly among Orthodox Christians, although there is some evidence that Lutherans from the same area also lamented.[19] Karelian wedding laments, now nearly extinct, were sung in the context of Christian weddings and, like the laments in the Greek tradition, accompanied many aspects of the wedding preparation.[20] Their performance was an opportunity to comment on the intricacies of the rituals and served also to confer efficacy on the ritual acts. At the start of the preparations for a wedding, a lamenter *olallinen*—an older female relative or a professional—moved into the house of the bride. Many of these lamenters were skillful in singing runes, sections of the *Kalevala*, which is now considered the Finnish national epic.[21] They were also experienced performers of wedding songs, which were generally sung in a fixed structure with a soloist and chorus. Laments, on the other hand, were a more extemporaneous outpouring of grief with texts based on common metaphors and textual formulae but strung together with words, melodies, and sighs created to reflect the emotions of the moment.

The bride herself did not necessarily lament officially until just before her departure from her family with the groom, although it was a credit to the bride if she could hold herself together well enough to sing her own laments.[22] There is no indication in the literature that skill in lamentation was deemed essential for all women in Karelian society as it was in Potomia in the 1980s, but the fact that brides were to sing at least one lament in their wedding preparations suggests that all women were expected to have some capability in lamenting. The first lament was sung at the betrothal ceremony, and others were sounded at subsequent points in the ritualized process, for example, at the preparation of wedding food, beer, and gifts and at the formal farewell to the bride's relatives and friends.[23]

Beloved woman who carried me
treasured one who bore me
shining one who brings my hems.

You should have suffocated me, you who
crooned to me, you should have struck me
on straw, you who carried me,
dunked me in the marsh, you who reared me,
with your hand you should have moved sand,
you who soothed me, with your finger,
plucked gravel, you who readied me.

You should have put me into warmer sand,
you who gave me warmth, pressed me into
gravelly swamps, you who soothed me.

I would have lain, you who brought me to earth,
warm in my sand, you who gave me warmth,
in the protection of gravel, you who soothed me.

Then you, too, would have been untroubled,
you who cared for me,
unpained by my familiar form, you who bore me,
you who washed me after my birth.[24]

In this Karelian bride's lament, actually sung during the betrothal ceremony, the singer suggests that the mother of the bride, who is described with increasing praise throughout the lament, would have done better to abandon her baby—now the bride singing the lament—in any of various places in the forbidding, soothing—in this context—outside world.[25] Such hardships and even death would have been preferable to the pain both mother and bride feel at the impending departure of the daughter to her husband's family home. The persistent contrasts of the harsh but benevolent—in comparison to the torture of separation—gravel, sand, and straw with the soothing, warming nurture of the mother propel the emotional trajectory of the lament forward, ending, as it were, at the beginning, with the most intimate and bonding of moments, the first bathing after birth. As in many wedding laments, mourning is interlaced with anticipation of various sorts, since it can be expected that the bride herself will experience that same bonding moment, with her own baby, in the near future.

Like the Greek laments, Karelian wedding lamentation is constructed of melodic gestures that descend only a small interval—in this case a fifth—with multiple shorter descents inside each phrase. The melodies of the funeral laments are almost inaudible due to copious sighing, sobbing, and voice breakings, not only at the beginnings and ends of phrases but throughout. In contrast, wedding laments are performed by some singers with a near-steady pulse. The melodic arc of the descending gesture is abundantly audible, as are the delicate elaborations that occasionally ornament the internal notes. Some wedding-lament performances, especially those by women born in the late 1870s and recorded between 1939 and 1950, do have audible sighs and small sobs with tremulous vocal timbres, suggesting an aesthetic shift from the late nineteenth century, when those women learned to lament, to the mid-twentieth century, when they and other younger singers were recorded.[26]

The Karelian wedding lamentation tradition was already well in decline in the 1980s. All of the women still singing at that point had learned to lament in rural settings prior to World War II. It is likely that the wedding ritual traditions were already changing at the beginning of the twentieth century since the Kalevala Society, an organization devoted to the nurture and documentation of Finnish cultural traditions and literature, saw fit to film a reenactment of a Karelian wedding in 1920. The film was shot on location in Suojäri, Finland, with local volunteers performing as the cast.[27] The film shows the ritual welcome of the (in this case) male matchmaker and then the groom's family to the bride's home, a traditional wooden house. Members of the groom's party offer money to the fireplace in the house and bring a token bride price to show their commitment and good intention. They are given cloths and bolts of linen in exchange, and a dialogue takes place.[28] The bride is asked if she agrees to the proposed marriage. Once she gives her assent, and after various rituals involving bread and salt have been performed, the groom's party leaves. The bride's mother performs a lament when the bride is awakened on her wedding day. Lamentation is represented on screen throughout the ritual bathing and other preparations for the bride's departure with the groom's family. The lamenters are shown to cry with a white cloth clutched to the right side of their faces, covering their open mouths in order to prevent evil spirits from entering. The bride herself is shown to lament kneeling on a pelt while pitching her face into the lap of her mother after her hair has been symbolically unbound by her godmother and a cloth placed over her head. She is then bidden farewell by everyone in her family, each of whom raises a loaf of bread over her head three times. Gesturing with long tree boughs, people draw protective circles on the ground around the wedding party as it departs. Multiple horse-drawn buggies return to the groom's house, whence his party had come. The carriages pass through purifying fires lit at the entrance to the groom's family land. The arrival of the bride at the groom's family home is a happy moment. No lamentation is sung at this point. Instead, the groom's family welcomes the bride by performing the same actions earlier performed in the bride's house, albeit in reverse order. Bread is raised over the heads of the bride and groom before they enter the groom's house, and the bride throws money into the fireplace of what will become her new home. The bride's hair, previously unbraided by her godmother is now re-braided by her mother-in-law, who twines her braids around her head in the manner worn by married women. After these events, feasting begins and there is dancing.

There is no suggestion in the film of a blessing or ritual of approval conferred by any church authority, although the bride's hair is ritually unbraided by a woman identified as her godmother, suggesting a Christian context. Christianity had already been deeply embedded in Finnish culture for nearly eight hundred years by the beginning of the twentieth century. The first successful attempt to convert the Finns to Christianity was during a crusade led by King Eric of Sweden in 1157 CE, and they became predominantly Lutheran during the Reformation. Perhaps the reenactment in the film was an attempt to highlight the elements of the wedding ritual that were determined to be essentially folkloristically Finnish, as in pre-Christian, although the technological developments, the clothing and the comportment of the actors represented in the film clearly date from a time long after the introduction of Christianity into Finland.

Beyond the lamenting by women throughout the film, the only representations of performance are in one scene in which a man plucks tentatively at a three-stringed dulcimer of some kind[29] while awaiting the first arrival of the groom's party, and in several scenes, occurring throughout the various stages of the wedding, in which people are shown to be dancing in modulating pairs. This dancing suggests that lamentation is only appropriate for those who will experience the changes wrought by the wedding directly; for others, it is important to represent the joyous, celebrative aspects of the wedding.[30] The presence of wedding lamentation in such a reenactment and the maintenance of knowledge of the performance of wedding laments by women into the 1980s are potentially indicative of the significance of lamentation in the wedding rituals of previous centuries. This significance is echoed in the *Kalevala* itself. The folklorist Elias Lönnrot, who at the end of the nineteenth century constructed the first written narrative of the Finnish epic, wove the poems and words of women wedding singers, from whom he had collected songs, into the runes themselves. The majority of the runes in Poems 19 and 20, which describe Pohjola weddings, were collected from several women rune singers of White Sea Karelia who were themselves performers of wedding songs and laments.[31] Many of the women lamenters with whom Elizabeth Tolbert worked in the 1980s were skilled in this full range of performance genres, from wedding laments and bridal songs to extemporaneous outpourings of grief using traditional metaphors and runic singing, the storytelling technique recounting the epic tales of the *Kalevala*.

Wedding Lamentation in Traditional Orthodox Communities

The two wedding lamentation traditions discussed so far occur within Orthodox Christian communities. In both Greece and the Baltic areas other varieties of Christianity are also practiced, yet lamentation is not an important feature in those Christian communities. What is particularly Orthodox about lamentation? It could be that these lamentation traditions are persistent because they occur in rural communities, but not all rural communities around the world—or in the region, more specifically—have lamentation traditions. In Christian contexts, lamentation traditions have left their traces wherever the Eastern Orthodox Church has spread—mostly through eastern and southeastern Europe. Wedding laments have been documented in some detail in Romania, parts of Russia, Lithuania, and Bulgaria. Although there appear to be few detailed ethnographic studies in common scholarly languages, in addition to their performance in the locales specifically addressed here, women's lamentation traditions in Christian Orthodox communities are known to have existed in Hungary, Slovakia, Albania, and Croatia as well.[32]

It is striking that these Orthodox lamentation traditions are often discussed without mention of their connection to Orthodox Christian contexts. It is true that the tradition has roots reaching back well beyond the beginning of Christianity: Greek women performed lamentations at funerals and weddings throughout the region during the Greek classical period and likely long before.[33] But it is not common to find this kind of lamentation in Orthodox communities beyond the limits of the political control of the Greek and Roman empires. Whatever the historical, political, and economic connections between these dispersed communities, they all share a history of Christianity connected to localizing of the Eastern traditions. Lamentation traditions may have existed before and in parallel to the practice of Christianity, but we must be wary of assigning too radical a distinction between the two. As is evident from some of the recordings made by Danforth, priests perform last rites for deceased members of the community while women lament the approaching death within earshot. Even as women lament each event in the marriage process, the couple still sojourns to the church for a Christian blessing and religious consecration. The women described here identify as Christian. They lament at events that require the involvement of the church, involvement that includes officiation by local village priests.[34] Just like the official Christian activities surrounding funerals and weddings, women's lamentation is precisely focused and lies outside everyday practice. It would be misleading to characterize the relationship between lamentation and Christianity in these communities as distinct. It should also be noted that the Orthodox Church has crafted elaborate lamentation traditions for both Jesus and Mary, the structures and performances of which parallel women's laments to some degree.[35]

The early Byzantine Church was tolerant of the myriad pagan and mystical traditions that had gradually been incorporated into Greek culture through the expansion of the territories during the Hellenistic period; beginning in the third century BCE Pagan and Christian elements were both present at the founding of Constantinople in 330CE. By the fourth or fifth century CE there had been little change since antiquity in the religious practices of towns and villages, and the situation remained largely unaltered through the twelfth century. This continuity favored the survival of lamenting rituals and their incorporation into Christian contexts, for the business of death and marriage had been and continued to be a community concern primarily located in the domain of women.[36] Regarding the situation in twentieth-century Greece, Margaret Alexiou noted that the church had no need to take a hostile attitude toward what had once occasionally been viewed as pagan; the two were thoroughly integrated. Popular culture, she wrote, had accommodated itself to Christianity, and the church had agreed to tolerate elements that it had discouraged at various points in history.[37]

The wedding laments performed in these Orthodox Christian communities are used to articulate sonically the many prescribed and ritualized acts in the process of marriage as practiced locally. They sound the step-by-step separation of the bride and groom from their positions in their birth families and the gradual incorporation of the two, both individually and as a new couple, into the fabric of the community. In a funeral ritual, laments for communication between life and death, the past and the present, the physical and the metaphysical are sung. The lamenter is a mediator between the living and the dead. Her voice accompanies the soul of the dead while confirming the continuance of life for those still living. The lamenter influences the entire community through her performance because "the poetry is not merely descriptive or expressive but effective as well."[38] The lamenters at a wedding mediate between the familiar and the foreign, the innocent and the mature, and the present and the absent while aiding the progress of the bride to her new status and location. The strong, forceful tone of their voices excludes the possibility of hearing the wedding lament as just as definitively sorrowful as a lament at a funeral, despite the pangs of loneliness and fear that may afflict mother and daughter. Through lamentation, Orthodox women connect one life-changing rite of passage to another, modulating the effect of the performances while aurally conveying the experiences of the women and family involved to the community at large.

Early Appropriations of Women's Lamentation in Greek Literature

Representations of lamentation in early Greek literature go back as far as the fifth century BCE. Greek tragedy appropriated the passion and potential destructive capabilities of performed sorrow by incorporating the language, music, and gesture of traditional women's lament. Aeschylus's play *The Persians* ends with a complicated scene in which the foreign prince Xerxes serves as leader of the lamenting chorus as he tells the story of the defeat of his army. He enters into the frenzied madness of performed public lament, rending his clothes and exhorting the chorus to respond to his wails. The representation of extreme collective grief, usually performed by women in Greece, is here embodied in a foreign, failed military leader. He is feminized and disenfranchised as a male leader. This construction of lamentation can be seen as negative commentary on foreign "barbarians," but it can also be read as a subtle decentering of the potency of women's lamentation. In embedding lamentation into a play, Aeschylus simultaneously provided an emotional outlet for men in the audience to experience the violence of grief, as performed by male actors, while denying women any public role in the aesthetic representation of the ritual drama they customarily created and appropriating any political and social power that could accrue to women's public lamentation.[39]

Gail Holst-Warhaft argues that Aeschylus was the first to suggest in a written format the threat posed by female mourning to the state and to male authority.[40] She states that through the development of classical Greek tragedy, "we are witnessing the transformation of Greek, perhaps of western art in general, from an art where women's voices are heard in all the remembered force of their pain and anger as they addressed the community over the bodies of the dead, to one where their rhetoric is only a memory of dubious significance."[41] This damning appraisal of Greek perspectives on women's public lamentation is based on an examination of Greek tragedies that spans the history of the ancient genre. Batya Weinbaum describes the influence of lament on Greek literature from another angle, arguing that "lament poetry, as sung by women, who were responsible for spiritual mediation of burials and grieving, actually gave rise to the feel, structure, and texture of the poems known as the *Odyssey* and the *Iliad*." She proposes that the public expression of the great sorrow of these epics finds its source in the lament poetry sung by the women of early Greece.[42] Either way, the structure and affect of women's lament permeates Greek literary works and history.

Women's lamentation in Greece and elsewhere may have had a similar effect on the development of localized traditions of Orthodox Christianity.[43] Greek Orthodox Christians practice what they understand to be the original ancient traditions established by St. Paul and the apostles. In nondoctrinal matters, however, the church absorbed practices from local Middle Eastern, Slavic, and Greek cultures, believing that scripture does not determine practice but that the biblical texts came out of tradition. According to Orthodox doctrine, humanity is rooted in two distinct characteristics—matter and spirit—the relationship of which generates the possibility of transcendence. When a person dies, the soul is only temporarily separated from the body. Before body and soul are reunited at the final judgment the state of the soul can be affected by love and prayers from the living.[44] The idea of an individual with a unique soul that requires personalized tending reverses an earlier Greek philosophical tendency to understand the individual by reference to the collective; the concept of the individual was peripheral or eccentric. That which was individual and specific to one person could not be used to illuminate human nature.[45]

The Orthodox understanding of the relationship of the soul to the body may help explain the persistence of lamentation in Orthodox Christian communities. Although lamentation is a collective process, properly performed by many women communally, ethnographic evidence from Loring Danforth and Margaret Alexiou suggests that the performance is intended to accompany the deceased on its journey and ease the pain of separation for those who remain, especially those individuals who are most afflicted by the loss. This connection between the focus on the individual lost and individual loss is a synergy between local practice and dogma that may have fostered the maintenance of lamentation in Orthodox communities around the world well into the twentieth centuries, while similar traditions in places like Finland—which embraced Lutheranism in the Reformation—have faded.[46]

It is frequently proposed that the Orthodox Churches may have been more lenient in their acceptance of the emotional excesses of women's lamentation traditions than the Western Catholic or later Protestant Churches.[47] But, as Alexiou notes, the Greek Orthodox Church has also intermittently tried to suppress lamentation much in the same way as Aeschylus and his fellow dramatists.[48] Yet, as far back as the sixth century, the sorrow of Mary on Jesus's crucifixion was deemed worthy of ecclesiastical lamentation, with many hymns describing the scene using images of Greek female lamentation.[49] There are traces of women's laments and mourning rituals in early Easter, Passion, and Lord's Supper traditions in the Orthodox traditions. Angela Standhartinger suggests that mourning rituals and lament traditions are presupposed and theologically reflected upon by some of the early Easter and Passion accounts. In particular, she finds resonances in descriptions of the care for Jesus's body, which is anointed with oils, as were the bodies of other deceased loved ones, as well as in the visits to the Tomb, where the conversations suggest the role of laments as mediators between the world of the living and that of the dead.[50] The patterns of women's lamentation traditions are embedded in descriptions of the major events described in the Bible. These patterns localized the practices of the first Christians and have continued to function as localizing forces throughout Orthodox Christian history.[51]

Bihari Hindu Wedding Laments: Tuneful Weeping and the Creation of a Voice

Lamenting traditions were once spread widely across northern South Asia from Bangladesh to Rajasthan and into Pakistan. James Wilce suggests that the pressures of urbanization, Islamization, and Christian missionizing have had a muting effect on this—formerly prominent—culturally diverse, women's expressive tradition in the region.[52] Research by scholars investigating relatively new rituals—no more than a century old—performed by Shia Muslim women during the mourning month of Muharram in Punjabi communities in Pakistan suggests that lamentation is something that is current. Gatherings called *majalis* in which women sing lamentation songs called *marsiya*, hear sermons by female preachers on Muslim piety, and beat their chests while singing *noha*, or mourning couplets that recall the tragedy at Karbala, are an important part of the month-long annual mourning period.[53] The authors do not mention whether the songs sung at these mourning rituals bear any trace connections to older forms of lamentation from the period when the community was better integrated with the Hindu community less than one hundred years ago, although they do note that there was use of "Indian beats" in some of the songs.[54]

Writing in the late 1990s, James Wilce notes that "South Asia has recently begun to undergo a privatization of grief paralleling the privatization of feudal lands and, more recently, of India's industries."[55] Despite the long history of the public expression of grief and vocal communal support for grievers, a number of scholars have found an increasing rejection of those (primarily female) expressive genres.[56] At that time, however, some lamentation traditions did continue, but in the more rural areas of the region. One such tradition documented by Kapil Muni Tiwary involves a form of wedding lamentation practiced in the region in Hindu Bihar, in Northeastern India. In the communities Tiwary studied, it is the bride who must leave her familial home, moving to live among her husband's family, a group of people she may not know well. Once it becomes certain that a girl will be marrying and a date for her departure from her home has been set, women in the community who are closely associated with the bride-to-be begin to practice what is called tuneful weeping.[57] The women of the village start visiting the bride: "She greets them all by crying on their shoulders. The visitor and the girl sit down with one's head on the other's shoulder, their arms enfolding each other, and weep tunefully."[58] The weeping session "may last from five to fifteen minutes. . . . [T]he more affectionate the bond between the weeping partners," the longer the pair weeps. The older woman of the pair is responsible for stopping the weeping, and she usually has to spend a few minutes engaged in persuading the younger woman, who is most often the bride, to stop. The bride will also weep with her family members in a similar pattern. The weeping, however, is organized and coordinated. "The weepers weep out well-made statements; their weeping is tuneful; their wept statements have a marked structure. Every statement ends with a refrain which is made up of the term of address which the girl uses for her weeping partner [Aunt, Father's Sister, Sister, Grandmother, etc.]."[59] There is a hierarchy of aesthetics for tuneful weeping. "Some weepers sound more tuneful than others," and some exhibit a "greater artistry and effectiveness," adjudged by the emotional impact on the audience. "Women comment on each other's ability to move people deeply by their weeping."[60] Young girls begin weeping training early, by enacting weddings with their dolls and practicing their tuneful weeping when the doll bride is carried off to the doll groom's home.

While both women and men in these communities weep from sadness and cry when injured physically or emotionally, only women weep in this tuneful, organized way in anticipation of the departure of a bride and when reunited with those whom they have long not met. Their wept statements may contain references to past moments when the weeping pair lived together without threat of separation; fear of "an unknown place"; "apologies for not having been as dutiful or respectful" as one might have been; requests for forgiveness for past failings; and pleas to never be forgotten.[61] Women do sometimes engage in tuneful weeping to men, often their brothers, fathers, or uncles, but men never engage in tuneful weeping in response; instead, they try to quiet the weeper with advice and soothing words. This is suggestive of the male preference for non-expression of emotion publically, the trend that has gradually expanded through the region reaching out from the urban areas.

Tuneful weepings always take place in public. While the weeping is certainly addressed directly to one's weeping partner, the concerns voiced are meant to be heard and understood by others as well. Hence, tuneful weeping can also be used as an effective lobbying tool, especially given the propensity of men who are wept at to calm the weeper and restore the peace. When a bride's male relatives come for the customary visit to her in her new abode, the bride may take that opportunity to weep as one would on meeting someone from whom one has been long separated. The respectful bride, abjectly clasping the feet of her male natal relatives, may talk about how much she misses "the loving kindness of the kin at her parents' [home]" and describe the differences she experiences in her new house. She may focus on the treatment she receives from her mother-in-law and how she perceives her own, certainly lower, situation in the new house. While her male kin soothe her, the new bride also has a moment in which to articulate her complaints about her aspects of her new living situation, an opportunity that would not otherwise be available to her. This kind of weeping can also be used in conflict resolution. A woman engaged in an argument may stop arguing and start lamenting. Tunefully weeping alone, she may express her grievances and complaints about the men and/or women with whom she has been arguing; she may also threaten and outline possible paths to consensus.[62] The opportunity to express an oppositional opinion in public is not usually available to newly married girls. The public resistance of girls to their new contexts or the choices others have made for them can have a destabilizing effect within the community. It should be noted that like the other wedding laments mentioned in this chapter, the lamentations of the Bihari women have a parallel performance mode that expresses the grief of the lamenter and of the community when someone dies.[63]

Unlike the wedding laments in the Orthodox Christian examples, the wedding laments of Bihar do not sound the particularities of the progress through a series of ritualized steps even as they sonically identify the relationship of the weepers to one another with their duration and intensity. Although they do gradually prepare the way for the separation of the bride from her family, friends, and home, they resound throughout the community in daily, often impromptu, interactions in any place in the village. People who share the expectation of the imminent departure of someone they hold close will meet and express their grief, anticipation, and joy about that separation. In the street or in homes, the weepings can happen anywhere and anytime and so sound the emotions and fill the spaces around the wedding preparations rather than the wedding events themselves. The spontaneous nature of tuneful weeping may suggest that in the Bihari world, women's emotions flow freely, encompassing both female and public spaces and perhaps even forming a background to most public engagement since the possibility of tuneful weeping as a form of dissent is persistently present. Other examples of women lamenting the departure of new brides and others abound in the region. In the Kangra region, in northwestern India, several genres regularly sung by women, in particular by the bride's girlfriends, focus on the departure of the bride to her new home and the general sadness of departure. Kirin Narayan reports that one of these genres, *suhāg*, is associated with melancholy and women generally weep while they are singing. The songs are often sung around the bride in a relatively continuous manner from the beginning of the three-day wedding ritual.[64]

In noting that women suffered enormously under the modernization processes brought to northern India by the British, Sumanta Banerjee suggests that it was British colonial interference in local performance practice that spelled the decline in the acceptance of the public expression of women's grief.[65] She points out that prior to the end of the nineteenth century, public lamentation, both for funerals and weddings, as well as the singing of religious songs by women, was a common occurrence. She examines two kinds of religious songs performed during the annual Durga Puja. One type, *agamani* songs, welcome Durga who is constructed as a domesticated Bengali bride. Durga's arrival each year is "visualized as the homecoming of the bride. In the agamani songs, the devotees' longing for an audience with the goddess becomes the palpable craving of a lonely mother for the company of her long lost daughter. . . . [T]he vijaya songs express the mother's sorrow at the departure of her daughter: the immersion of the goddess Durga becomes an excuse to give vent to the pangs of separation that every Bengali mother suffers when her daughter leaves for the home of her husband."[66] Durga is domesticated, treated as a daughter who returns to her natal home for a short time and then must depart again. The songs performed for the puja lament the distance between mother (Bengali women) and daughter (Durga). One song translated and quoted in Banerjee scolds the daughter's husband for selling away her dowry in order to enhance his own pleasure.

> My Gauri [another name for Uma/Durga]
> is a precious bumble-bee.
> All the clothes and ornaments of Uma,
> That bounder has sold away
> To smoke his hemp![67]

While there is no record of these songs being sung as laments at weddings, that Durga is imagined as a bride and laments are sung at her departure for the return to her "husband's family home" suggests that the idea of lamenting at weddings is familiar to these nineteenth-century Bengali women.

Interpretations of women's public singing, whether in Bihar, Kangra, or Bengal can be further enhanced by reference to the stories of the female characters that populate well-known epics such as Radha, the milk-maid consort of Krishna, or

Sita, the wife of Rama, who follows him into exile. Examining the ways in which women elaborate on those stories, branching away from the main events, to present their own interpolations is particularly revealing. Banerjee notes that in the Bengali *kavi* songs, once again the gods and demi-gods are "deglamourized" as Krishna and Radha are depicted as "a rustic young couple" who are "in a daring adulterous and incestuous relationship—expressing the same fears and hopes, wounded pride and blissful consummation that are the lot of ordinary mortals in love."[68] These songs are part of a long Bengali tradition, visible in the nineteenth-century British record, of using the Radha-Krishna tale as a vehicle for airing the grievances and desires of women by poets and everyday women, women of high caste and low, rich or poor in their various traditions.[69]

The patriarchal social system of Indian literary epics has little room for women's desires of any sort, however. Desire is a flaw that can lead to serious consequences. In the *Ramayana,* Sita is abducted by Ravana, falling into this terrible situation because of her desire for a beautiful golden deer, actually an evildoer intent on entrapment, who passes by their forest encampment. When her husband Rama reluctantly agrees to chase after the deer in order to satisfy Sita's desire, he leaves Sita in the protection of Laksmana. When they "hear" Rama's death cry, Sita insists on sending Laksmana to save Rama. The cry was a ruse designed to create a situation in which Sita would be alone without protection. Approached by an old man seemingly in need of aid, Sita is convinced to step outside of the magic circle Laksmana drew to protect her before he left, and Ravana manages to steal Sita away to his kingdom in Lanka. War and many deaths follow as Rama and Laksmana struggle to rescue Sita. Once their quest has been successful and Sita is returned, physically unscathed, to Rama, doubts about Sita's chastity arise, not in Rama's mind (depending on which version one is reading) but in the minds of others, the sharp-tongued, schadenfreude-craving public. To save the kingdom, Rama is forced to cast Sita into exile back into the forest, where he occasionally joins her. She bears two children while she is in exile. Finally, in order for her to return to society, Sita must demonstrate her purity by allowing herself to be burned. If she is pure, she will not burn and will be vindicated.[70] The selection of which elements from this outline are featured in any given rendition depends on who is telling the story, and the ending can be interpreted variously. But one of the basic morals of the story is always the idea that because Sita wanted something unusual, she and her whole family were punished for many years.

The construction of gender roles in the *Ramayana* has been used not only to establish ideals for both men and women but also in Indian nationalist discourse of the twentieth century relating to issues of dedication and loyalty to the government and community of "Mother India."[71] The high valuation of Sita's personal strength in choosing to join her husband in his initial exile in the forest, in bearing up stoically through her own exile (even though it was ostensibly caused by her own weakness) after being rescued from Ravana's kingdom, and in her unwavering commitment to her husband—despite his being cowed by the opinions of others with respect to her chastity—is confirmed in television shows and theatrical performances over and over again. There are female characters in other Indian epics who are individually more effective and powerful than Sita. In the *Mahabharata*, Drupadi is the loyal wife of the five Pandava brothers, heroes of the epic. Despite their prowess in most things martial, Drupadi knows their weaknesses and hastens to point out where they are wrong, either before or after the fact. That the independent-minded, polyandrous Drupadi has not been elevated as a womanly ideal in Indian social and national discourse is not really surprising. While many goddesses are worshipped around Hindu India, the position of women in Hindu communities is muted in some ways and controlled by men and other women—mothers-in-law—in men's contexts.[72]

That the *Ramayana* epic is known by nearly everyone in India cannot be disputed. But not everyone has the same relationship to the epic and not even all Hindus are inclined to interpret the fate of Sita in precisely the same way. Individuals elaborate the stories in their own minds on a daily basis and relate them to their own situations. Bengali poet and scholar of epics Nabaneeta Dev Sen explores the retellings of Sita's story in the work songs of Marathi and Bengali village women.[73] She notes that the stoicism of Sita, exorbitantly lauded in the national discourse on women's place in "Mother India," is replaced with an emphasis on the lamentable aspects of Sita's individual and very female suffering. The songs focus on the minutiae of Sita's life and have her speaking (something she rarely does in most retellings of the epic) to herself and to the listener of the song. In one work song depicting Sita's daily life while in exile, Sita addresses the trees for lack of anyone else. In several songs, Sita wonders what sort of woman she is. Who is she, given to her husband before she could take care of herself, let alone others, and now banished to the forest with only trees for companions? In one Bengali song Sita laments her solitude and her abandonment. Even though she is a royal personage from a family of renown, in the song Sita sings,

> I have no father, no mother
> I was found at the tip of a plough [an orphan]
> I don't know who my parents are
> Like moss in a stream I float.[74]

Another Bengali song queries the way Sita's fate was cast by Brahma.[75] Yet another wonders about the sexual exile Sita suffered during the twelve years she was banished from Rama's kingdom, ignoring the elements of the story in the Sanskrit version that tell of the details of Sita giving birth to Rama's sons while sheltering with Valimiki, the author of the *Ramayana* text, an episode that is more usually recounted. A Marathi song describes Sita's birthing her child alone in the forest:

> Sitabai has given birth
> Where will Sita find nourishment?
> There is no one to cook her a meal.
> There is no cradle for her babies.
> Sitabai has given birth
> The hills and forests are rejoicing
> She has no one else to call her own.[76]

According to Dev Sen, these songs are sung by women at work on a communal project or hummed by a solitary singer as she prepares food, washes clothes, or carries out other daily activities. The singing is intended not for an audience or for public performance but for the singers alone. The uniformity in attitude toward Sita's position is a striking feature across this collection of work songs; similarities can be found even in the form of specific phrases evident when songs in the three different languages chosen by Dev Sen—Bengali, Marathi, and Telugu, which range from northeastern India to the mid-southwest—are compared.

Although there is evidence that women retold the Hindu epics in songs and literature as far back as the sixteenth century (and likely further back), scholars have only recently begun to consider this material seriously.[77] Women have not preserved the particularities of the social mores of the nationalized *Ramayana*. Instead, they give Sita a voice by allowing her to comment on and lament about her life experiences as they, the singers, imagine themselves into her life. These retellings hint at the dissonance between the idealized construction of Sita as the perfect wife and the real-life experiences of everyday women. They imagine Sita as having normal human responses and the temerity to speak her mind about her condition through their own voices.

The delicious rebelliousness of the traditionally "perfect" Sita saying what she thinks is a pleasure most Indian women are denied, at least in public. It should be noted that the songs of these sorts are sung alone or with only other women and that in the songs Sita is herself alone. Nevertheless, that the texts are sung at all reflects mild resistance to social restrictions and solidarity that emerges between the singers and Sita and is of a different sort than that offered in the national narrative.[78]

The rarity of women speaking their thoughts and expressing their desires publicly is precisely what makes the tuneful weeping of the women in Bihar compelling as an expressive tradition. In the context of a marriage and the rupturing of an aspect of the world as they know it, women appropriate the ability to speak publically—often in a mixed-gender setting—for themselves. They articulate their concerns and worries, lament the departure of their own, and—by giving voice to their concerns—hope to affect their own situation or that of a loved one in a significant manner. India's national Hindu construction of the role of women and wives is narrowly focused on the properly modest and docile conduct that is apparently preferred by men, and many women, as being the correct way to ensure auspiciousness to any situation. But in transitional moments like marriage, situations in which women's roles are undeniably at the center, norms can be disturbed. Women take advantage of the possibilities for destabilization in order to make a difference in their own situations and those of others.

Amplifying Italian Catholic Wedding Laments

The last case study for women expressing their sorrow about the changes wrought by the wedding plans of their family in the form of a lament is found in a historical Italian musical tradition that has died out in contemporary Italy. The wedding laments of Catholic Italy are no longer to be found today, with some exceptions perhaps in the far south of the peninsula,[79] but the tradition of wedding lamentation is inscribed in the composed music of several centuries. A cultural and musical map of Italy might be drawn with northern and southern halves, but Marco Sorce Keller suggests that rather than include a sharp line drawn across Italy at the Appennino Settentrionale mountains, we might better imagine a continuum in which Italy is a bridge leading from Europe to the Middle East by way of the Mediterranean. He finds *canti lirico-monostrofici* throughout Italy but ballads, or *canti epico-lirici*, primarily in the north, a result of what he terms the Gallican connection where Celtic languages were once spoken.[80] He points out that the south was once an integral part of the Greek world and southern Italy was "in all respects part of Greece; long after the Roman conquest, Greek remained the everyday language."[81] Given this several-millennia-long connection to Greece and the maintenance of Greek expressive traditions in Italy,[82] there is a logic to the continuation of a strong lamenting tradition in some places in southern Italy despite the negative assessment of lamentation by the Roman Catholic Church, which may have had greater practical effect than the less stringent complaints of the more accepting Orthodox Church. In short, it makes sense that there are vestiges of the lamenting tradition in the areas of Italy that were effectively still culturally Greek after the Roman invasion. In the north, however, the traces of lamenting traditions could still be found in the early seventeenth century, even if they are no longer present.

The most studied northern Italian wedding lament, albeit crafted by a man and thoroughly composed, is that found in the Mantuan court extravaganza at the 1608 springtime wedding of Francesco Gonzaga and Margherita of Savoy, an event burdened with significant political implications for the Mantuan court, the

Gonzaga family, and local hierarchies of power, not to mention a complicated history of family allegiances. The musical performances created for the celebrations were part of this social and political complexity, and many of the creators involved, including composer Claudio Monteverdi and poet/librettist Ottavio Rinuccini, had been employed by the court for a previous royal wedding some ten years earlier and were therefore familiar with the intrigues of court life. The events of May 1608 in Mantua have engendered myriad interpretations not only by modern scholars but also by participants and official historians of the event.[83]

As was common at aristocratic weddings of the time, themes of abandonment, abduction, and general female despair were prominent in performances over the several wedding weeks. Monteverdi's opera *L'Arianna* was one of four presentations featuring these subjects.[84] These themes reveal a persistent connection between funeral and nuptial events in the classical world and in Italy at the time. They also resonate powerfully with issues raised in lamentation at weddings in the Orthodox Christian wedding traditions discussed above. Some have read the tears of women at weddings as a sign of women's awareness of their new subjugation as they transition from being daughters and sisters to being, in the first place, wives and only secondarily daughters or sisters.[85] As shall be suggested here, the representation of a weeping woman at marriage entertainments could also have had other meanings, including latent ritual significance.

Analysis of performed lamentation at the Gonzaga event tells of an import that reaches beyond the pro forma presence of this genre. Anne MacNeil has noted that the connection to classical tales of women who had been deserted on the point of their own marriages—Arianna (Ariadne) sings her famous lament after running away with Teseo (Theseus), who subsequently deserts her when he is called to arms—would likely have had a double effect: it would have both conveyed subtle advice to young women present and neutralized perceptions of impropriety that might have resulted from having a notorious professional female actor—Virginia Andreini—as the affecting lead lamenter in the role of Arianna.[86] Tim Carter describes lament as a site of women's empowerment in a most practical sense. Virginia Andreini herself had a role in urging Monteverdi to include the now famous Arianna's lament in the opera, as a vehicle for her own dramatic and vocal virtuosity. Perhaps this lament was added to the score in exchange for Andreini's agreeing to perform at the last moment, replacing Caterina Martinelli. This addition would also have enhanced Rinuccini's libretto, which was criticized as dry by another powerful woman involved in Gonzaga court life, Duchess Eleanora Medici-Gonzaga, the wife of Vincenzo Gonzaga since 1589, mother of many children and a woman fully engaged in the marriage preparations.[87] A third perspective is provided by Suzanne Cusick's comparison of Monteverdi's Arianna with a later Arianna from 1618 composed by Francesca Caccini. Cusick reveals in Caccini's work a woman who is in control of the stages of loss, rather than tossed about as in Monteverdi's lament. For Caccini's Arianna, there is no despair, no attempted suicide, no outrage or hurled curses; instead, she commands the tropes meant to contain emotions, as is all the more evident when we recognize that Caccini has chosen a form and overt harmonic motion that do not suggest the lament tradition followed by Monteverdi's *Lamento d'Arianna* in which the lamenter is singing because she is rendered nearly mad by grief. Caccini's Arianna performs the control of her grief through the careful repetition, stanza after stanza, of melody, a place where a woman's subjectivity, not her subjugation, might find voice.[88]

Across these three commentaries on Monteverdi's *Lamento d'Arianna* there is not so much disagreement as confirmation of the multiple meanings of the act and image of women lamenting. Arianna is not only deserted and despairing; she is also empowered as she curses Teseo and his offspring. Cursing recalls an older power of woman as shaman and invokes the danger of a woman unhinged. Like the female lamenters who sing at weddings and funerals in the traditions discussed in this chapter, Arianna performs the ripping of the social fabric caused by a departure in an embodied and sonic way and for the benefit of the rest of the community. As compelling as the piece is, Monteverdi's representation of Arianna causes the lamenter and the public act of lamentation to be reduced somewhat as a cultural statement. Arianna as the weeper for her own sorrow, a sole female left on a rock, is different from the groups of professional women who perform laments in Greece or Karelia or southern Italy and, perhaps by cultural connection, in Northern Italy. Alone, she cannot relieve or be relieved by the performed grief of others and so the representation of lamentation on the stage is a personal rather than communal expression by an individual who has lost her loved one. But Arianna also serves as a "community" lamenter expressing grief on behalf of the bride, Margherita of Savoy, and her female relations. MacNeil is right in that the role of lamentation at weddings is deeply cultural and a ritualized means of dealing with departure and change of state for both the bride and the groom. But Carter is also right, for lamenting is an empowering act reserved for women. The image of the helpless Arianna disguises part of the true nature and effect of weeping at departure, women as lamenters, and the act of lamenting, which can also involve the hurling of abuse and curses at the departed in an effort to distance the pain and express one's thoughts. Cusick, too, is right, in that women not only tailor the tropes to their own needs, as did Caccini, but craft their own texts and performances to be appropriate to the situation. They control the potentially destructive power of the grief of the community, dealing with departure by taking into their own bodies the despair of those most directly concerned.

The beautiful and affecting representations of lamentation that were heard on May 28, 1608, were part of a long tradition with roots that date back at least one-and-a-half millennia (using the *Heroides* from which Rinuccini took the story for the opera as an arbitrary endpoint). Hints of the more complicated, richly textured nature of lamentation in Italy as part of the Greek Mediterranean—indicating that Italian lamentation is not just a performance of sadness at impending subjugation—are present even in the moralizing representations from the wedding of Francesco Gonzaga and Margherita of Savoy. Although Arianna sings her own lament alone, it is actually a public performance, for she sings in front of a group of fishermen in the presentation, not to mention in front of the adoring listening public at the 1608 event. This public singing is reminiscent of singing through the rituals that make up the preparation for a wedding. Even though we are invited into the private pain of the character, she is also a public performer who sounds the separation of bride and groom from their parents and natal homes.

With respect to the text of the lament, Rinuccini has skillfully woven together the sorrow and rage of a particular abandoned woman with tropes commonly found in Greek lamentation generally and that also resonate to some degree with themes from marriage laments around the world. For instance, the one who is abandoned can only sit and experience the pain of separation, imagining the process of the departed.

Table 1: Text from the fourth section of Monteverdi's Lamento d'Arianna.

O Teseo, o Teseo mio, se tu sapessi, o Dio! Se tu sapessi, ohimè!, come s'affanna la povera Arianna, forsi forsi pentito rivolgeresti ancor la prora al lito. Ma, con l'aure serene tu te ne vai felice, et io qui piango. A te prepara Atene liete pompe superbe, et io rimango cibo di fere in solitarie arene. Te l'uno e l'altro tuo vecchio parente stringeran lieti, et io più non vedrovi, o madre, o padre mio!	Oh, Theseus, o my Theseus, if you only knew, oh God! Alas, if you only knew the terrible fear poor Ariadne is suffering, perhaps you would relent and point your prow back to the shore. But, you leave with joy on gentle breezes, while I lament here. For you, Athens is preparing joyful proud ceremonies, and I remain food for beasts on these lonely sands. You will again joyfully embrace your happy aged parents but, oh mother, oh father, I will never see you again.

Fourth section of Monteverdi's *Lamento d'Arianna*, translation from http://www.operafolio.com/libretto.asp?n=L_Arianna&language=UK&print=y (accessed 28 January 2018)

Arianna points out the increasing pain and suffering she endures, trapped and abandoned on the rock while thinking of Teseo as he moves away from her. Her pain increases as she imagines him imagining the pleasures awaiting him on his return to Athens. The contrast between Arianna's stillness and Teseo's motion parallels the movement tropes in some laments collected by Loring Danforth in Potomia: "You are a man. You walk and the pains pass. But I am a woman. I sit and the pains mount."[89] And in a lament sung during the exhumation of the bones of a young daughter who had died five years earlier, the lament has the dead daughter herself describe the inexorable draw of a new place and the difficulties of coming back: "Whenever I set out for home, I meet rain and mist; and whenever I turn back to that foreign land, I find sunshine and good roads."[90] Here the joy and pleasure that will be experienced by the person who departs is juxtaposed with the difficulties of the person who has been abandoned. Teseo never tries to return to Arianna; instead, he embraces the "foreign land with its sunshine and good road." The departed's destination must surely be more pleasant than staying, or at least sufficiently pleasant to "justify" causing the pain experienced by the person who has been abandoned. The many resonances between Rinuccini's text and the various lamentation traditions of the region suggest that the laments performed at the 1608 Gonzaga wedding were shaped by contemporary understandings of a lamenting tradition that once existed, and perhaps continued to exist, in northern Italy, or as part of Italians' then-ongoing rediscovery and appropriation of classical Greek stories and ideas.

Most of the sung laments from the (formerly) Greek Mediterranean, in particular those following the Christian Orthodox tradition, are constructed of descending phrases, the ambitus of which is often a fourth or an extended fourth usually of a minor quality. Although the piece employs multiple melodic gestures that arc downward, suggesting the sounds of the sighing and wailing of a lamenter, the melody of Monteverdi's *Lamento d'Arianna* far exceeds the narrow ambitus of the fourth or fifth common to the laments from Greece or Finland discussed here. In addition, Monteverdi does not use the descending minor tetrachord in the bassline that later became iconic with the lament and with representations of women lamenting in the Baroque. He does employ that descending tetrachord figure as a structuring principle in his perhaps equally affecting *Lamento della ninfa*.[91] Is it only coincidence that a natural sigh also arcs downward, often for the interval of some kind of fourth? It is tempting to imagine that the descending minor tetrachord used in Monteverdi's *Lamento della ninfa* and many other Baroque laments is an appropriation of the internal structure of sung lament phrases as they were heard in Italy at that time or in the memory of such lamentation. The descending tetrachord and the lament phrases in Greek, Karelian, and Russian laments also form the general ambitus of an enunciated sigh generated by either despair or fatigue. None of the recordings or transcriptions of lament that we have were made before the end of the nineteenth century. It is also possible that the women lamenters appropriated the falling tetrachord, increasingly iconic with lament over the course of the seventeenth century, sometime after that point.[92] Just as the lamenting tradition itself may have spread two millennia earlier, so too the representation of the sigh may have traveled, crossing boundaries between Catholic- and Orthodox-based cultures.

Conclusion: Lamenting and Lamentation as Control

It is primarily mothers and daughters who perform the ritualized lamentations addressed in this chapter, as they mourn their lost relationships with children and parents respectively as well as the end of childhood and lost virginity. Themes of loss, loneliness, fear, despair, anger, and hopelessness are found in all of these traditions—British-Pakistani Muslim, Greek-Orthodox Christian, Karelian-Finnish-Orthodox Christian, Bihar–Northern-Indian Hindu, and seventeenth-century-Italian Catholic. That the women of these communities express despair and lament the changes wrought by marriage does not mean, however, that they do not want themselves, their daughters, or their sons to marry. They anticipate the pleasures of children and grandchildren, nurturing the hope that the new household will be a successful and generative part of an extended family network at the same time as they mourn the changes wrought by the marriage. In addition, women take advantage of the intensity of the focus trained on their performances to critique their families, communities, and social structures, voicing their opinions in a context in which their statements cannot be immediately challenged. Lamenting is a form of empowerment for women. The power exerted by women in these contexts is apparent in the ways in which some religions have appropriated aspects of their performances into official practice. In none of the scriptural traditions of Hinduism, Islam, or Christianity is lamentation prescribed as necessary or, to my knowledge, officially observed as part of wedding ritual. Nevertheless, in the communities where wedding lamentation occurs, it is considered integral to the overall process and success of the wedding event, even if they were compelled to document it at that time because of an impending decline.

Lamentation at wedding events anticipates an audience and conveys more than the loss the singers mourn. In the Greek, Russian, and Karelian examples presented here, laments act as sonic markers for each significant stage in the marriage process. They are sung while greeting the groom in the bride's house, when waking the bride on her last morning at home, on the bride's departure to the church for the official wedding ceremony, and as she takes final leave of her family to travel to her new home. In Bihar, the performance of wedding laments is more informal, occurring whenever and wherever women involved in the marriage to any degree might meet. There is also a competitive element in the singing of these laments in Bihar. Those who cause true weeping in others, either their lamenting partner or observers, are considered to be more persuasive. It is not clear if they are necessarily considered to be in deeper grief. The bride actively laments in the Bihar tradition, crying with her female family members, friends, and acquaintances in the street, during prenuptial events, or at home. After she has married, the bride tests her own persuasiveness when she laments her new situation with her in-laws as well as the failings of her parents on the first visit of her natal family to her new home. The lamentation of seventeenth-century Italy is found in music composed by men for professional women to sing in performance at the marriages of aristocratic women. The performed grief of the characters is rooted in their having been left by lovers who have gone joyously to war—a marriage and a woman abandoned for the male, certainly ephemeral, pleasures of war. In the representations of lamenting women in Greek literature, the lamenters rage against war and its usurpation of their men. Anger mixes with loss, and the lamenting women are empowered to deal with their grief through the act of singing their laments. Through their despair they find strength to voice their opposition to their situations. Borrowing from performative traditions for dealing with loss, wedding lamentation does articulate anticipated loss, but it is a loss caused by change that can eventually be a little kinder than death. The lamentation performances are altered to reflect this difference.

The first of the epigraphs at the head of this chapter suggests that the experience of offering one's daughter in marriage is a sacrifice greater than any other. The second epigraph reminds the listener that tears accompany the entrance and exit of the daughter to and from a family: tears because she is not a son; tears because of the costs involved in convincing another family to take her in as their daughter-in-law; and tears because one comes to love a daughter and mourns both her departure and the turmoil and trouble that will accompany her adult life, as they have one's own. Wedding laments both provoke and soothe fear; they anticipate anxiety and joy; they articulate and intensify emotions. They are an externalized expression of those emotions and represent the possibility of controlled social dissolution and recovery. The sonic presence of laments articulates grief and separates it from those who are grieving, while at the same time laments sound the social order, a structure that keeps the grievers aware of the community and themselves within it. Loss of the self, in a personalized way, is prevented. Even while one's body is occupied with other tasks, the sound and words of the lament fill space and time. The aural expression of sorrow slows time down, for space must be made for that expression to be heard.

Women dominate the rituals connected to life-cycle events. Their connection to these events allows for their enhanced engagement with secret rites such as magic and witchcraft, as communities strive for assurances of prosperity and continuity. There is danger in moments of transition, and women control and wield that danger through their bodies. Segregated domains for male and female activities render men socially but not culturally dominant and establish a complete network of balances within the community.[93] Women obtain power in society through their control over bodies in birth, marriage, and death. Those powers can be usurped and re-appropriated to domains that are controlled by men. The tension that arises between female and male control of these powers is articulated in the appropriation of Hinduism's idealization of Sita as perfect woman by women who recast Sita from a woman's perspective as well as by the appropriation of lamentation traditions by the Greek Orthodox Church or Greek tragedians. In the Indian context, women find themselves empowered to critique the structures Hinduism has created to curb their independence—the tuneful weeping of Bihari women at weddings is an embodied example; in the Greek context, the power of women's lamentation is understood to pose a potential threat to the stability of society, secular or religious, and therefore must be controlled and redirected. In each case, women's performance practice helps shape and determine the parameters of the development of community or the practice of religion. If weddings are moments of transition and transitions are moments when fissures develop, the singing of lamentation at weddings in the contexts discussed here is also a sonic invocation of other ground-shifting, transitional moments in which departures change everything. Lifetime transitions are seized by women as moments in which change can be wrought through the power of their performance.

CHAPTER 3

Demeter's Lamentation and Baubo's Mockery

Responses to the Marriage (Abduction) of Persephone

This interlude is situated between two chapters that explore articulations of the complex emotions women experience at their own weddings and at the weddings of others in their family or community. The narrative thrust of the classical myth of Demeter and Persephone, on which this section focuses, is propelled forward by events and emotions that resonate with the previous chapter and its exploration of wedding lamentation performed by mothers and daughters—evocations of death, unrelenting solitude, inability to control one's fate, a ripping of the fabric of community. However, the turning point in this myth echoes not with tears and wailing, but with laughter and taunts. Mockery and jest, the subjects of the next chapter, are also integral to Demeter's story.

The Abduction Marriage of Persephone and Hades

In ancient Greece the cyclic drama of the separation and reunification of Persephone and Demeter formed the narrative of renewal festivals dedicated to ensuring and celebrating fertility and successful harvests. Here, in outline, is that story. After young Persephone is abducted, Demeter—Persephone's mother and Goddess of the Harvest—seeks news of her whereabouts.[1] Nine days pass before Hekatê reports that she heard a piercing scream at the time of Persephone's disappearance and joins Demeter on her search. They find Helios, who, thanks to his all-seeing sun eye, tells them he saw Persephone abducted by Hades, King of the Underworld, the brother of Persephone's father, Zeus, King of the Gods—who had given Hades permission for this deed. On discovering that the abduction was a family affair sanctioned by the authority of Zeus—a decision by men and for men—and that there is little she can do, Demeter is rendered utterly bereft and miserable. She wanders the world grieving and searching for new meaning since her old life as goddess of earth's fertility and harvest now has none. She decides she will offer herself as a nurse to a willing family. In her fruitless wanderings Demeter meets the four beautiful daughters of Keleos at a well and asks them if someone nearby might need her services as a wet nurse. They declare their mother has a new son in need of care and invite Demeter to follow them to their palace. Their mother, Metaneira, welcomes Demeter into the palace and recognizes that, despite her deflated demeanor, Demeter is much more than an old, itinerant servant. Metaneira offers Demeter a beautiful couch on which to sit, but Demeter declines the couch in favor of a low, small stool, similar to a birthing stool, that is given to her by Iambe, a local servant. Demeter's grief is unquenchable. She sits for a long time, her veil covering her head. Urged to eat in order to ease her suffering, she does not respond. Finally, Iambe begins to jest in front of Demeter. She makes merry jokes, mocking comments, and gently insults Demeter.[2] Gods normally anger when insulted by humans, but Demeter begins to laugh.[3]

The mood-jolting mockery of Iambe helps Demeter recover her sense of mission. She gladly takes on the role of caring for Metaneira's son, whom she endeavors to turn into a god. Metaneira inadvertently halts the deification process of her son by peeking in at Demeter's activities and "rescuing" her son from the empowering fire in which Demeter has laid him. Although Demeter is enraged and curses Metaneira, through the rage she finally determines the means she will use to force Zeus to allow Persephone to return home. It is the therapeutic laughter generated by the jesting mockery of Iambe that is ultimately the catalyst that returns Demeter to the world and to herself. She is once again a whole being with purpose. She reconfirms her continuing role in the world and her undiminished powers of life. Hiding her fecundity in the dark of a temple dedicated to her by Metaneira as an apology for interrupting the deification of Metaneira's son, Demeter cruelly starves the earth of the elements that allow for the production and sustenance of life. She hides all the seeds in the soil, willing them not to germinate and rise up. Once the cries of the starving, despairing humans become unbearable, Zeus demands that Hades allow Persephone to return. In her joy at the thought of meeting with her mother again, Persephone is tricked by Hades into eating four pomegranate seeds.[4] For each of those seeds, she is required to spend one month a year with her "husband," Hades. Every year during these four months Demeter mourns and hides her fertile presence from the earth, causing the earth to mourn in sympathy, thus providing an origin story for the cycle of decline and renewal that is contained in the yearly process of seasons from autumn through winter to spring.[5]

Connections between death and marriage in ancient Greece and traces of those connections in the twentieth century have been well documented.[6] Likewise, the equation of marriage with death as a primary theme of the Demeter/Persephone story has been noted, not to mention the theme of marriage as a form of violent abduction.[7] But associations between the Demeter/Persephone narrative and the images conveyed by wedding lamentation, not previously articulated in literature on wedding laments, are also well worthy of attention. Demeter's despair and mourning are evocative of the lamentation sung during the preparations for marriage in Greek weddings, as a mother anticipates the departure of her daughter to the house of another. Persephone, too, leaves her mother, descending into the underworld, where Hades rules over the dead. Persephone's abduction can be likened, albeit in an extreme form, to a young Greek girl's marriage.[8] She embodies the kind of death described in wedding laments. She is reborn and returned to her mother but is changed, as are all daughters when they become wives. Persephone has responsibilities to her husband and home that alter her position in her natal home. That they were forced upon her through the auspices of male authority in her family and society is paralleled in some of the imagery of Potomian wedding lamentations.[9]

Demeter was the central figure in the ancient Greek Thesmophoria, festivals held across Greece, Italy, and Asia Minor and dedicated to ensuring/celebrating fertility and successful harvests and to marking women's connection to them.[10] Thesmophoria had roots in the oldest and most important agricultural and fertility rituals known to ancient Greece, all of which were celebrated and controlled by women. There is also evidence that the Thesmophoria served as a location and moment for women's initiation rites.[11] Mockery was an important element in the generative, chaotic, inversion-laden, wild abandon associated with the fertility festivals. Men were forbidden to enter the scene. Grain and other items symbolic of fecundity, such as pig heads or even whole piglets, were cast into the depths of a crevice in an effort to magically reignite the fertility of the earth. Lewd jesting and bawdy actions were performed to ensure that, following the myth, Demeter was awakened from her despair-induced malaise in order that she would return fertility to the earth.[12] Unlike wedding lamentation, the mockery that serves as the catalyst for the resolution of Demeter's paralyzing misery when her daughter is abducted does not have a parallel in contemporary or even recent historic Greek marriage practice, although mockery of similar sorts is present during weddings in many other places in the world. It should be noted that the orderly legal connections of marriage are not to be found in the ancient rituals celebrating Demeter, although such themes can be found, instead, in the celebration of the Thesmogamia, a festival devoted to Hera, the legitimate wife of Zeus. Demeter is seemingly positioned against the order and process of official marriage and the hierarchies upon which it relies. She strives to prevent marriage for her daughter and was never properly married herself, having engaged in relations with many gods. Unregulated by male society, Demeter represents an abundant fertility.

Women's cultic patterns in ancient Greece stressed the simultaneity and mingling of oppositions, a contrast to the dialectical relationship of thesis and antithesis that was characteristic of Greek logic and speech.[13] In the narrative, Demeter embodies all the iconic states of a fertility cycle. She is simultaneously old and ever young; infertile and fecund; a childless mother and an old woman who can suckle a child; tragic and satirized. Demeter has passed this capacity to embody oppositional states to her daughter, who is both living and dead or at least passes repeatedly and cyclically between those two states. The Demeter/Persephone myth can be read as an ancient articulation of the emotions women, mother or daughter, may feel at the prospect of marriage. But in the context of the Thesmophoria, the myth tells of a women's world, one not penetrated by men and outside of the rules and orderly control of male-dominated society for the duration of the festival, a fertile, female context that strives to ensure fertile productivity and the sustenance of the life of the community. Lamentation at funerals, the expressive source for wedding lamentations, also fell outside of the parameters of an orderly society. Performed publically only by women, lamentation in ancient Greece was viewed as dangerously emotional and possibly destructive.

The Power of Expressed Emotions in Ancient Greece

Loring Danforth has documented Potomian women actively attempting to control and mute the emotive wailings of extravagant funeral lamenters in their midst. The women he interviewed also stated that the singing of laments is preferable to wild shouting and wailing as a means of expressing grief at death rituals. Aware that people can get hurt when lamentation is uncontrolled, the Potomian women urged the grievers among them to calm down, scolding them when they were unable to regain their composure.[14] Here women simultaneously enforce the (male) cultural norms while watching out for the health and safety of lamenting women. These restrictions, self-imposed or otherwise, on women's lamentation map on to broader, long-standing cultural worries regarding the public expression of women's emotions and their habits.

The performed texts of Greek lamentation, whether ancient plays or rural women's laments in the twentieth century, regularly contain sharp critique of the people and elements blamed for causing the death and subsequent pain experienced by the griever. Concern that extreme lamentation has the potential to threaten the structures of Greek society can be documented as far back as the sixth century BCE, when legislation aimed at restricting immoderate and extravagant performances of lament, in particular by women, was enacted in Athens and the larger city-states.[15] Regularly performed in public, lamentation ensures that the words and thoughts of the lamenter will be heard not just by their families but by the community as a whole. Witnessing individuals rendered mad with grief can have a destabilizing effect on their loved ones as well as the larger community. More pertinent, when lamenting lost loved ones killed in war, women articulated—directly or indirectly—their criticisms of the male leaders of the community. Gail Holst-Warhaft argues that the development of the male-dominated genre of funeral oration, in which the heroic deceased was to be praised rather than mourned, and the pointed rhetoric of restrictive legislation suggest that women were becoming too disruptive of male order, too powerful in their lamentations.[16]

Awareness and fear of the possible destructive effects of the strong emotions brought on through lamentation is rendered palpable in theatrical representations. For instance, the dangers of excessive female mourning can be found represented in Aeschylus's *Agamemnon* in the character Clytemnestra, who despairs at having been duped into allowing her daughter to be sacrificed at Aulis in order to ensure the departure of her husband's revenge venture to retrieve Helen. A war she does not condone is begun through the sacrifice of her daughter and lasts a decade. Clytemnestra's ten years of mourning her daughter—ruing her own mistake, her daughter's selflessness, and their combined lack of control in the face of male manipulation—are not spent languishing. Instead, empowered by her grief, she seizes control over the city of her husband, takes a hapless lover who does her bidding, and either organizes or performs the murder of Agamemnon on his return with his war-trophy bride Cassandra. Whether Clytemnestra is interpreted as weak and submissive (as in the *Iliad*) or vengeful and manipulative (as in *Agamemnon*), her excessive mourning shakes the very foundations of her city and its power structures, challenging the authority of its male hierarchy.

Women in ancient Greece were understood to require control because, unlike men, they were not self-regulating. D. M. O'Higgins argues that it was thought that their worrisome natures[17] inclined women toward rule-breaking behavior such as overt obscenity and unfettered speech, acts that could have influence in society—acts that were denied to men. And since the rules governing speech were more stringent in the case of women, the power released by women breaking those rules was proportionally greater.[18] It has been suggested that women's public lamentation, despairing the loss of their loved ones, might have generated the desire for society-altering revenge in their male family members or have induced the women themselves to turn against the state.[19] The existence of their critical performances—transgressive verbal and physical acts such as lamenting, the lewd jesting and insult that wrenched Demeter from her self-destructive malaise, the mocking of men and male prowess in the contexts of fertility-ensuring, prenuptial celebrations—provides performers and their communities with perspectives that are different from the male-centric focus of their worlds. The possibility of alternatives—real alternatives that might threaten societal structures—disturbs and decenters the hegemon without rupturing it, as the next chapter will explore.[20]

The classical myth of Demeter and Persephone helps demonstrate the longevity of "wedding" lamentation and mockery—both present in the myth, albeit without music—as women's expressive genres that are catalytic elements in the fertility-confirming, human-sustaining narratives of the ancient story and of those of weddings around the world. Even while they conjure and confirm fertility and the continuation of society, women's expressive genres challenge, test, but ultimately confirm male communal order.

Figure 1: Baubo Figurines, Glyptoteket Museum, Copenhagen, Denmark. Photo courtesy of Evelyn Aschenbrenner.

CHAPTER 4

Revelry and Resistance

Prenuptial Performances of Mockery and Ridicule

As it is, the bride is very tense. So that's why we have the friends and relatives sit by, sing songs, tease the bride, talk about in-laws, tease the in-laws and try to cheer up the bride and make it a big happy occasion. The truth is, before the wedding is the only time when you can tease the in-laws, call them names and make fun of them. It's just to cheer up the bride to say your husband is like this and your mother-in-law is like that. Calling them foolish, pointing out that they are illiterate and making fun of them. It just makes everyone laugh and nobody minds it. After the wedding the bride steps into reality. You start a new life. You can't call anybody names and you can't tease them.

—Shenaz Hooda, *The Painted Bride*

Mockery and ridicule—words or actions intended to deride, scoff at, jeer, taunt, goad, or humorously imitate another with either benign or malicious intent—immediately impose a distance or separation between the mocker and the mocked. While mockery can occur between two individuals, mockery that is performed in front of multiple people is the concern of this chapter. In a group context, those aligned with the mocker may feel a burst of inclusivity and affirmation, a confirmation of their collective position of usually ephemeral empowerment in the context. The distance created—an us-and-them phenomenon—enhances the relationships between those doing the mocking. Temporary affirmation of the collectivity may be the most important effect sought by the mockers and their audience, although the experience of the mocked may be otherwise.[1]

The mockery and ridicule performed at weddings around the world induces similar experiences of inclusivity and exclusivity at events that involve the conjoining of two previously distinct in-groups through the marriage of their children—a society-maintaining act that simultaneously demands the rearrangement of the two in-groups. In this chapter I address women's use of mockery and ridicule in prenuptial performance from the following cultures: Hindu Trinidadians and Biharis; Canadian-Moroccan and Bulgarian-Israeli Sephardic Jews; Romanian Orthodox Christians; and professional Muslim Tuareg smith praise singers. In these case studies, mockery is directed toward the family and community of the marriage partner and other powerful personages in the community. As recounted in the epigraph to this chapter, mockery can be performed at gatherings of the bride's female family members and friends. It can also be part of the official encounters of the two families, as we shall see in the Romanian case study.

As this chapter will demonstrate, mockery as an act of resistance actually defines the continuing power of the larger structures and expectations operating in the background. This function is similar to inversions performed in pre-Lenten carnival festivals in many Catholic communities or during Holi in Hindu communities. Less obvious are similarities with varieties of resistance practiced by peasant and other dominated subgroups within societies around the world. In his work on peasant resistance, James Scott notes that it is rare for dominated groups to engage in successful revolutions; even failed rebellions are few and far between.[2] The intense focus on these political moments in both scholarly historical discourse and myth telling among the resisting and resisted groups belies their limited historical reality.[3] Far more common, but significantly underreported, are varying forms of everyday resistance.[4] James Scott theorizes the ways in which the process of domination generates a hegemonic public conduct and a "backstage" discourse among both the dominating and dominated groups.[5] Societies are not, generally, overthrown by means of everyday backstage resistance from the dominated. Instead, everyday resistance allows for commiseration with others who are enduring similar situations. Everyday resistance is momentarily liberating and confirming, suggesting the possibility of a life without the oppression of the hegemonic structures but without expectation for living that life. It can serve as a temporary release of tension and also as a method of reducing the potential for more serious threat. Further, the existence of resistance can remind those in power of the potential of the dominated to resist as well as providing a means by which to measure the level of commitment embodied in the resistance. These forms of resistance push against and, most often, simultaneously assure the continuation of the status quo. Scott explores the nuanced reasoning as to why the dominated do not usually revolt against the hegemonic. He argues that the separation between dominated and dominating groups gradually comes to form the identity—an "us versus them" construction—of the two groups such that disrupting the hegemony necessarily involves a radical shift in identity politics for both groups. The hegemonic structure has inertia that draws the two (or more) groups into developing distinctive subcultures that are powerful forgers of social identity. Scott suggests that the constant dialectic between everyday resistance and hegemonic structures actually confirms and strengthens the identity of the dominated group as much as it voices protest and raises ire against the hegemonic group.[6] There are resonances to be intuited when contemplating the position of some women in their respective societies and the dominated, resisting groups Scott analyzes.

As Scott notes, mockery is a primary mode of resistance among dominated groups.[7] Mockery can insinuate the possibility of real change while suggesting that imagining such change is farcical, a mockery in and of itself. In the epigraph at the beginning of this chapter, women sing mockingly of their soon-to-be-in-laws. However, daughters who are to be married, mothers who are to relinquish their daughters, and aunts, sisters, female cousins, and friends of brides do not necessarily want to overthrow the system into which they have been born, a system that constructs significant elements of their identity and into which they may be inclined to socialize their own children. This is not to make a direct equation between the categories women and resistant peasants. After all, women are part of the dominating classes just as women are members of dominated groups. Further, most women participate actively in the construction and maintenance of the inequalities of their own societies writ large.[8] Instead, I am suggesting a continuum of resistance such that women's wedding songs mocking the physical and fiscal capacities of the soon-to-be-in-laws can be understood as having effect parallel to the everyday resistance of peasants as Scott has described it, albeit on a smaller, even more local, community. Their performed mockery and ridicule supply commiseration opportunities for members of the in-group, bolster their convictions about the hegemonic structures of their society, and assure continuation of the status quo while suggesting the possibilities of more radical dissent.

Mockery and Ridicule in Indo-Trinidadian Matikor

> We arrived at dusk. The drummers, all women, had already started. Not a man was in sight. Two older women crouched at the side of the house where the soil had been freshly dug. They mixed together ghee, earth, sugar, salt, and some petals on a broad leaf, wrapped it tightly and buried it. Bess whispered that this signified the start of another household. The women formed a circle, taking turns to dance to the centre of the ring, simulating the sex act in various ways, angry, fierce, tender. There were games as well, older women knotting their skirts into phallic forms, running races while holding eggplants clamped firmly between their legs, frolicking and teasing the younger women. The songs were wonderful, varied in rhythm and so unlike the lushly arranged Bombay film songs that blared out in the markets and maxi-taxis. The wedding night songs were held fast by their own beat, an underbeat it seemed to me, nasal and piercing at times, yet whispering, as if secrets were being passed from woman to woman. An ancient aura surrounded these women, a oneness with their past and present that showed in every ripple of bare flesh, every beat of their bare feet against the mud-daubed earth.
>
> —Ramabai Espinet, *The Swinging Bridge*

This description appears near the end of the novel *The Swinging Bridge*, by Ramabai Espinet, in which the main characters—Canadians living in Toronto—wrestle with the emotions of recovering their roots as Trinidadian Indians. The scene depicted above is a *matikor*,[9] a women-focused ritual that begins the final three days of preparation for a wedding in the Hindu Indian community in Trinidad. The practice was imported with the Indians who came as indentured servants to Trinidad in the nineteenth century from several districts in Bihar state and other states in northern India. The first immigrants, who departed in 1845 on the ship *Fath Al Razak*, were predominantly men (198 men and 29 women) and they, like their successors, tended to be from a variety of castes. Without women to maintain the rituals specific to the various castes and because Hindu marriage was not yet recognized as a legal bond in Trinidad, the caste system virtually broke down in the early days of the Indian Hindu community in Trinidad. While it was possible for a man to offer his own bride to another for a large bride-price because his own marriage was not legally binding, it was also possible for a woman to have more than one husband because of the shortage of women. Nevertheless, women played an important role in the continued performance of folksong as part of ritual ceremonies. As Tina Ramnarine has noted, "Just as women in India sing wedding songs that are central to folksong traditions, Indian women in the Caribbean are seen as the preservers of tradition with regard to the music and dance of wedding rituals in particular."[10]

Still practiced in a variety of ways in twenty-first century Trinidad,[11] the *matikor* ritual was and in traditional contexts still is primarily an all-female event, performed at the bride's family home.[12] At the beginning of the first day, the oldest and youngest female members of the household prepare and, with the help of five married—hence auspicious—mothers, carry a tray with various items that include propitious leaves, vermillion (*sindur*), and sweets to a nearby clean source of running water. Once there, the women place the tray on the ground and light a candle beside it. The mother of the bride digs the earth and mixes it with water from the clean source, along with the vermillion and other items on the tray. The married women are anointed with the mixture at the chakra on their foreheads, the place where women traditionally wear the dots of powdered *kumkum*.[13] The rest of the guests are invited to eat the sweets on the tray, and they start singing and dancing to the accompaniment of the *tassa* drums. At this point men are not allowed to dance at all, but younger men and boys may be permitted to do so later in the evening.[14] The singing and dancing continue on the way home from the water source.[15] Once the party has returned to the home of the bride, the dancing becomes more exaggerated and boisterous but also more humorously erotic. The male drummers stand "at a discreet distance," averting their eyes while the women sing lewd songs ridiculing the young, the old, the soon-to-be-married, the future in-laws—just about everyone involved in the wedding process. They also perform mock erotic dances, "perhaps using an aubergine (eggplant) to imitate a phallus, or inserting a pillow in their blouse to look pregnant."[16] Dancers gyrate their hips with varying degrees of subtlety, approaching one another provocatively from the front or backing up and rubbing into one another and laughing hilariously as they mime sex acts of various sorts. The dancing involves the raising of one arm seductively over one's head while keeping the other low, rotating one's wrist by the hip or reaching out toward another dancer and then gracefully switching the arms around. Although they are a distinctive part of Trinidadian dance genres, these moves can also be connected to folk-dancing patterns in India.[17]

While her friends and family are dancing, the bride is taken inside her childhood home under the shelter of her mother's head shawl. She sits on a small stool, and rice (a symbol of fertility) is poured into her cupped hands, after which the *pundit*, usually a male Hindu official or priest called in only for this part of the event, performs a *puja*, or ceremony of offering. The bride is then covered with a saffron paste that gives a yellowish hue to her skin. The saffron smooths and conditions her skin. The resulting golden tint is considered beautiful. Then, the youngest girl present, as the purest female individual in the house, performs a ritualized cleansing of the bride by anointing her with more saffron, using a swatch of *doop*, or long grass. She touches the toes, knees, shoulders, and areas above the bride's head with the saffron and grass five times. Once all of these steps have been completed, the bride is considered purified and is ready to rejoin her friends and family members in singing, dancing, and enduring with good humor the sexual jokes that her older family members make at her expense as well as at the expense of her in-laws and men in general. During the same evening the bride and all her girlfriends will have their hands and feet adorned with mehendi (henna). While girls can take courses to learn how to apply mehendi, it is most often a skill learned through repeated observation of practiced family and friends. The tassa drumming and singing continues through the whole evening. Once the henna has been applied on all the girls, the musicians go home and the party breaks up.[18]

The pundit is also present occasionally on the three days of the wedding, and especially on the day on which the last official stages of the rite are performed. That he is present for so many of the women-centered events, in particular at the maṭikor to perform the puja at the purification of the bride in her mother's home, suggests that the events are ritually important for the whole community. His presence there connects the event, including the bawdy nature of the songs and dancing, to representatives of official Hinduism as practiced in Trinidad, which suggests that the mockery and ridicule performed at the matikor are tolerated, condoned, or otherwise acceptable and appropriate to the patriarchal structures of the community despite their lewd nature.

Some of the songs sung at Hindu weddings in Trinidad are sober and unaccompanied, performed in accordance with the more somber, nerve-wracking moments of the wedding ritual: the arrival of the groom at the bride's house; the greeting of the groom; the exchange and assessment of precious gifts; the giving away of the daughter; the transfer of the bride's allegiance from her father and family to her husband and his family in a ceremony in which the groom traces the bride's hair part with vermillion; and the entrance into the ritual bedroom. Known as *byah ke git*, these serious wedding songs recount some of the events from the most iconic and tragic of Indian love stories, the *Ramayana*. Byah ke git equate the new couple with Rama and Sita, the perfect yet dharma-crossed romantic couple around which the *Ramayana* stories revolve. Like the wedding laments used in the orthodox Christian lamentation traditions examined in chapter 2, these byah ke git are used as sonic articulations of the various stages of the ritual. They mark the arrival at important moments in the transformational process that is the wedding: the joining of two people into a new, adult relationship; the transition of a female person from girl to woman and from the responsibility of one family to another; the bonding of two families.

Helen Myers documents the text of one song sung at the end of the wedding, when the bride and groom process into the marriage bedroom:

> In the evening the clouds come in the sky
> At midnight it starts to rain [a sign of fecundity]
>
> Mother, open the sandalwood door.
> Let Rama enter the *kohabar* [the room in which wedding rituals are performed]
>
> Mother, open the sandalwood door.
> Let Sita enter the *kohabar*.[19]

Myers notes that these more serious, ritual-articulating songs may well be in decline in Trinidad, a result perhaps of the whittling away of the elaborate, time-consuming, and expensive traditional formalities of the wedding through increasing urbanization and globalization.[20] Myers points out that the bawdy, mocking lachari songs sung at matikor events seem, however, to continue to thrive. The distinction between the two types of Trinidadian wedding songs, byah ke git and lachari, is similar to that made between two kinds of songs sung in the northeastern areas of India, where the unaccompanied ritual songs are called *vivaha* or *vivah* (*byah* is the Trinidadian cognate) and the bawdy and ribald songs are similarly called *lachari* or *lachi*.[21]

Trinidadian lachari songs tend to be in duple meter and the lines of the texts, which are in Bhojpuri occasionally mixed with English, are repeated in a responsorial manner. In *Are Nadiya Kinare* a bride is jealous of her sister-in-law, against whom she sings in the text of the song. While describing him as a king and saying she loves him so much she cannot even blink at him (she only can stare), she accuses her husband of loving someone else and casts a spell of night blindness on him (so that he cannot go out at night seeking other women). Only the one who has cast the spell can lift the fever it has brought on, but she feigns inability as she tries, unsuccessfully, to relieve the fever with different delectable parts of her body. She asks,

> Oh how can I dispel night blindness?
> All day and night this spell does not break.
> Oh my husband will suffer from night blindness.
> How can I sweep the place [that is, do her daily chores with her concerns for her husband on her mind]?
> Oh with my breast I will dispel night blindness!"

Later in the song, the sister-in-law also gets the fever because the mother-in-law has only a small place in which the whole extended family must live and hence it is easy for diseases to pass from one person to another. Once the sister-in-law gets night blindness too, the bride's husband is then miraculously freed of the illness. The bride singing the song describes this joyous moment in the following way:

> My husband will then be free from night blindness.
> Oh I will give him a Panama hat.
> He puts a beautiful hankie around his neck.
> Oh he is walking down the road with his balls swinging!
> O I love him.[22]

In just a few simple but humorous verses, this song both conveys humiliating accusations that the bride's in-laws might be poverty stricken or, just as bad, miserly, and tells of the bride's feigned incapacity to provide solace to her husband, which contains further threats of avoidance of duty to her in-laws. It also contains exaggerated plaudits of the private features of the bride's husband, who is, the comment insinuates, no longer as beholden to his mother and other female family members as he now is to his new wife, who knows all about his balls and dares to talk about them, an indication of her empowering intimacy with her husband and general unwillingness to be cowed by her in-laws. In a traditional context, this kind of insubordination by a new bride would be impossible. Laced with hierarchy-busting innuendo and blatant sexual references, the song imagines an amusing and temporarily empowering inversion.

From Lachari to Chutney: Reinterpreting Mockery and Ridicule at Matikor

In addition to providing opportunities for intrafamily political commentary and critique, what do these kinds of songs and this kind of event do for the Hindu women and girls who sing and participate? How can such songs be interpreted?

Baksh-Sooden proposes that matikor is likely a privilege that was "probably fought for centuries ago by Indian women [in India] to express their sexuality collectively within Hinduism," thus suggesting that matikor is an act of resistance arduously earned by women who perceive themselves trapped in a man's world.[23] Baksh-Sooden's statement implies that the women who created matikor had no agency in their own culture until they created matikor. Given the good-humored, light nature of the mockery and the general acceptance and ritual importance of matikor in the Trinidadian Hindu marriage process, this construction seem more like a latter-day feminist reinterpretation of matikor than a description of the intentions of the generations of women who developed and participated in the practice both in India and in Trinidad. Sara Bergman also intuits a strain of resistance through sexual independence in the actions of the performers at matikor, writing that "*matikor* reflects women's assertion of their independent sexuality and resistance to control."[24] The staff writers for Triniview.com have a related perspective:

> Maticoor [alternative spelling] night is an important zone of female empowerment. The almost exclusively female-centered ritual is meant to instruct the Dulahin (bride-to-be) on sexual matters through humour, dance, song, and role-play. It was in this zone that Hindu women throughout the centuries found a safe haven where they could express themselves without the prying eyes of men, pass on valuable traditions from mother to daughter and be free to be sensual, ribald, and spicy without judgment or censure.[25]

The Triniview.com description captures the multifaceted nature of the event—ritual purification, sex education, humorous send-up, bonding through mockery, experimenting with sensuality—but suggests that women would not be able to do these things in front of men for fear of censure. All three of these writers understand matikor as a zone of resistance, as female empowerment in the face of male objectification of women. While these analyses capture the way some contemporary Indo-Trinidadians perceive and value matikor, other coexisting interpretations are also possible, rendering any single analytical take on the nature and meaning of matikor less nuanced and complete than it needs to be.

The idea that matikor is solely a scene of women's empowerment outside of the view and participation of men is likely false. Even in the most traditional of contexts, many of these songs are sung within earshot of men, in particular the tassa drummers, but also other men in the families of the bride and groom and not only the young and adolescent sons who are living in the home of the bride and regularly attend the events. In the rural, north Indian Bhojpuri-speaking villages from whence the Trinidadian matikor tradition derives, women actually sing mocking and ridiculing songs to and at the men of both marrying families, including the groom, and in the presence of the Hindu officials during some of the most important moments in the ritual process during the three-day marriage event. The participation of the pundit in the puja that takes place during the matikor event in Trinidad indicates that the matikor is clearly not solely a hard-earned "feminist" escape from the patriarchal Hindu hegemony.

Over the course of the late nineteenth and twentieth centuries more Indians, both Hindu and Muslim, migrated to Trinidad. Among the Hindu population, caste and class distinctions became more solid, especially after the rise of the concept of India—Mother India—as a homeland for its diasporic populations after Independence, in 1947. At the beginning of the twentieth century, Indo-Caribbean women did not dance with men at weddings, although they did dance in the presence of men. Women who danced with men were generally regarded as not respectable. Professional dancers were, however, invited with increasing frequency to perform at Hindu weddings as entertainment. These dancers, part of the relatively small community of Indians in Trinidad, paved the way for the general loosening of intergender communications in public, particularly because they were present at community daily events given the small size of the community, unlike professional female dancers in India. Around midcentury, changes in gender restrictions accompanied ongoing creolization processes and the decline of various ancestral traditions in both Indian and African communities on Trinidad, and the last fifteen years of the twentieth century saw a renewed interest in "authentic" Indian and African home cultures.[26] One result of these cultural shifts for the Indian community has been the normalizing of men and women dancing together at weddings, at both matikor-type events and during the celebrations after the final wedding ritual, most often to chutney music.

The musical legacy of chutney comprises elements of many of the oldest musical forms that Indians brought with them to the Caribbean, in particular the simple refrain-verse-structured songs from rural North India with lewd Bhojpuri texts that are heard and danced to most prominently in matikor. A style of dance called *wining* is accompanied by chutney music. Wining "combin[es] graceful hand and arm gestures with sensuous pelvic rotation. . . . Often, one hand is held behind the back and the other is upturned on top of the head, in a posture clearly deriving from Bhojpuri-region folk dance."[27]

Sara Bergman explores shifting gender constructions in Indo-Trinidadian public dancing over the course of the twentieth century. She notes that interest in learning Bollywood and classical Indian dance forms such as Odissi dance are part of a reaching back to long-left India for an ethnic authenticity in gender construction. She argues that while matikor and chutney may have opened up options in the realm of public performance for Indo-Trinidadian women, classical dance forms have gone further, creating new public spaces for women to gain respect and increased independence through their mastery of classical forms as part of the renewed interest in Indian cultural forms among Indo-Trinidadians, whose identity is pulled equally by contemporary constructions of Indian and Indo-Afro-Trinidadian identities.[28] Oscillating between the gender constructions of classical

Indian dance styles and those of chutney, not to mention those of other Caribbean genres, Indo-Trinidadian women skillfully maneuver among them, claiming and embodying them all in different contexts.

The songs and dancing of matikor rest at the roots of Indo-Trinidadian women's construction of their contemporary positionality. The mocking nature of dance and song performance in matikor has filtered into chutney dancing by men and women alike, as well as into the chutney texts. The lewd gestures and texts performed by women as they mocked and ridiculed men and women in the intimate circles of their family and soon-to-be in-laws during matikor have been absorbed and generalized. That wining, with its roots in female-focused matikor, has become a mix-gendered, contemporary popular dance performed not only at weddings but also on weekends, can be interpreted as an embrace and normalization (appropriation?) of Trinidadian women's expressive culture, not only in Trinidad but throughout the Caribbean and beyond in the Trinidadian diaspora.

Whether the normalization of a women's performance genre is disempowering for women is an open question. In its older female-focused context, the lewd mockery and jesting ridicule of matikor provided precisely the kind of hegemony-confirming, identity-building everyday resistance that Scott theorizes. Women bonded together to assure and bolster the bride and her female relatives before the wedding, taking the opportunity to teach, taunt, titillate, and remind one another, and those surreptitiously listening, that subordinate women can imagine an inversion of male hegemony, a process that both confirms the status quo while temporarily empowering women during the performance and strengthens their identity as Hindu-Trinidadian women. The most radical aspect of chutney performance today is that while it actively works within normative gender constructions of contemporary Trinidad—woman as sensualized object of male (and sometimes female) gaze—it intersects directly with the inversions of those norms in the mockery common at matikor events, resulting in a playful, sensualized atmosphere at contemporary Chutney wining events. The aura of the traditional, raucous Hindu marriage ritual hovers behind contemporary chutney performances, resonating with old Indo-Trinidad as well as imagined India. In Trinidad matikor has shaped the iconic performance genre of twenty-first-century Indo-Trinidad while localizing the practice of Hinduism in the diasporic community.

Women and Split Imagery: Documenting Mockery at Weddings in Hindu Bihar

Many Indo-Trinidadians originally migrated from northern rural India, from the region now contained by the states of Bihar, Uttar Pradesh, and Rajasthan. The area has been continually studied since at least the middle of the nineteenth century, when Sir George Grierson—a native Irishman who was a career servant in the Indian Civil Service, rising as high as magistrate and collector at Patna and opium agent in Bihar—published his collected information on the material and ritual lives of the peasants of Bihar.[29] Grierson was also in charge of the colonial Linguistic Survey of India (appointed in 1895) and his texts, in true British colonial style, are replete with extensive examples of local script as well as the transliteration of local words and their meanings. He collected information on many aspects of prenuptial and wedding events in which Indian residents from many different religions participated, invariably providing notes on the myriad stages of ritual activities surrounding marriage in each religion. For the Hindus of the region he includes information about "the ceremony called *matkorwa*." He recounts a series of events similar to that found in Trinidad, with "women of the family and their friends" singing their way to a well, where they "level a piece of ground . . . and smooth it" with clay and water. The minute details of the physical process and even some of the significance of the acts are recorded, but there is no indication of the nature of the texts or the sound of the songs sung during the process.[30]

William Archer, another British colonial servant working in India in the late 1930s and 1940s, specialized in Bhojpuri poetry. He published a book on Hindu marriage rituals and texts performed during the various stages of wedding events.[31] Archer was particularly interested in the visual and literary representation of symbolic elements, and in addition to documenting hundreds of songs texts, their symbolic references, and their uses in marriage events, he explored the depictions of these symbols in the *Madhubani* wall paintings that the women of Mithila and surrounding areas created to prepare rooms and houses for marriage and other festivals. He wrote,

> The women paint the courtyard walls of the houses of the bride and groom with images of protective and exemplary deities which vary according to season, date, caste, family and astrological predictions. [. . .] The most elaborate paintings are reserved for the *kohbar* or marriage chamber where the bride and groom spend the first few nights of their married life together.[32]

The designs include multiple manifestations of fertility and fecundity, such as the lotus flower circle and the bamboo. These plants are iconic references to fertility because of both their rapid growth and their visual analogies to female and male sexual organs—the bamboo shoots are often depicted piercing the lotus flower.

Other motifs include images of amorous god couples—Vishnu and Lakshmi as well as Rama and Sita or Krishna and Radha (both of these pairs are incarnations of Vishnu and Lakshmi). These same godly couples are referenced in the songs texts documented by Archer, embedding the bride and groom by analogy in the religious context as well as imbuing the occasion with grandeur and auspiciousness.

A cup of sandal
A case of betel,
O Rām, take the betel
From your mother-in-law.
O mother in Janakpur
I will give Rām my blessing
The turban of Rām flashes on his head
Lovely is Sīta's sari
With its gold border.
O mother in Janakpur
I will give Rām my blessing
The wedding suit of Rām
Shines on his body
Lovely is Sīta's vermilion
Beyond all praise.
O mother in Janakpur
I will give Rām my blessing
The stockings of Rām
Shine on his feet
Lovely Sīta's painted toenails,
Beyond all telling.
O mother in Janakpur
I will give Rām my blessing[33]

In this song, the physical attributes and the accouterments of the nuptial couple are directly compared to those of Rama (Rām) and Sita. The song is addressed to the groom's (Rama's) mother by the bride's (Sita's) mother. Both human mothers are elevated and made more auspicious through this comparison, as are also the bride and groom. The bride's mother is simultaneously signaling that she supports the marriage of her daughter to the groom.

Some of the scenes depicted in the Madhubani paintings include women dancing together and images of brides being conveyed to weddings and also other imagery with explicit references to marriage. The dancing often depicted in those images—women with arms raised who gyrate their hips in close proximity while gazing intently at one another—suggests some similarities with the dancing women perform at matikor events in Trinidad as well as with mix-gendered wining in chutney dancing. Scenes of various marriage processions, in particular ones in which the bride is carried in a sedan chair on route to the groom's house, are also depicted. The opulence represented in the scenes is characteristic of one in which Sita, a queen, would be found. Analogies to Sita connect the bride to the mythic figures of Hinduism and especially to Rama and Sita's long-lasting idealized marriage.

Edward Henry also researched the musical cultures of the Bhojpuri-speaking groups, but in the middle of the twentieth century and therefore later than Archer.[34] In the midst of documenting songs from every conceivable context—from mendicants to processionals for weddings, harvests, fertility festivals, and so on—Henry devotes a whole chapter to women's wedding songs. He reports in great detail on song texts and on the actions they accompany and articulate, providing descriptions of the structures of the songs and sensitive assessments of their connection to Hindu myths. Together these three collectors, Grierson, Archer, and Henry, have created an invaluable compendium for a gendered approach to song and mockery as they are used in Bihari weddings.

Whether the detailed data from sources like Grierson, Archer, and Henry warrant it, scholars who focus specifically on gendered aspects of Indian women's performance can fall into the trap of rendering women as either defiantly sexualized and empowered or pacifically pure and dominated. Gloria Raheja and Ann Gold identify this dualism as the split female image which, "variously characterized, . . . is generally grounded in two linked perceptions" of women: as possessing a "sexual potency" that, if untamed, will be "dangerous" to men and the community; and as "procreative and nurturing" of children and society.[35] This tension is best represented in the "contrasting forms" of Shiva's consort in which the "solitary and wild dance of the blood-drinking, gruesome, and disheveled Kali threatens the cosmos [while] stately, beautiful," devoted, and fertile Parvati soothes and supports it. They are both manifestations of *Shakti*, the female energizing force of the universe.

Fusing the Split Image in the Construction of Hindu Women

At the root of the split image of women are their "strongly contrasting [lived] roles within the kinship system." Women as mothers and daughters are empowered and in charge of ensuring prosperity through ritual in the home and family; indeed, they materialize and maintain the structure of Hindu society through their caste-specific daily offerings and prayers. But simultaneously they are also wives and son's wives—marry-ins—who are subservient to all other family members but their husband's younger brothers.[36] Women must be fertile, and hence evidently fertile, but they must also be chaste in order to show their fidelity. They must also be demonstrably reticent about engaging in sexual relations or discussing sex or lovemaking in any way, whatever their personal desires and despite the voluptuous depictions of sensualized femininity in myth, epic, film, temple adornments, and even the Madhubani paintings of Mithila women.

Women's roles are not discrete. A newly married woman who has recently moved to her husband's family home must appear to be modest and ashamed of any suggestion that she is sexually active when communicating with her in-laws. At the same time, she will feel pressure from both families to become pregnant as soon as possible. The birth of a child, preferably male, will ensure the continuance of both families, but equally important for the new bride is that the birth of that child will gain her a foothold on the ladder of authority in the family. Only as an evidently fertile, and hence auspicious, woman can she remove herself from her odious role as child-like and subservient daughter-in-law. Yet, another piece of her authority in her new house is determined by her ability to please her husband sexually and draw him away from the influence of his female relatives. The son/husband is also caught by this split image, trapped between his mother and his new wife, both of whom hope either to gain or maintain authority by demonstrating more extensive control over him, each in her own respectively appealing manner. The position of each person in such a Hindu ménage à trois might be perceived as unenviable, even if there is a persistent overlay of patriarchal privilege. The relevance of an event like the matikor becomes more apparent when the multiple, seemingly irreconcilable positions occupied by a new bride are identified.

Raheja and Gold are not claiming that the embodying of multiple positions simultaneously is unique to Hindu women.[37] Their goal is to understand the ways in which women negotiate their progress through these multiple life roles, how they experience and fuse their various identities. Women "do not necessarily perceive [their roles] as ultimately conflicted."[38] It is likely that the split image approach is one that derives from a male viewpoint. In order to access a female perspective, Gold examines texts for women's songs sung during weddings and at births and at other events in which women sing in single-sex groups. In these songs, Gold does not find oppositions between "murderous, sexual[ized] females" and nurturing mothers. Instead, in songs like *Gali of the Small Husband* she finds a "merged anticipation of sexual pleasure and motherhood from the bride's viewpoint."[39] *Gali* are wedding songs sung by the women in the family of either the groom or the bride at the men, and occasionally the women, of the other family in semi-formal greeting situations. *Gali* means insult in general, but "sung *gali*s are always sexually oriented."[40] The *Gali of the Small Husband* states,

> On the cross-path grow those plants whose poison leaves are yellow
> Ram Kishan had a son, a floppy-eared fellow.
> Take down my full water pot, small husband dear.
> Small, small what's to be done?
> See the male wonder:
> In nine months, I'll feed a son.
> Daughter have a lot of fun.[41]

This song points out that the "'miracle' of phallic growth" is a "male wonder" even small men enjoy and that the bride will have a good time and then fulfill her obligation to her new family by producing a son. Here sexual pleasure and fertility leading to motherhood are combined while a groom is mildly insulted.[42] The bride is also reassured that even if the husband chosen for her is "less" than she had been hoping in any way, he may still be enough. Mockery and insult are not reserved only for men but may be sung for anyone in the groom's family. *Gali* songs insulting the groom's mother are sung when the groom enters the bride's house for the first time. In one, the groom's mother is accused of having no genitals:

Black sheep's not woolly
Bridegroom's mother has got no pussy

In another, the groom's mother, who is supposed to hide any interest in sex and refrain from sexual activity is described as actively seeking and enjoying sex:

Bridegroom's mother asked for a sugarcane stick.
Take this one, a piece of prick.
Oh, but it's sweet!! I'll plant more quick,
In my cunt I'll plant that prick.
In my cunt I'll plant that prick.[43]

These two songs are generally sung in alternation and together suggest that "only if she had no genitals—as natural to women as wool is to sheep—would she, with her taste for sweets, be able to give up sex."[44] Although the groom's mother is a mature woman and about to be a mother-in-law, her sexuality is married publically to her role as a mother. In these women's songs, fertility, sexuality, and motherhood are persistently united, not rigidly separated as in the male-constructed, split-image perspective on embodied womanhood. In addition, the singing of this kind of mocking song about the new authority figure in a bride's life just as she is entering the house of the bride has the effect of combining, on one hand, disrespect for the mother-in-law (mothers are not supposed to be identified as sexual beings) and, on the other hand, the bride's competition with her mother-in-law, sung on the bride's behalf by her relatives. These sentiments are enhanced statements of the everyday resistance that will characterize the new relationship of the bride with her mother-in-law.

In another wedding song, *The Song of the Seven-Colored Wrap*, documented by Gold, a new bride—who should be shy, subservient, and reticent about speaking—describes herself as craving a gorgeous luxurious wrap or shawl.[45] While a shawl is equated with the bride's modesty, her desire for the wrap is connected to her ability to convince her husband to do her bidding and to fulfill her every craving for certain foods and to her inability to sleep—all taken as signs of sexual desire. As the groom offers to bring the bride increasingly delicious items, only some of which she has asked for, she starts to turn him down, saying she could not enjoy what her husband brings her because she misses her younger brother, a suggestion that she would like to go home and visit her natal family. Finally, when the groom agrees to get the carriage, ever contrary, the bride declares that she could not go because she would miss her groom.

Here the pleasantly demanding and desirable bride has her own sexual interests and controls those of her husband, as is demonstrated by his capitulation to her request that she be able to visit her brother. Her final thoughts about missing her husband suggest that even though she wants to return to her natal home to visit her little brother, she does actually enjoy her intimate life with her husband. The many desires expressed in this song reveal a convincing panoply of possible emotions for a newly married bride, emotions that can be expressed openly and will be affirmed by the responses of her groom. This song does not portray a mute, retiring, subjugated bride, but rather an affirming, curious, emergent, appropriately modest (she searches for the beautiful shawl) wife, a wife who is sexually interested, and hence likely fertile, which means she might soon be an auspicious wife with child and her groom a successful husband. These images fuse aspects of both Lakshmi (nurturing and attentive to appropriate behavior) and Kali (interest in sex and wild expression of desires). The two representations exist not in conflict but in an ongoing embodied synchronicity.

Raheja and Gold hear the women's "voices portray shifting, polychromatic self-images."[46] A focus on the multiple representations of women in the texts of songs they sing at weddings reveals characteristics from across the spectrum of female ways of being that coexist inside individual actors who demonstrate agency, seek pleasure, and confidently maneuver their ways through these multiple constructions, all the while poking fun at and mocking men, women, propriety, and the proper order of things. This is not to suggest that all women are to be found happily existing in their multiple locations, unburdened by the pressures of in-laws or barrenness or unhappiness. Rather, at marriages—singularly important moments in the life-trajectories of women and their families—women choose to sing about their culturally inscribed roles in ways that disrupt dominant narratives with bawdy, confrontational sexual themes while insulting everyone. The mockery, ridicule, and insult conveyed in Bihari wedding songs are performed at moments in which old familiar boundaries are reconfirmed, but with new actors in the established roles. The hegemony of these boundaries is imposed on all parties, and all take turns resisting it through performance. Mockery and insult here articulate a kind of everyday resistance to those limits, even as the mockers are settling into their new roles within the hegemonic structure. Whether one assumes the split image perspective on women and female sexuality or adopts a more synthesized, embodied, and experiential perspective, the boundaries suggesting those two interpretations persist. Mockery and insult performed in wedding songs both test and confirm those boundaries.

Finding similar themes, issues and cultural solutions in women's wedding songs in both Bihar and Trinidad—with culturally related, though long-separated populations—demonstrates that women's performance traditions are enduring, at least in these instances. Such maintenance reveals a relative cultural importance and suggests that women's practices, despite the fact that only a few women were included in the original migration to Trinidad, have been and continue to be instrumental in localizing and bringing to life the practice of Hinduism in both Bihar and Trinidad.

Double-Edges: Backhanded Praise in Sephardic Jewish Women's Wedding Songs

Sephardic Jewish communities are spread throughout the world, with large communities in Israel, France, New York City, Buenos Aires, and Montreal. Sephardic Jewish women are the main conservators of wedding songs in their communities and of the traditional Hispanic poems called *romances*, whose roots can be traced to the epics and chronicles of medieval Spain. Scholars have noted that Sephardic Jewish women sing throughout the wedding period, sometimes performing songs to articulate specific acts, known as "songs of the bride" (*cantigas di novia*).

Among Jewish families in Bukhara, Uzbekistan, the women of the families of a bride and groom play a game called "The Singer and the Drink." The hostess sings a song while holding a full glass. When she finishes, she passes the glass to the next woman in the circle, who can decide to sing another song or drink.[47] The event is designed to allow the two families to become familiar with one another and to bolster the spirits of the bride-to-be, as well as everyone else who is drinking. Among Sephardic women in general, musicologist Amnon Shiloah notes a corpus of songs for cursing. These songs are ostensibly meant to entertain the women by introducing a light atmosphere. "Two singers exchange juicy curses for the edification of all those present. These songs are usually concluded with conciliatory verses in which the singers ask for forgiveness, express contrition, and try to end on a . . . note of good will."[48] In addition to defaming other women present, these songs may also poke fun at or complain about elements in their community of which they, as a group, do not approve, such as "old men who want to marry young women—either as a first wife or to replace an older one"—or families who are not generous.[49] Shiloah does not present any texts, nor does he delve into the specifics of who is insulting whom in these songs. As in the Indian and Trinidadian wedding contexts, the insults do surely bring a certain amount of levity to what is otherwise a difficult, if exciting and auspicious, event for all. There is probably more to insult trading than simple humor, however.

Among the Bulgarian Sephardic Jews living in Israel in the late 1970s, women could still sing the songs of mockery and insult that once were an integral part of their traditional wedding rituals. Songs were performed in order to give an account of the bride's trousseau, which once prepared, was evaluated publicly when presented to the groom's family.[50] Songs were also performed during the bride's prenuptial purification performed in the *hammam*, her official reception by her mother-in-law-to-be, and when she departed from her mother and family with her husband and his family.[51] Other songs were sung to help the wedding families get to know one another and to familiarize the bride-to-be with the family into which she was to be married.

Working with primarily older women immigrants, Susana Weich-Shahak documented eighteen wedding songs, several of which include insult and mockery. In a song sung by the women in the groom's family, the bride's mother is criticized for providing a paltry dowry.

> How little you give her, mother-in-law.
> How little you give to your daughter, your beloved daughter.
> I will give her seven dresses, one for her to change every day.
> This is still not enough, mother-in-law.
> How little you give to your daughter, your beloved daughter.
> I will give her seven blouses, one for her to change every day.
> Still little this is, mother-in-law,
> How little you give to your daughter, your beloved daughter
> I will give her seven pairs of drawers . . .

The song continues with the bride's mother mentioning golden necklaces, best wishes for the bride's life, and finally a young servant to help with her firstborn.[52] While the song is ostensibly critical of the bride's mother and the trousseau she has helped her daughter prepare, in fact it provides an opportunity for an explicit and detailed description of all that has been and will be given. This list, therefore, also serves to enhance the status of the bride's mother and her family, even as the text suggests the offerings are paltry. Before the bride goes to visit the groom's home for the first time, she must bathe at the hammam. In one of the songs sung by the bride and the women in her family at this event, a list of desirable luxuries is outlined. They sing of a sumptuous bathing experience, graced with expensive toiletries, two servants to help, luxuriant cosmetics to be applied afterward, as well as extended time in the steam bath—indicated by the bride's feeling faint—all of which would be expensive. At the end of each verse they sing, "Let my brother-in-law pay for it." Their words suggest that they can live it up at the expense of their new in-laws, but they also indicate that such grandiose expenditure is somehow necessary.[53]

When the bride finally departs from her parents' house with her new husband after a five-day wedding event, there is a certain amount of anxiety. To relieve the tension, insults are sung again. The following song insults the bride, the groom, and his female relatives.

> The king has one daughter
> fair and kind and blushing;
> One day, because of the heat,
> she stood by the window,
> no, it is not, it is nothing,
> the groom is taking her home!
>
> That lad
> with his short beard,
> used to make buttons
> (and) silver clips.
>
> Bride, when you see
> your mother-in-law
> pick up a slate,
> open her brow.
>
> Bride, when you see,
> your mother-in-law
> take her by the hand:
> Come, my new mother.
>
> Bride, when you see
> your sister-in-law,
> take up the shovel
> break her back.
>
> Bride, when you see
> your sister-in-law,
> take her by the hand:
> Come, my new sister.[54]

First, the bride is insulted as incautious, having attracted the attention of men, perhaps even intentionally, by standing underclothed in her window; her family too are implicated, for they should have trained her better or, failing that, ensured that she could not approach the window as she did. The verse implies impropriety, even inadvertent pregnancy, but then assures the listener that all is well because the groom has agreed to marry her. Then, the groom is accused of being a mere producer of simple household goods and likely very young, as suggested by his short beard. Because mothers-in-law and sisters-in-law have a reputation for ill-treating new brides in their families (despite the fact that they too were, or will be, in such a position), the bride is instructed first to be fierce and unpleasant with both her mother-in-law and her sister-in-law—the two people with whom she will have to deal on a daily basis, perhaps competing with them for influence over her husband—and then to show compassion after she has trounced them. The power she might amass in taking the upper hand in household negotiations is most likely imagined, at least partially, given the usual age and familiar hierarchies. That the subject is a topic that can, however, be laughed at and sung about publically in front of the people who fill all the roles noted in the songs suggests that the possibility of resistance may not be entirely imagined.[55]

Judith Cohen identifies four main themes in the wedding songs of Moroccan Jewish women from Canada: the erotic, the pragmatic, the frivolous, and the religious. These general themes are echoed in the mockery sung in most of the case studies presented here. Cohen points out that the same song can encompass several themes at the same time.[56] In many of the songs, the themes are explored with a humorous twist, often with a mocking or playfully insulting tone. In the song *Quando yo en ca de mi padre* (When in My Father's House) the singer states,

> In my father's house, I combed my blond hair;
> now in my husband's house . . . I spend my time looking in his wallet . . .
> the morning is good, but how much better the God who sends it!

This text suggests an image of the lovely bride-to-be infatuated with cultivating her own beauty, a task essential to her securing a good husband. Once married, she continues her pragmatic approach to life by closely monitoring her husband's finances. She is also aware of the presence of God over and above, or perhaps sensibly in conjunction with, her pragmatic approach to life. Both anticipatory concerns of a bride about living in her new home with her new husband and a bride's desire to preserve her own sense of self are similarly articulated in *La Cena del Despozado* (The Groom's Dinner):

> Give the groom his dinner, for he hasn't eaten;
> give the groom his dinner, a sardine; for the bride, a hen.

In other verses the groom is offered black bread and the bride white bread, and at the end the groom is told there is no bed, so he will have to leave love for tomorrow. The song ends, "Hold on, groom, leave love for tonight."[57] These two songs encourage the listener to imagine the life of the new bride, to think about her position and how she is going to improve her lot by thwarting the expectations of her new husband and his family. The bride's attempts to control her situation is a theme that links the texts but that control comes from an interruption and mockery of the expected order of things. Mockery of a bawdier, nearly erotic but also insulting, nature is found in *La Novia Destrenza el Pelo* (The Bride Lets Down Her Hair).

> The bride lets down her hair, the gentleman becomes faint.
> Who will go wake him, who will go wake the groom, who will go wake him?
>
> The clouds float in the sky, [clouds] that wet the groom
> Who will go to meet him, to meet the groom, who will go to meet him?
>
> Don't faint, young man, for I have the weapons
>
> Underneath his robe, Hasdai has a small bottle[58]
> Who will go to meet him, to meet the groom, who will go to meet him?
>
> Shawil puts on his boots and you can see his balls
> Who will go wake him, who will go wake the groom,
> who will go wake him?[59]

This song text moves from passably discreet to blatantly bawdy in a few short verses. The groom is "slayed" by the bride, faints, and needs to be resuscitated by the bride who has the "arms/weapons" to help him. The rather coarse depictions of male excitement contrast with the representation of the bride. She is in control and chooses to let down her hair, which begins the poetic cascade from male composure to male chaos. Here the bride does not doubt her powers or her poise; rather, she is actively controlling them to manipulate the men in her surroundings. It is not clear if Hasdai and Shawil are meant to be understood simply as everymen, perhaps representing grooms in general. Perhaps they are other men who are equally awed by the bride but Hasdai and Shawil are perhaps sturdier than the groom who, unable to contain himself, has passed out. If the latter meaning is intended, then the message of the song is multiplied and may serve also as advice for the groom. As in the case of the insults hurled at the mother-in-law when she is coming to visit the bride's house in rural Northern India, the insults to the groom here are backhanded praise as well. His inability to withstand the powers of his bride render the groom less potent than his bride. But a man who can claim a bride able to wreak that kind of havoc on both the groom and any number of others must also be powerful and successful in his own right. In all these Jewish contexts, the insult and mockery have a double-edged nature, insinuating positive commentary while delivering demeaning and humorous barbs.[60] Although the Sephardic Jewish brides are depicted as feistier than Hindu brides, in both cases a bride can succeed in the groom's home context by diverting existing power structures to focus on herself without generating undue animosity or disrupting basic decorum. This strategy echoes those of the subordinated groups studied by Scott that were discussed at the beginning of this chapter.

Romanian Strigatura: Mocking and Lamenting to the Same Tunes

Romania was a communist country for more than forty years, from 1948 until 1989. A national focus on urban industry, which was accompanied by rural male migration, meant that traditional Romanian culture tended to survive only in rural areas. The experience of women in rural villages did not change significantly: studies show a persistence of traditional patriarchal values and behavioral norms in these agricultural areas, even in the face of evident and dramatic modernization elsewhere.[61] Many Romanian Orthodox Christian wedding rituals were maintained through the communist period in Romania, including both lamentation and prenuptial opportunities to mock, insult, and otherwise heckle members of both wedding families.

> When you bore me, mother,
> How happy you were.
> You thought you had a son
> But you had only sorrow and longing.
> When you saw I was a girl
> Your whole body ached.[62]

This lament, in the form of a *strigatura*, comprises couplets that were composed by a young woman and performed by her at the wedding of another woman in 1979 in Ieud, Maramures County (a remote area of northern Transylvania), on which occasion the lament was recorded.[63] Wedding strigatura are shouted more than they are sung, performed by women over rhythmically organized music provided by men on violins and an accordion. The music and the text are organized to the extent that singers time the beginning and endings of their couplets to match the phrasing of the melodies as performed by the instruments, but there is no real melodic connection between that which is mostly shouted by the singer and that played by the instrumentalists. Strigatura are always sung to a particular person. In the text above, the singer contemplates the sorrow her mother must have felt on seeing that she had given birth to a girl instead of a boy. This sorrow is experienced primarily because a young woman might bring shame and calamity upon her family by getting pregnant out of wedlock. The onus of preserving a girl's virginity falls directly on her parents. If a young woman misbehaves when she is a daughter-in-law, the fault falls on the shoulders of her husband's family, in particular the woman's mother-in-law, since she is the authority figure in charge of running the household. A girl represents the possibility of trouble, grief, and shame, primarily for the women in her families, until she has borne children and is a mother herself. Kligman notes that women cry at all life-cycle events, stating that "any [Romanian] woman can tell you the basic reason. Women suffer, and rightly so. Eve sinned. Humanity's depravity is her fault, a deed for which women should atone."[64] Local religious training and participation also "teach a girl inherent shame."

The weaving of Christian original sin into the rationalization for lamentation at weddings and other life-cycle events contrasts with the enthusiasm and vivid enjoyment the same women have when they anticipate and engage in their own wedding and the marriages of other women. Gail Kligman quotes one mother as saying, "Don't worry, if she doesn't cry, I've got onions."[65] Her words suggest that the weeping and lamentation young women perform at their weddings are more important to the community than to the bride and her female relatives. There is a tension between the bride's pro forma weeping and any heartfelt mourning she and others might experience as they contemplate/remember/relive the loss of girlhood and a woman's passage into adulthood, with all its challenges and hardships.[66]

At least one and sometimes several *druşcă*—designated lamenters and general cheerleaders—accompany the bride and groom through every prenuptial and wedding event. Usually young women who are contemporaries of the couple take on the task of singing strigatura at appointed moments in the events. For example, just before the groom leaves his parents' home to go to the church, a strigatura is sung to him. In a room crowded with his family members and friends, a girl dressed in attractive yet traditional formal dress approaches the groom. They are both holding bottles filled with *horinca*, a triple-distilled plum brandy.[67] Accompanied by a fiddler and an accordionist, the druşcă begins her strigatura. The interplay between the singer and the instrumentalists is flexible. In performance, the strigatura is organized into five-line verses in which each line takes four beats to be chanted in a strident monotone.[68] The instrumentalists play a 24-beat repeating melody with a cadential phrase that does not necessarily line up with the end of the singer's verse, although there is a repeating pattern. This phrasing of cadential gestures allows the instrumentalists to expand or contract their melodies to accommodate extra-verse lines, breath-catching rests, and contractions of text composed and chanted by the singer. The older the singer the more likely she is to take her time with her verses. Younger singers tend to be more motoric in their text delivery, while older singers often deliver their strigatura at a more leisurely pace, but still with the intensity of a stern berating. The performer actively engages the gaze of the groom, compelling him to listen to her and to respond to her words. In her text the druşcă observes that the groom will leave his house an unmarried man for the last time. She begins by praising him.

May you live long, you, handsome bridegroom.
Let the world long to watch.
May the world be dear to you

As the fiddle is to me,
Now and all through the spring.

May the month has come again [meaning unclear].
You, bridegroom it is time to go to your proud one.
It's time to leave the house,
To go to the priest to get married.
Let the world long to watch.

May the month has come again.
You are leaving your farmstead.
Whether it will be good or bad,
Only God knows
Let the world long to watch.

May the month has come again.
If you are well-behaved and good,
No harm will come to you.
Let the world long to watch.

May the world be dear to you.
Before you go
To church to take the vow,
Stay here with your mother first.
May the world be dear to you.

[several unclear verses follow]

May the month has come again.
To ask for forgiveness,
Because she raised you.
May the world be dear to you.

May the month has come again.
Bridegroom go, go, go home
And join your chosen one.
May the world be dear to you,

May the month has come again.
May you be well with your proud one,
On the path you have departed,
Never sad.
May the world be dear to you.[69]

This performance of the strigatura lasts more than three minutes.[70] The groom stands awkwardly listening to the praise and nodding at the end of each verse, just managing not to look sheepish. When his debt to his mother is mentioned, he bows his head ever so slightly. Nothing more is required from those on the receiving end of the strigatura than to listen and accept. The delivery of the text on a monotone in a heightened and strident style of rhythmic speech converts the sound of authoritative women telling others what to do into a musical presentation in which family ties and obligations are outlined while multiple layers of human relationships are affirmed. The strigatura performed before the religious ceremony are closer to laments than mockery, and women can be seen daubing at the corners of their eyes throughout these performances. Once the bride and groom are officially married, the tenor of the strigatura changes.

After the bride dresses for the marriage ceremony at the church, she is given a crown of thorns by a young boy. A direct comparison with Jesus's trek to Calvary as martyr is intended. Accompanied by music and strigatura on the walk to the church, the bride is allowed to dawdle to show her independence. She should not linger so much that the groom and her intended mother-in-law become irritated, however. While the couple is married inside the church, their unmarried male and female friends dance outside the church. After the ceremony both families retreat to their own homes for a meal.[71] Each time the bride and groom move through their neighborhoods, they are accompanied by large, festive crowds and musical accompaniment similar to that used for strigatura. The exchange of the bride to the groom's family is still unfinished, although the church rite is complete.

The two families prepare to meet at the home of the bride's parents. To complete the exchange, the two families must engage in three more events, each of which involves a certain amount of role play. In the first event, the groom's family arrives at the bride's house feigning a search for the first spring flowers or sheep—depending on the time of year—both of which are white, signifying purity. A person acting in the role of father-of-the-bride brings two younger girls dressed in the traditionally colorful flowered skirts of girls from the village. Both young girls are declined for not being "white" enough, enraging the person acting the role of father-of-the-bride, who must be calmed down with a series of sung proverbs and good advice that is actually meant for the younger people in the room. After this dispensing of advice and some urging, he finally produces the "whitest flower," the bride, and she is accepted.

In the second scene, two older women—usually the cook who has been preparing the food for the feast at the bride's house and a woman from the groom's family—then engage in bartering for a hen, an icon of the bride. As they playfully negotiate in strigatura, they urge one another not to get angry in their bartering and start making sexual jokes in their verses.

> En route to the wedding
> I injured my thigh

If you don't believe me,
Well, godfather, lift my skirt and see for yourself!
Hey behave yourself,
Don't lift it from the front!

Another strigatura suggests that instead of money, the seller wants to have sex with the godfather of the groom. The response involves insulting the godfather and shoring up family relations:

My husband is a big scoundrel,
He doesn't desire just anyone,
He wants only me.
I'll give you money, land,
But I won't sell you my husband.[72]

In yet another verse, the singer offers to buy the hen for enough money that the hen's owner would be able to buy some underpants to cover up her genitals and reduce temptation. Other verses are more blatant about the sexual encounters to come, suggesting that the men involved will have gotten erections at the thought of the purchase of the bride.[73] All of these engagements are performed in strigatura verses. Once the purchase of the hen is complete, it is cooked and eaten, symbolizing the appropriation of the bride into her new family. The third mini-drama then commences. Women from both families taunt the bride with stories of future neglect and torment at the hands of her groom and her mother-in-law. The bride may break into tears at this point, as the moment of true separation from her family and natal home is nigh. Once she cries, with or without the aid of onions, ameliorating verses are sung and the wedding concludes.

In this example from rural northern Romania the tension and play between anxiety about separation and the excitement, exuberance, and good humor—not to mention bawdy insults generated by the nascent sexuality of the bridal couple—are strongly articulated. The theatrical and social aspects appear to be more prominent than any personalized relationship of the primary actors to the events. Beyond the dawdling of the bride on the way to the church ceremony, there are points in these activities at which individuals use the ritual moment to express their resistance to any form of hegemonic authority. But hegemonic power is not absent: while men dominate in the public world in Ieud, women dominate in the private world of the home, and they dominate each other.[74] Structures against which to mount everyday resistance exist, but the performance of wedding strigatura seems not to be the place for such resistance.

The performance of both mournful sentiment and raucous mockery to the same melodies and accompaniment style is unique among the examples in this study.

The use of similar melodies for wedding and funeral lamentation, as in the Greek Orthodox tradition, preserves a basic sentiment—the expression of mournfulness and loss. But the use of strigatura for both mournful solemn verse and mocking bawdy verse is a rare phenomenon. The sound of the strigatura appears to be the sound of a wedding itself rather than the expression of a particular sentiment, whether mockery or lamentation.

Professional Prenuptial Mockery: Resisting and Confirming Hegemonies

The prenuptial mockery described so far in this chapter has generally been performed by the people most directly involved or by their close family members and friends. Among the Tuareg noble families, it is performance professionals with deep knowledge of their employer's family life histories who perform prenuptial mockery. The everyday resistance that is worked out through their performances, however, is that generated by the life-long relationship between the professional singers and their patron families, rather than revolving around the individuals getting married or their absorption into roles defined as subordinate.

The Tuareg are a semi-nomadic Islamic people living predominantly in northern Niger, Mali, and other West African nations whose territories are associated with the Sahel. The Tuareg have slowly migrated south from the northern reaches of the Sahara, down through the Sahel, over the past millennium. Despite ongoing political and community-based changes, the rural Tuareg noble families and the group called the Tuareg blacksmiths (or smiths) still maintain a kind of patron-client relationship in which the "smiths act as go-betweens and mediators . . . both between Tuareg and the outside world of government functionaries and tourists, and within Tuareg society itself, helping to negotiate noble marriage matches and bride-wealth payments."[75] Both male and female smiths engage in praise singing, performances that involve both extolling and condemning their patrons, dancing sensually and sometimes erotically, and generally maintaining a jocular, often gently mocking relationship with their patrons.

Tuareg women have significant status within their own social ranks. They own and inherit property, and men and women have relatively free social interaction, with certain exceptions. Married couples may not be in close physical proximity to one another in public, and reserve is shown toward people who are considered affines, Islamic scholars, and elders of both sexes on the paternal side of one's family. This reserve involves refraining from eating together, gesturing broadly, or singing in each other's presence, and requires that men cover their nose and mouth with a veil.[76]

In addition to brokering weddings and bride-wealth prices—and occasionally serving as go-betweens for people involved in illicit relationships—blacksmiths also organize the evening festivals at the weeklong wedding celebrations. Under cover of night, many of the social restrictions described above are partially lifted, especially during wedding festivities. Men pinch women as they walk by, and suggestive remarks are made by both men and women, well within earshot of both the intended object and many others. All of this is in strong contrast to the Tuareg concept of *tirriza*, or shame, which is in operation at most other times in public. Both men and women perform during these wedding festivals, usually at different times but often in close proximity and occasionally for people of the opposite gender.[77] They also sing in choral groups and serve tea and other ceremonial foods.

Within the context of wedding festivities in which there are many types of music and dance, both male and female smiths perform praise singing and dancing for their patrons. Here I will focus on the performances of female smiths only. When the bride and groom have their separate ceremonies for the application of henna to their hands and feet, women smiths sing and drum during and after the rituals. Soloists engage in comic repartee in which they insult their patrons and each other. In response to both the praise and the comedy, the nobles offer presents of money and millet, and indeed praise singers regularly receive their payments in grain as well as money. According to Susan Rasmussen, both nobles and praise singers view this kind of dancing as a form of begging. Self-denigrating gestures performed during dance include the mimed plucking of lice out of their hair and the raising of their hands above their heads in submission to Allah but also to the patrons who are present, perhaps signaling an unstated comparison.[78]

After a bride or groom has henna applied to hands and feet before being wed, a group of smith women, who have participated in the henna ceremony themselves, performs a *tebateq* dance as they leave. They accompany themselves on small hand drums called *acanzam* and the *tende* drum made from a large mortar for crushing grain, a reference to the importance of grain in the community and women's connection to the growing and preparing of that resource. Amid the dancing, a soloist sings praises and inserts mocking comments and jokes about her noble patrons for whom she is performing. She calls out the names of people who give her money or presents or squirt her with perfume. She also identifies those who are not generous. The performers and the audience know each other very well, and there is give and take in verbal jousting as the soloist performs her praises, mockeries, and jokes. By demeaning herself in the performance but also by knowing her audience well, the soloist engages that audience in dialogues that address topics ranging from the everyday and the political to the aesthetic and the mockingly ludic.

In one tebateq performance a smith woman by the name of Nana sings more than one hundred lines of improvised text as she interacts with the many different people within listening range.[79]

1. This cloth [on which nobles place millet for payment] refuses to set itself down because it does not know the installation [suggesting it needs something—gifts—to hold it down]
2. This is like a promise
3. It is medication against death
4. You the impolite ones [addressing the other assembled smiths]
5. The people have arrived
6. at the place of eating
7. You are not happy
8. Isn't anyone going to chase the marriage bull in this courtyard?
9. Consider a marriage bull.
10. What happiness for someone who is among nobles!
11. You must give it to us, we'll eat but you understand
12. you keep well your business.
13. You want to tire us
14. May God not push me before the Prophet
15. For ten days I have not prepared the porridge. Go, I am going to chat
16. and pour [the millet I receive].

.

.

28. [Of] all the smiths he who does not shout
29. has eaten the sexual organ of his father
30. The son of Akawa [who gave her money]

.

.

55. I am going to the *marabout* [to visit the shaman for a protective amulet]
56. [for] that's a lot of money, I must be protected [against sorcery]

.

.

69. That is greasing my throat
70. Boubacar who greased my throat
71. M̄ouha, son of Abdou, but it was not only him that brought him
72. into the world, there was also Habsu [his mother]

.

.

96. Asalama, these jewels are mine

.

.

100. Timana, Anta the daughter of Aka she gave that to Saidi, son of Kader, son of Kader and Zeinabou.

Nana mocks the smiths in line four but at the same time she points out that while smiths are impolite, they have the power to speak their minds and thoughts in a way that others, in particular their own patrons, do not. Speaking also draws attention to mouths and food topics that are considered to be shameful. Nana speaks of eating directly when, at line ten, she says she has not cooked millet in ten days. Meanwhile she has run in a wild manner around the circle of the audience, staring directly into the eyes of many nobles, particularly the patrilineal ones, and simultaneously breaking many of the behavioral restrictions mentioned above. Nana's mention of the marriage bull insinuates an imagined paucity of the gifts that have been offered to her at that point, insulting the father of the family of the groom. But eating meat is also a euphemism for sex among the Tuareg. The layered suggestions continue to mount up. At line 28 she insults the male smiths, perhaps her own patrilineal relations, who are listening, telling them that if they do not give her some shouts of approval, then they must have had oral sex with their fathers. Then she acknowledges Akawa, who gave her grain. The mixture of insult and praise is destabilizing or jarring and amusing for everyone around. It generates a desire to see how far she will pursue the insults and also perhaps a desire to avoid being the target of the insults, hence the financial effectiveness of this kind of praise singing for the smiths. Tuareg smiths of both sexes control noble men's reputations through poetry and song full of commentary.[80] On receiving a good quantity of grain from one patron, Nana declares, in line 55, that she is going to have to go to the Muslim scholar/shaman, or *marabout*, in order to obtain an amulet that will protect her from thievery. "Greasing" her throat, another invocation of mouths, bodies, and possibly sex, is how she describes the gift of Boubacar, in lines 69 and 70. Then, in another reference to sex and the equal necessity of both men and women for the continuance of life, she points out that without Habsu, his mother, Mouha, son of Abdou, would not be present, simultaneously referencing sex and marital affairs and the importance and power of women as at least equal to those of men. Nearing the end of her performance, Nana receives a piece of jewelry. At line 96 she identifies this fact and claims it. The Asalama mentioned is the smith woman in charge of keeping all that the smiths receive for distribution later, and as Nana has received a piece of jewelry, she wants to ensure that it is hers.[81] These products, the grain, and the money are divided among the smith women who attend the application ceremony. Nana is reputed to be an excellent performer of tebateq at henna ceremonies precisely because of her ability to weave together artfully insult and praise alike. Other performers who merely joke around or whose insults are not thoughtfully constructed are not valued to the same degree as Nana.[82]

The Tuareg nobles seem to possess all the wealth and political power while the smiths live almost as paupers. The smiths are supported, not owned; empowered, but not in power; they are endowed with deep knowledge of their patrons and networks, necessary to the efficacy of many community and personal rituals, and considered to be magical—hence somewhat unpredictable and dangerous—because of their connections to blacksmithing. "Most Tuareg describe transformations effected by smiths in terms of their alleged mystic powers; in this sense, the praise definitely affects audiences and performers powerfully, by advertising the content of their relationships 'off stage' [non-ceremonial situations]."[83]

One way to interpret the power of smith praise is to understand the implications of the very possibility of insult and mockery. Here is James Scott's everyday resistance rendered public, not a hidden transcript but a practice acknowledged by both dominating and dominated groups. As Rasmussen notes, "The ludic and clowning aspects of these performances make a clear statement about power, hierarchy, the reciprocal obligations of superiors and subordinates, women, and men."[84] The relatively low social position of the smith praise singers with respect to their patrons is, paradoxically, precisely the aspect that allows them to speak the truth, to tease, goad, and playfully mock their patrons at important life-cycle moments while testing the strength of the social boundaries.

As their traditional networks have been eroded through migration, some Tuareg smiths have found gainful employment in urban areas, working as masters of ceremony for wedding halls and in radio and television broadcasting. In these contexts, they are valued for their skill with words and their connections to rural magic. Without the social structures that they are allowed—indeed encouraged—to contest in rural contexts, however, smith women can only praise in these urban contexts. They rarely criticize their customers, who have paid for a performance, not for the status confirmation the smiths can conjure and sustain in rural contexts. The relationship of mutual dependence common in rural contexts is not present in the urban setting. Rural patrons support women smith praise singers with food and gifts during performances, and they offer the praise singers specific forms of honor because their own reputations are only truly protected through the mouths of these performers and their goodwill. Mutuality is the key to understanding the participants' encounter with both the praise and the mockery performed.

Palliative or Galvanizing: Prenuptial Mockery from Iambe to Nana

As suggested by the effectiveness of Iambe's jesting and mild insult of Demeter in chapter 3, mockery can be instrumental as a means of motivation, especially in situations wherein strong emotions might be temporarily paralyzing. Mockery and ridicule mediate anxiety and despair during moments of tension and transition. This chapter has discussed women's use of mockery and insult in prenuptial performance by Hindu Trinidadians and Biharis; Canadian-Moroccan and Bulgarian-Israeli Sephardic Jews; Romanian Orthodox Christians; and professional Muslim

Tuareg smith praise singers. In these case studies, mockery and ridicule are used to ameliorate the possibility of upset and anger since they often serve as indirect praise. They are instrumental in familiarizing soon-to-be-joined families with one another. They articulate and facilitate intragender relations while bolstering the emotions of brides as they move toward their new roles. They contest the power of new in-laws, husbands, and social boundaries, while allowing for the exploration and increased anticipation of new sensualities. Some of the events discussed here incorporate the presence of male religious officials (Trinidadian matikor and some Romanian strigatura); others are performed within an entirely female, non-public space (Pakistani Mehendi performance in the epigraph at the beginning of the chapter). Trinidadian matikor occur inside an imagined, private, female space that happens also to be populated by male drummers and the young male children of the family. The performances by Tuareg smith women are conducted in mixed-gendered contexts in which mockery, ridicule, and omnipresent sexual innuendo effectively generate a sensualized tension.[85] In all cases, the excesses of mockery, insult, and ridicule contribute to the pleasurable side of wedding events while, following van Gennep and Turner, such tactics aid in moving the bride (and groom) through a liminal state in which she is not yet married but has progressed beyond the confines of her role as daughter.[86] The impermanence and transitional nature of the bride's prenuptial position allows for the testing of boundaries and resisting of religious and social norms—symbolic actions that are not usually part of the daily self-construction of the bride and her companions.

Performances of prenuptial mockery are complex cultural phenomena. As is the case for most compelling humor—as uproarious as the mockery in these performances may be—it is not uttered simply for a laugh. Prenuptial mockery plays an important part in the marriage processes described here. Rituals have often been theorized as constructing stability in families, communities, and societies.[87] Yearly festivities draw extended families together, create and confirm expectations for the events, and foster a sense of continuity between generations. And irregularly occurring events such as marriages, funerals, circumcisions, and maturational celebrations such as confirmations, circumcisions, and bar/bat mitzvahs can be understood to have a stabilizing effect on communities and individuals for the same reasons. Yet rituals inevitably destabilize individuals within communities at the same time, especially those rituals in which people's lived experiences are altered dramatically. When those changes will result in power shifts that will mark the lives of the participants forever—even if the outcome is reasonably predictable—apprehension is likely to be felt. From this perspective, the performed contestation of communal norms, with all its appealing and comforting inversion and insult, can be seen as an outlet for such anxieties. The very act of resisting confirms existing understandings of the individual and of the community.

Marriage is a primary element in the maintenance of a society. It is associated with fear, anticipatory anxiety, departure, and loss, but it is also associated with sex, fertility, sensual pleasure, status, and the negotiation of power. From a purely pragmatic perspective, mockery performed at prenuptial events talks to many of these functions. It provides an opportunity for women to bond with one another as it articulates—sonically and spatially—a female space that will be just memory after the marriage, but which is, for the nonce, a place for bolstering spirits and reassuring nerves, sharing pleasure, demonstrating competence, and exploring the aesthetics of living well. It can also conjure a gender-neutral space in which women and men, whole extended families, witness the merging of the families of the bride and the groom, ensuring all will be well for the couple by observing and participating in a testing of the boundaries of politeness, hospitality, and trust. Mockery mediates the discomfort generated by the impending change, the passage of time, the rite of passage itself. Private performances of mockery, like that described in the epigraph at the beginning of this chapter, create an us-against-them context that shores up the emotions of the bride and her mother while helping to normalize the changes that are bound to occur. Public performances of mockery, like those engaged when the families of the bride and groom meet in Sephardic Jewish communities or the Romanian Orthodox contexts, ensure that the doubt-generated anxieties are articulated publically, just in case it is necessary, in the future, to admonish poor behavior by the in-laws. Through all of these contexts, mothers, fathers, and grandparents on both sides may recall their own passage through these transitions, their own stint as new bride or groom. The community-structuring aspects of boundary-contesting mockery are readily apparent.

In this chapter I have suggested that James Scott's analysis of the relationship of groups to their larger political societies and the hegemonic forces within them can also be used to illuminate interpersonal and interfamily relationships within their immediate communities and larger society. Dominating and dominated groups mutually constitute one another, but that mutual engagement is dynamic, constantly reexamined in varied pitches. The goal is not necessarily transformation; inversions and overturnings can be imagined without imperiling community structures and the essential identities they mold. But the expression of the potentiality of a challenge is heard by both dominant and dominated. Marriage is disjuncture, but it is also opportunity. New roles are adopted, already written, but with gestures, costume, and lines that require rehearsal, while the audience expresses its confidence in the player, its fears for the performance, and the potential risks which all recognize. The expression of words in music can change their everyday meaning. The musical and presentational context of the performances of the mocking, insulting, and ridiculing words renders them simultaneously more potent and less hurtful. The impact of performed insult is therefore distanced and enhanced when compared to the experience of insult delivered as a spoken word. In these prenuptial contexts where mockery is performed, the mocker is safe from retaliation, and the mocked can laugh and shrug off the insult as all part of the performance. Hegemony is resisted by being ruffled and reminded of the possibility of rebellion, but nothing has really shifted structurally. The individuals involved, however, have moved inside the structures and made radical changes in their own lives. They have participated in events that define their community, as these performance traditions of resistance are viewed as iconic.

The existence of women's traditions of prenuptial mockery in local forms in four world religions in different places around the world suggests that within the constraints of patriarchal religious cultural contexts, like the peasants Scott observes, women seek ways of contesting the hegemony that binds them. But they do not seek to destroy those structures, for their identities are defined by the same hegemony, which they also help to construct through the socialization of their children and their own lives lived.

CHAPTER 5

Girls's Poetry and Social Critique at Muslim Berber Weddings

I am going to wash my fringed headscarf (tasebnath);
I shall hang it on the fades bush:
Take your sugar away!
You and I aren't good together
—Berber Girl's Couplet

This chapter focuses on the poetic performances of Berber girls in Riffian communities in rural Morocco, examining the ways in which performance context offers individual girls the opportunity to speak their minds on issues and concerns that matter deeply to them and about which they cannot speak in any other context. In the process, I examine the polemics of musical performance in Islamic contexts and explore feminist interpretations of some Islamic constructions of gender. The ethnographic material on which this chapter is grounded is drawn from fieldwork performed by Terri Brint Joseph before the 1980s. From more recent work on Berber communities around Morocco, including the seminal works of Katherine Hoffman and Jane Goodman,[1] it is clear that the ethnographic snapshot provided by Brint Joseph is now altered significantly in everything from gender relations and opportunities for younger people to move between urban and rural contexts to educational opportunities for children and the revaluation and essentializing of Berber culture as a national icon for Morocco. The point of using Brint Joseph's ethnographic data here is as an example of a performance context, historical or contemporary, in which women use the opportunity of performance to assert agency and generate change for themselves.

Unmarried Riffian Berber[2] girls compose poetic couplets[3] and then perform them in front of all the village during the wedding celebrations of other girls.

Their performances take place around an open fire "in front of the houses of the bride and groom or on a central patio located inside the walls of the house." While the bride and groom are formalizing their marriage, the crowd gathers around the open fire at sunset and listens intently, cheering and ululating. Wedding festivities generally last for at least three days, and the performances fill the nights, continuing until sunrise. The performers are all girls of marriageable age who are normally shielded from public view in daily life. They sing several times each evening, presenting many different couplets. In their texts, the girls address unwanted (but sometimes prospective) marriage partners, Berber migration to Europe, problems and inequities wrought on their communities by tourism, discontent with government policies, and their own hopes and desires for marriage and families. The girls perform in groups of four, accompanying themselves with tambourines and small drums called *tabours*. They walk out to the performance space and began a shuffling dance, stepping side to side in a line. They take turns singing. Each girl leads the group when singing her own couplets, with the other girls responding by repeating the sung melodic lines in unison. Couplets round off with the sounding of a refrain that can be repeated until the next girl is ready to begin singing one of her verses. The audience, made up primarily of men and boys, with young girls and older women in the back, is often responsive, enthusiastically and lustily shouting "*Yallah*" to encourage the singers to perform the chorus again. When this happens, the tempo increases and the girls move into the *shidih*, in which "they undulate, moving their hips, waists, and breasts in circular movements while the audience shouts more encouragement."[4] "Dressed in their finest floor-length gowns, [the girls wear] dark glasses," ostensibly to disguise their identities. The political and social impact of their poetic messages would be diluted, however, if their identities were actually hidden. The glasses act as a "fictive mask" that "make[s] it easier for the girls to step beyond the role ascribed to young women of the Rif."[5]

Since the middle of the nineteenth century, Berber culture has been under the lens of anthropologists and linguists working from a variety of perspectives, and much has been written on Berber marriage ceremonies.[6] The Riffian Berbers form a distinct linguistic and ethnic group within the larger world of Islamic Morocco. Indigenous to the area, they engaged with Christianity when it first reached the Maghreb and gradually converted to Islam—through both commerce and conquest—between the seventh and the eleventh centuries. Amongst the poorest communities in Morocco, Rif Berbers farm barley and other grains on their steep mountain terraces, relying solely on erratic rainfall for irrigation. They supplement these staples with fruits and vegetables grown in irrigated gardens near rivers and with meat from small herds of goats. Women's lives are saturated with the daily charges of childrearing, food preparation, and home maintenance. The myriad tasks are distributed in accordance with age status. Berbers practice seclusion (*purdah*) of women who are of childbearing age.[7] But seclusion does not mean that Berber women—married or of marriageable age—are exempt from physical, outdoor labor, only that they labor in places where they cannot be seen by men who are unrelated to them.

In traditional contexts, Riffian Berber women do not customarily veil themselves, and therefore the females who move through public spaces, collecting water and performing other necessities outside the home and family land, are generally young girls and older women, people on whom the stringencies of seclusion are not as strict. The latter travel around in public, often out of their villages, visiting neighbors, women's markets, and participating in religious sisterhoods. The privileges claimed by older Berber women are similar to those of urban Moroccan-Arab women of all ages, who often have at least one servant to provide relief from the daily drudgery of running households. Moroccan-Arab women veil themselves in public, yet women of all ages regularly travel outside their homes, visiting the mosque and baths as well as friends and neighbors on a regular basis.[8] Whether the differences in the mobility of Moroccan-Arab and Berber women are a function of the difference between urban and rural living or suggest that Berber women are somehow more traditional, however "traditional" may be defined, is not possible to discern from the ethnographic data; each interpretation may well be valid in particular circumstances.

Girls near or of marriageable age in Berber communities are not generally allowed to be seen by men from outside their immediate families. They are encouraged neither to speak their minds and criticize their elders publically nor to dance suggestively, titillating their audience with immodest bodily undulations. Crossing so many boundaries regulating appropriate behavior for Muslim Berber women, not to mention several Islamic restrictions pertaining to musical performance (especially that concerning dancing for pleasure and with a strong beat), the performances of these girls might seem to compromise both their own futures and their families' standing in their community. And yet, they do not. Their audience is ardently appreciative and admiring, contemplating these girls favorably as daughters, sisters, or friends, even considering the girls as brides for their own sons and cousins or for themselves. The honor of the fathers and families responsible for protecting the girls remains intact during and after the performances in spite of the many morality boundaries that are breached.

In what follows I will introduce the debate on musical performance by women in Muslim communities, contextualize Berber women in the broader discourse on women in Islam, and propose ways in which the performativity of these events mediates the possibility for negative assessment of the position of the girls who perform at marriage ceremonies.

Women and Musical Polemics

The performance of music and, in particular, of women performing music and dance has been continuously contentious throughout the history of Islam. However, no age or region of the Islamic world has been without either organized sound, avoiding the term music, or Muslim women performing in some capacity. The most common form of organized sound in Muslim communities is religious chanting, *qira'at*, the sound of which has been heard throughout the vast reaches of the Muslim world for more than fourteen centuries. Some non-qur'anic chants, like the *adhan*, or call to prayer, and the chants/rites of pilgrimage (*hajj*), have, theoretically, undergone only modest variation over time, most of which are thought to stem from individual and regional style differences. Numerous works written over the centuries have endeavored to prevent the assimilation of indigenous or local musical habits and styles into the adhan, the sound that is generally understood to be iconic with the practice of Islam itself. The pilgrimage chants are learned and sung from texts while preparing for or on the hajj itself, but other forms of recitation have been more susceptible to localization and interpretation.[9]

With the exception of the chants used during pilgrimage, it is rare to hear religious recitation performed by Muslim women in public. People such as Maria Ulfah, an Indonesian women's rights activist, scholar of women and Islam in Indonesia who is much sought-after for her qur'anic recitation skills as both teacher and performer, run counter to this trend. Associated for much of her professional life with the Institut Ilmu al-Quran (IIQ) (Institute for Quranic Studies) in Jakarta, she is also a graduate of the special program for female reciters at the IIQ. Winner of many recitation competitions, Ulfah has traveled across the world teaching and leading sessions that integrate qur'anic recitation with interpretation. She has invested much of her scholarly efforts in writing about the differences between the Indonesia *ummah*, or community, and the various ummah of the Middle-East, in an effort to articulate why it is that women are respected and valued as reciters of the Quran in Indonesia.[10] It is, nevertheless, still safe to say that in many traditionally Islamic contexts, the recitation of Islamic religious chant is primarily the domain of men.[11] Indeed, the recitation of Islamic religious chant, like many other performance genres accepted as legitimate within Islam, is not necessarily considered by Muslims to be "music."

Beyond the basic patriarchal structure of Islam itself, the fact that women rarely perform religious chant in public is tangentially related to what might best be described as the "problem" of music in Islamic society. While no society is monolithic in its perspectives, the antagonism between music and morality is particularly strong and well-articulated in Islamic discourse across the world. Music is openly appreciated and nurtured in most Islamic societies, as is demonstrated by the many highly developed art musics and the much-loved popular genres and international stars found throughout the Islamic world. Still, music is simultaneously reviled as dangerous and despicable in many of those same places. The practice of, and pleasure generated by, music has fostered the production of reams of polemical writings and censure for performers and listeners alike over the centuries. Islamic commentators through the ages have regularly noted that because of the visual and aural pleasures involved, musical performance by people of either gender tends to be associated with a relaxing of morals. This loosening of morals is thought often to cause a breakdown in the proper public demeanor of listeners and performers alike, either spiritually or in an embodied way. A breakdown of demeanor in turn disrupts the proper relationship of the individual to society and to Islam. When women are involved in performance, it is commonly assumed that they are not pious. Indeed, their presence in the company of men outside their own families is cause enough to justify this castigation, in particular in communities where purdah of any degree is the norm, irrespective of how the female performers themselves perceive and enact their own piousness and morality. Male performers are not immune from castigation and opprobrium, but they do not contest as many cultural and religious mores when they perform, and therefore the net effect on their position in society is often not as great as for female performers.[12]

Insisting that the polemical aspects of the discourse on music are both unhelpful—not based on either the Qur'an or the Hadith—and more political than anything else, Lois Ibsen-al Faruqi suggests the adoption of more precise terms when debating the position of music in Islamic society. She presents a taxonomy of music in Islamic communities that ranges from the most *halal* (acceptable), which is non-accompanied chanting without meter, through instrumental unaccompanied, unmetered genres, to the more controversial genres in which there is a mix of sung and instrumental, metered and unmetered contexts and to the music that is considered *haram* (forbidden), that is, metered dance music. The debate about music is actually focused on metered genres that might induce listeners to lose their self-control and dignity by being tempted/provoked to behave immodestly. The remaining genres are acceptable to varying degrees around the Islamic world.[13] Irrespective of the fact that men also perform and appreciate metered musics, women are the ones associated with these forms of illicit musics and, hence, the ones who are judged more harshly.

The separation of women from general society was present to varying degrees in Islamic areas long before Islam began. But the embrace of this separation, as well as the vigorous debates about it, by some leaders of Islamic communities over time has served to articulate and enhance the "difference" of women from general—read male—Islamic society. Islamic women must constantly reconfirm and actively demonstrate both their acceptance of and their adherence to the restrictions that "other" them, articulate their difference from men within society; to do otherwise is to risk the perception that both they themselves and their families are improper in some way. Although there are real differences between Islamic societies with respect to issues of women and performance, in most Islamic communities female performers are assumed to be immoral to some degree.[14] Whatever their lived reality, all female performers merge at some level in the public imagination with courtesans and prostitution, with other forms of public and private entertainment found in different Islamic communities, and with women performers and women in general in non-Islamic communities. How, then, is it possible for the young women of the Riffian communities to perform in public, singing to music with a steady beat, moving their bodies seductively? Why are they not considered to be like dancing girls or prostitutes? Why is the honor of their fathers and brothers not besmirched by their performances in front of all those other appreciative boys and men? That they are not professional performers may mediate the situation to some degree, but the young Berber women are still crossing many of the limits of appropriate behavior for marriageable young women and their families.

The Veil and Women in Islam: Interpreting Muslim Female Sexuality

From some perspectives, women seem to have a secondary role in Islam and Islamic society. Women and men worship in separate areas of the mosque, usually with the women behind a screen of some kind and either off to one side or at the back of the prayer hall. Additionally, traditional Islamic practices such as veiling and seclusion (purdah) remove women from direct communication with people outside of their families, confining them to private worlds, while men can have face-to-face contact in both public and private worlds. Neither veiling nor purdah is specifically required in the Qur'an, although in Surah 24:31 of the Qur'an both men and women are instructed to dress and behave modestly. Traditions of veiling and seclusion were part of pre-Islamic Arab and Mediterranean cultures in general.[15]

The originally protective provisions described in the principal scriptural sources (Qur'an, Sunnah, and Hadith) of Islam—articulated for the tribal cultures prominent in early Islam—were gradually transformed into strict patriarchal structures emphasizing female seclusion and gender segregation. These changes were instantiated through exegesis of scriptural sources that resulted in narrowly defined concepts of female modesty, in particular as Muslim societies started to move from tribal to urban organization.[16] Starting in the twentieth century, Muslim social reformers argued against these and other practices such as polygamy with varying success, at the same time helping to generate reactionary movements around the world. Many Muslim women have attempted to reconcile religious tradition with their modern lives by combining an active public life with outward modesty.[17] Veiling styles range from the *burqa*, a black cape which hides the individual's body completely, to the various styles of *hijab*, which generally cover just the head and shoulders, leaving the face visible but may be as loosely cloaking as a scarf draped casually over the back of the head. Perhaps more significantly than men, Muslim women are caught in ongoing debates inside Islamic communities that turn on the intersection of modern and traditional constructions of gender. Yet, even wearing the veil does not always signal a traditional perspective on women's roles. For college-aged Muslim women or women living in predominantly non-Muslim places, their wearing of a veil of some sort suggests that they are to be taken seriously, as an intellectual equal in both the classroom and the world.[18] The multiplicity and diversity of Islamic veil traditions found around the world, not to mention that many Muslim women choose not to wear a veil, is indicative of varied interpretations of gender-appropriate behavior that are constructed as women negotiate their own relationships and local relationships to universal Islamic traditions. Such local decisions and traditions are in constant dialogue with the universal, and restrictive, interpretations of women's positions within the ummah.[19]

According to the Qur'an, in the gender-blind eyes of Allah all believers are equal. Surah 33:35 reads,

> For Muslim men and women, for believing men and women, for devout men and women, for true men and women, for men and women who are patient and constant, for men and women who humble themselves, for men and women who give in Charity, for men and women who fast (and deny themselves), for men and women who guard their chastity, and for men and women who engage much in Allah's praise, for them has Allah prepared forgiveness and great reward.

This verse outlines practices that articulate almost all the five pillars of Islam[20] and that there is equal opportunity for all who fulfill those acts to receive the rewards that Allah has prepared, irrespective of gender. The relationship between women and Islam, however, is determined not only by interpretation of Islamic texts but also through the complicated interrelationships of scriptural interpretation and the history and contexts of particular cultural groups that happen also to be Islamic. In some Muslim societies, the equality of men and women before Allah is disrupted by what is understood as the dangerous sexual appetite of women.

In the introduction to the 1987 revised edition of her landmark study, *Beyond the Veil: Male-Female Dynamics in Modern Muslim Society*, Moroccan feminist Fatima Mernissi notes that distinction must be made between what people actually do or seek to do—their decisions, aspirations, patterns of consumptions—and "the discourses they develop about themselves," especially those "they use to articulate their political claims."[21] The first dimension is about life lived, but the second is about culture represented, internally and externally. There is a distinct tension between these two in the public discourse about women in some Islamic communities. Mernissi argues that Islamic restrictions and rules about marriage and women in public arose from a fear of what she describes as an "active" female sexuality.[22]

In her brilliant if controversial work, Mernissi attempts to articulate Muslim concepts of female sexuality. She addresses the work of George Murdock, who hypothesizes that with respect to sexual mores, societies fall into two sorts: in one, regulation involves an internalization of prohibitions; in the other, external precautionary safeguards are instituted. Murdock argues that Western societies are of the first sort and that societies practicing veiling and seclusion of women of childbearing age are of the latter sort.[23] Mernissi argues against Murdock, suggesting that these differences reside not so much in any mechanism of internalization but rather in the societies' perspectives on female sexuality. Using the theories of sexuality articulated by Imam al-Ghazali (1050–1111 CE) and Sigmund Freud (1885–1939 CE), Mernissi determines that female sexuality is passive in the writings of Freud and active in those of al-Ghazali. Acknowledging the differences in their intentions—Ghazali was trying to revitalize what he understood as true Muslim belief, while Freud was trying to derive a universal theory of psychosexual development—and the periods in which they were writing, Mernissi seeks to "highlight the particular character of the Muslim theory of male-female dynamics, and not to compare the condition of women in the Judeo-Christian 'West' and the Muslim 'East.'"[24] Working through Freud's 1909 *Three Contributions to the Theory of Sex*, Mernissi notes Freud's analysis of male and female sexualities as active and passive, respectively. She argues that this polarized perspective enlightens an interpretation of human sexuality in al-Ghazali primarily because there such polarization is missing entirely.[25] Instead, al-Ghazali conceives of both male and female sexuality partaking of and belonging to the same kind of energy and substance.[26] In his *Revivification of Religious Sciences*,[27] al-Ghazali argues that male and female are equal in their embodied sexuality and their desire for fulfillment. He says that men and women each have a liquid, both of which are necessary for progeny. Both men and women have ejaculations but the "difference in the pattern of ejaculation between the sexes is a source of hostility whenever the man reaches his ejaculation before the woman. . . . The woman's ejaculation is a much slower process and during that process her sexual desire grows stronger and to withdraw from her before she reaches her pleasure is harmful to her."[28] Al-Ghazali is intent on encouraging his readers to engage in foreplay since a "woman's pleasure necessitates a lingering at the intermediary stages, the believer should strive to subordinate his own pleasure, which is served mainly by the genital union."[29]

Al-Ghazali's analysis and suggestions are motivated by the idea that ministrations to women's pleasure are necessary in order to subdue their dangerous sexual appetites. If left unfulfilled, women might wreak havoc on society. Mernissi interprets al-Ghazali as suggesting that in addition to her own active sexuality—or perhaps because of it—the Muslim woman is endowed with a fatal attraction that erodes the male's will to resist her and reduces him to a passive role. He must give in, as her attraction to an individual man is like that of Satan's irresistible power over human beings.[30] Here woman is equated with Satan, albeit with influence only on an individual level. Women's active sexuality, the embodiment of disorder and destruction, generates fear not only for individual men but also for society. These fears make it necessary to remove women from public where their presence could inadvertently generate chaos either by the rendering of men as passive or through their own destructive tendencies if left unfulfilled. The subordination of women to fathers, uncles, brothers, husbands, and brothers-in-law ensures that their sexual energy will be controlled and contained. Polygamy, seclusion, veiling, chastity, and non-equal access to divorce through repudiation are therefore theorized as acts that protect not only men and women but also communal wellbeing and order. These rules and restrictive habits, while not specifically articulated in the Qur'an, have been developed through interpretation of certain passages in the Qur'an, in particular Surah 4:34, in which the possibility of resistance against authority and what to do about it are addressed.[31]

Feminine Beauty, Feminine Subordination, Feminine Rebellion

> *Men are in charge of women by [right of] what Allah has given one over the other and what they spend [for maintenance] from their wealth. So righteous women are devoutly obedient, guarding in [the husband's] absence what Allah would have them guard. But those [wives] from whom you fear arrogance—[first] advise them; [then if they persist], forsake them in bed; and [finally], strike them. But if they obey you [once more], seek no means against them. Indeed, Allah is ever Exalted and Grand.*
>
> —Qur'an 4:34, *Sahih International Translation*

> *Men are supporters of wives because God has given some of them an advantage over others. So the ones who are in accord with morality are the ones who are morally obligated, the ones who guard the unseen of what God has kept safe. But those whose resistance you fear, admonish them, and abandon them in their sleeping place, then go away from them; and if they obey you surely look not for any way against them; truly God is Lofty, Great.*
>
> *—Qur'an 4:34, Sublime Quran Translation*

Gender theorist Fatna Sabbah argues that

> the ideal of female beauty in Islam is obedience, silence, and immobility, that is, inert passivity. Far from being trivial characteristics and not limited to women, the three attributes used to describe ideal female beauty and behavior are the same as the three qualities required of the true believer vis-à-vis God. The believer must dedicate his life to obeying and worshipping God and abiding by his will.[32]

Men and women are in a similar state with respect to obedience, the only difference being that men must surrender to Allah and women to both men and Allah. The possibility of rebellion against this feminine surrender is a disobedience imagined for women in the Qur'an only with the concept of *nushuz*—disobedience or rebellion against one's husband's wishes.[33]

This issue is explored in Surah 4:34, presented as the epigraph to this section, in which men are acknowledged as more responsible and more obligated than women, who should therefore obey them. The two translations of Surah 4:34 above[34] agree up to this point. The first translation is a standard English translation. The second is a translation by Laleh Bakhtiar, the first translation of the Qur'an by an American woman. The variations arise in the interpretation of what is to happen when women are disobedient. Bakhtiar disputes the common interpretation of the Arabic root *d-r-b* suggesting that it means not "to strike," not even "to strike lightly," but rather "to go away from."[35] She cites several other instances in the Qur'an in which different words are used with the meaning of the transitive verb "to strike" (*d-r-b* is never used in those contexts) and points out that the Hadith—citations of Muhammad's life acts through which Muslim law is determined—demonstrates that Muhammad never struck anyone and always advised against striking.[36] Bakhtiar argues that the elaborate culture of violent male dominance that has been cultivated in Islamic communities around the world is baseless, that it cannot be argued that the Qur'an supports this behavior. Historiographic work by Manuela Marín demonstrates systematic misinterpretation of the Qur'an and the Hadith with respect to this particular Surah starting as far back as 871 CE, by Hûd b. Muhkim al-Hawwârî.[37] The evidence amassed by Bakhtiar and Marín against fourteen hundred years of traditional interpretation of Surah 4:34 is not uncontroversial, but there is still a compelling argument that fear of female disobedience, either in daughters and sisters or wives and in-laws, may be one important element in the drive to find justification for physical dominance of men over women in the Qur'an.

Possible reasons for fear of disobedience, of nushuz, by women in early Islam can be intuited from the story of Sakina, a beautiful first-century Islamic aristocrat with a fiery temper. Sakina was a patron of poets and sat at the table of the Quraish Nobility Council, the ruling body of the Quraish tribe, the tribe of Muhammad the

Prophet. She lived in a century of turbulence, as conversion and adjustment to the new religion and religious leaders generated change in the lives of many. Sakina refused to veil herself and to be quiet in the presence of men. She rejected the idea that her husband should be allowed to harm her in any way or to have more than one wife. Before one of her marriages, "she stipulated that he would have no right to another wife, that he could never prevent her from acting according to her own will, that he would let her elect to live near her woman friend, Ummu Manshuz, and that he would never try to go against her desires."[38] Her husband acted against Sakina's will, spending one weekend with his concubines.[39] Sakina took him to court in Medina, where she is said to have shouted at him, "Look as much as you can at me today, because you will never see me again!"[40] There are also stories of several women selected to be the bride of Muhammad who, on the first ritualized meeting with him, told him they were seeking refuge in Allah from him. They repeated this phrase three times, repudiating him as men repudiate and divorce their wives.[41] These historical women's beauty, status, and wealth were their most important assets when they sought to thwart the new religion's emerging rules regarding women's behavior and independence.

In the context of first-century Islam, a community demanded the subservience of the individual to the group. Women's modesty and submission were constructed as indicative of an organized and well-run community. Independent women threatened Islamic communities because they represented the possibility of disobedience that might, ultimately, topple the nascent religious world. The connection between fear of nushuz and Muslim men's fear of women and their active sexuality is natural: women who rebel against men in any way can be understood as threatening the integrity of the whole Islamic community. The sturdy and comforting parallel dependency whereby women are subordinate to men as men are subordinate to Allah is disrupted. The breach caused by these women suggests that rebellion against Allah is thinkable, which threatens the ummah, which is itself constituted by those mutually agreed laws.

Interpreting Berber Girls' Performing

The historic memory of these rebellious women suggests that the specter of aristocratic women flouting the emerging laws of Islam was certainly noteworthy and possibly even exciting, for later historians spend time describing their beauty, heat, and potency. Perhaps they were so noteworthy because their protagonists were women or aristocrats, or because the emergent Islamic patriarchy had succumbed to the protagonists' power in a way that after the fact was unthinkable, or because the protagonists' self-determination as women was frightening as it suggested the possibility of self-determination outside the mutually agreed terms of Islam. Any, perhaps all, of these rationalizations is possible. Can the enticing visage presented by the Berber girls as they dance sensually and sing their own compositions criticizing their parents and their community be interpreted as an embodiment of nushuz?

The songs of these young unmarried Berber women and their performances are sanctioned by the authorities in their community, the majority of whom watch with pleasure while encouraging the girls on with enthusiastic shouts. Yet with their performances the girls are, if not toppling, then at least pushing at the power structures of the community. Exuding sexual energy, their clearly provocative dance movements in concert with their accusatory or even insulting texts expose them to public scrutiny. Terri Brint Joseph argues that

> the songs serve the vital function of a rite of passage for these girls within the framework of a larger rite of passage, the wedding itself. While the bride and groom are being initiated to their new status as married adults, the girls who sing at the wedding, like debutantes in Western societies, are being "presented" to the community as young women who have come of age and can be scrutinized by the parents of prospective grooms as well as by the young bachelors. . . . [T]he girls performing are setting in motion a train of events which may determine their own weddings.[42]

Joseph's primary analysis is located in the functionality of the performances. She suggests that in the context of a male-dominated society—in which the girls are expected to resume their docile and obedient demeanors once they stop singing—the wedding performances are a singular opportunity for the girls to speak their thoughts and voice their discontents with a bold openness, relegating their own fathers and the whole community to a passive, almost subservient role. It may be one of their only chances to have an effect on the determination of their futures.[43] Understood as an attempt to disrupt the social order or an act of resistance aimed at bringing change, the dancing can simultaneously be a confirmation of that same social order: the girls are participating in their own construction as marriageable young women. Dressed up in their most beautiful garments, dancing provocatively, they present themselves for the viewing pleasure and amusement of all, young and old, men and (some) women.[44]

The dancing of another group of women is also common at Berber weddings, that of the *shikhat*, or prostitutes. Shikhat manipulate and breach gender boundaries, often smoking and sitting with the men for whom they have been performing.

> The poetic publication of privacy in song lyric and bodily movement establishes the shikha as public property; that is, her commoditized vulnerability serves the purpose of society as she is appropriated as a symbol of immodesty and becomes an emblem of shame. Yet the performance of shikhat exposes the values of the

> dominant culture to challenge by speaking a different attitude . . . into being. They "reflexively comment on those patterns and alter a society's awareness of itself." Poesis, bodily and lyrical, becomes a means of self-revelation, social reflexivity, and subtle resistance.[45]

While the resistance performed by shikhat at Berber weddings is not identical to that performed by the young Berber girls, they are related. The shikhat perform gender ambiguity by willingly appropriating both male actions and the familial and personal shame generated by extreme immodesty. This ambiguity generates a societal awareness, a self-reflexivity that particularizes the normative, rendering it actively present rather than simply part of the unarticulated background. Like cultural difference in the midst of a society, this reflexive awareness decenters the normative, allowing the possibility of difference in multiple manifestations.

The music and dance, and even their sunglasses, bond the girls as they perform, disguising them and eroticizing them in ways similar to the henna applied to a bride's body that both reveals and "hide[s] [her] sexuality in layers of other socially significant meanings, like that of 'tradition.'"[46] They are momentarily separate from the rest of the community, of it but also outside of it. The protective, sonic cover of their music emboldens them to step in front of their families and friends to communicate that which they cannot say or do in ordinary moments. The potent critical texts and the boldness of their performance confirm the idea that women harbor within them wildness, an unpredictable sexuality that is perennially poised to erupt and disturb the equilibrium or the community. The women performing are intentionally enticing, yet they are still girls; they are sensual, but until recently children—young daughters and sisters. Their sensuality is created through bodily movements culturally defined as sexy—organized by melodies sung and pulsations from the tabours repeatedly struck—but also through the simple act of standing in front of people and drawing their attention in an act of intentional, if temporary, immodesty. The sensuality of the girls is thrilling, but the pleasure and excitement remind the viewers of the unrealized dangers the girls represent. The music enhances the movements and the enjoyment, as well as the possibility of fearfulness. The performance confirms women as less than men by reminding observers of the potential for wildness and indecorum that theoretically and—in the performative moment—apparently resides inside women, albeit in the bodies of girls whose wildness has not quite fully matured. Understood in this way, the analysis may then corroborate the idea that men are to Allah as women are to men, appropriately maintaining the subordinations necessary to ensure the hierarchies and privileges on which society is constructed.

The texts the girls sing add to the imagined potential disruption to society should women and their fierce, active, and as-yet-untamed sexuality be let loose. Yet the texts also have a publically acknowledged potency, since they speak to the plans, situations, and concerns of the community, in addition to the needs and preferences of the girls. The texts represent months of work on the part of the singers. The community laughs at the innuendos and at the individuals impugned while calculating the impact of messages. This efficacy, then, suggests that none of the boundaries accentuated through these performances is simply confirmed. The music articulates the boundaries in a process that blurs these limits. To do so in a mixed-gendered public performance disturbs the imagined fixed nature of those boundaries within public discourse. It also complicates the construction of women as subservient, docile, reserved, and demur, disturbing not only the ways in which women are received but also the cultural matrix designed to restrain them.

Pleasure, Fear, and Ambiguity—The Performances of Berber Girls at Weddings

For the Berber girls at weddings, their performances involve moving outside their usual gendered ways of being in order to effect some kind of difference in the future for family, self, or community. Their breaking away from normative behavior is justified, perhaps essential to their hoped-for result. The girls are using a ritualized and extraordinary yet familiar way to communicate their preferences, both contesting and influencing the future. It is unlikely that all of these women experience their performance as a form of resistance. Yet that possibility is present. In this event, these girls articulate intentions in a way that is not possible through everyday behavior. That the setting is performative provides a certain amount of cover for the male members of their family and community, in that transgressions can be excused as part of the celebrations and the festive moment. Families can be assured that the participants will return to their usual demeanor once the event is over. Although it is sanctioned, the dissonance between appropriate behavior and the performers' public actions is a reminder, and a confirmation, that female entities have the potential to disturb society's norms—in keeping with the tradition of female disobedience in the beginnings of the Muslim ummah. There is a circularity in the relationship between women operating in public as performers, even in ritualized situations, and the perceived need to have strong restrictions on women's behavior in these two communities.

One pleasurable aspect of observing or experiencing inversion is that it enacts the dissolution of the norm while confirming its very existence. Music and dance in these contexts lubricate the imagination of the performers and the audience alike. They not only enable and embolden the women to perform their offerings, critiques, and transgressions but also, because of the ephemeral nature of performance, confirm that the situation is merely temporary, part of a passing ritual celebration in which non-usual gendered actions are temporarily acceptable. The ritualized sounds of the performances allow women to embody a subversive resistance to, or at least a divergence from, gender norms without actually threatening them. This controlled representation of disruption may recall the possible dangers of real subversion or resistance and the fear of such acts, but pleasure at subversion either observed or engaged is present as well. Sensual and yet distant, demure and submissive, performative and individual, breaking and confirming social mores, the performances of the women validate the need to observe, restrict, and control women and the order of the gender hierarchy while simultaneously reminding everyone involved of the exhilaration of disruptiveness. Although the performances of Berber girls are appreciated, even required and desired by their communities, the act of performance positions the women in an alternative space where, according to some cultural parameters, they are exceeding the boundaries of appropriate behavior. The tension between appreciation and the potential for opprobrium reflects the ambiguity that is embedded in the constructions of women in the community. The containment of the event, the boundaries produced by ephemeral nature of the performance, ensure that the structures that hold the community together are not seriously jeopardized by the revealing of either the girls or their thoughts about their futures.

CHAPTER 6

Transgression and Tarantella among Catholic Women in Calabria

Beautiful Virgin, open the doors,
For your devotees are arriving,
And we come singing and dancing.
Mary of the Mountain, I commend myself to you.

—Madonna della Montagne Pilgrimage Song

This chapter focuses on two manifestations of the tarantella tradition in Catholic southern Italy, exploring not only the connections between them but also the ways in which performance mediates the ambiguity of the social positions of the women who dance tarantella in their different contexts.

Nestled at the bottom of a deep gorge some 865 meters above sea level and surrounded by the steep and craggy sides of the Aspromonte massif in Calabria, Italy, the Sanctuary of Our Lady of Polsi, La Madonna della Montagne, was, until recently, accessible only by foot. Despite, or perhaps because of, the difficulty of accessing it, the location has been the site of shrines and festivals associated with fertility since pre-Roman times. Votive clay artifacts (*pinakes*), likely associated with a fertility cult of Demeter and Persephone and manufactured in the nearby Hellenic colony of Locri, have been found by archeologists at several sites in the area.[1] Basilian monks following the Greek Rite founded a hermitage there in the seventh century honoring the Madonna. Roger II of Sicily founded the sanctuary itself in 1144 CE, and the Latin Rite was finally imposed in the late fifteenth century, as Rome expelled the Basilians.[2] The shrine has persisted and celebrations of the Madonna at that site continue to the present. The site has been associated with fertility and female auspiciousness through several different religious cultures and for more than two millennia.

The festival honoring La Madonna della Montagne occurs during the last days of August and the first days of September. On the night of September 2, 2012, people begin to settle themselves on the stone tiers that form an amphitheater around the cobblestone plaza outside of the sanctuary. A tall young man dressed neatly in a black shirt and pants serves as emcee located on a small, low, permanent circular stage. While directing people to sit down with his arms, he begins to sing a melody with the lyrics, "Hosanna, hosanna, hosanna in altissima." The swelling crowd increases; what was about one hundred people is gradually three times that many. Two white-clad nuns encourage the crowd to stand up and people begin clapping in time and humming along with the singer. After the recitation of Ave Maria prayers led by one of the priests who also leads several songs, an empty pedestal is brought to the side of the stage. As the crowd grows and anticipation builds, a woman takes over the microphone, singing a melody that is familiar for it has been repeating in the background of the soundscape since the beginning of the event. Suddenly, in the sonic distance the slap and strike of a tambourine and the reedy pulsing of an accordion are audible, sounds associated with the accompaniment for the tarantella dance that is iconic with the festival. The audience suddenly cheers and begins clapping vigorously. Led by three priests, a large crowd accompanied by two musicians emerges from a small lane that rounds the corner of the sanctuary. Surrounded and supported by stoic men in everyday dress, the statue of the Madonna and her child is moved into the center of the square at a surprisingly brisk pace. The crowns of the statues glitter as they catch momentary illumination from the lighting around the plaza. The eyes of the blue-clad Mary and her naked baby Jesus stare with a loving fixity out toward the crowd that has now grown to some five hundred people.

A quick ninety-degree turn and the statue is backed up and placed gently on the waiting pedestal. The rushing tarantella accompaniment and the slower hymns sung by the crowd merge and collide, continuing until the statue is secured on its new mount and the people gathered welcome the statue with a hearty round of applause just before the priests begin the prayers appropriate to the moment. Video cameras and iPads capture the scene for both personal and media use, while the formal aspects of the event continue with different parts of the printed service read by local young women, alternating with songs praising the Madonna. A local bishop delivers a brief sermon, and a final Ave Maria is recited by the crowd. The young emcee, joined by an electronic piano and a chorus of young girls—many of whom have taken their turn reading parts of the Mass—sing pop-influenced songs for the Madonna to an appreciative audience. The charismatic local priest begins an energetic interactive segment seeking audience responses; loud applause greets each suggestion. Then, with some final, more formal words of parting by the bishop and a recitation of the Lord's Prayer, the event concludes. The Madonna and her child are lifted once again by their stoic bearers. Accompanied by salutary banners, the Madonna is processed once more around the sanctuary and returned to her loft inside.

This description is based on a video series of some fourteen installments posted online after the 2012 celebration of the Madonna.[3] Other excerpts capture large crowds in the sanctuary during a daytime Mass in which Communion is offered. At the end of that event the crowd organizes itself into crushing lines in which each person approaches the statue of the Madonna and child. Reaching out with a hand to touch the base of her pedestal, occasionally bringing a flower to add to the floral offerings that surround the base, supplicants kiss their fingers while reaching to and from the Madonna, sealing their prayers by crossing themselves reverentially and moving on. Abundant videos from other years can also be found as well as compilations from 35mm footage shot in the 1960s and descriptions and photographs from the many years before then. The advent of roads has meant that most people do not take the long walk down the winding pathway to the sanctuary, nor do most pilgrims spend one or several nights in the area at the bottom of the gorge, picnicking and sleeping out under the September stars as part of the activities as they used to do. Tarantella music and dance, however, have remained a constant for as far back as anyone can remember.

Tarantella and the Pilgrimage to the Madonna della Montagne in Polsi

Before roads were laid into Polsi in the late 1960s, all pilgrims arrived by foot. Although men and women alike offered their bodies and time to the Madonna through the pilgrimage, and both men and women danced the tarantella, women were more likely to make dancing a specific part of their offering to the Madonna. Women might vow to dance down the entire route if they wanted to ask for a favor or give special thanks to the Madonna.[4] In a description from 1912, the young Corrado Alvaro writes, "Girls thus dance along the entire route, and will be dancing night and day for the hours that they have specified in their vow, until they will collapse on the ground or need to lean on a wall while their feet are still moving. . . . They have cast-iron legs, and dance all night long to the dismay of even the strongest among the peasants."[5] Even with the advent of roads and the resultant shortening of the endeavor, pilgrimage is still a communal event. People travel together in minivans and small buses in which they sing and trade pilgrimage songs and stories.[6] Brass bands, singing, and tarantella ensembles consisting of accordion or bagpipe and tambourines were, and are still, the central musical elements of the festival.

When people perform tarantellas to pass the time and add to the general festivities during the pilgrimage, they form a tight circle of dancers, musicians, and onlookers called *rota* or *ronda*.[7] In more organized situations, one person serves as the leader and is responsible for inviting people into the center of the circle to dance, gently shepherding them out, choosing who will dance with whom and when while carefully monitoring the social ramifications of each partnering.[8] Dancers move in and out of the circle in a steady flow, often dancing for a few phrases, edging out of the circle, and occasionally returning to the center of the ring for another few phrases. In situations where no one is in charge, dancers negotiate entrances with their heads, eyes, and bodies, gesturing desire to enter by engaging the gaze of those already in the ring, and then moving into the space, physically willing the others in the ring to move over. Dance turns evolve as a dynamic, embodied conversation: flirtation, contestation, physical challenge, friendship, irritation and other emotions are all conveyed through subtle interpretations and manipulations of basic tarantella moves and the use of space inside the dancing ring.

Once they begin, the music and dance are persistent, never pausing until the entire event is finished. The tambourine and accordion players set a driving pace in a skipping triple meter known as the *pizzica*. Musicians occasionally step in to spell one another, carefully joining at the end of a phrase so as not to disturb the pulse and the disjunct, hopping melody. The dancers move into and out of the circle and so are afforded breaks to recover their breath and ease. Male and female forms of the tarantella dance are based in the same arm gestures and foot patterns, but (at least in couples' dancing in the video footage from Polsi over the years) women's interpretations tend to be slightly more restrained than men's movements, with arms raised only to the waist rather than above their heads, delicate hand movements rather than arcing hand gestures, feet kept close to the ground with small steps (rather than big steps starting at the knee, as is common for men), and evasive tactics and actions—turning away from a male co-dancer as though to block his approach. The nature of the gender differences in these dance moves resonates with long-standing, commonplace characterizations of Calabrian women (and Mediterranean women in general) and gender relations: women are shy, reserved, quiet, demure, and their honor must be maintained and protected. In the past it was the case that even though men and women danced together in the same ring in pairs, they never touched one another.[9] As with all stereotypes, these characterizations only partially describe reality. The lived nature of gender roles is naturally more complex and varied. Goffredo Plastino points out that Calabrian peasants and shepherds have traditionally gotten "close to and touched one another while dancing, even hitting each other's buttocks . . . gaz[ing] at one another purposely, challenging each other to resistance and seduction. . . . The way in which Calabrian people danced tarantella had already been described in a number of books in the nineteenth century; yet the model whereby women are kept under strict control by men has been amplified and underlined to such an extent that it has become a commonplace."[10]

Plastino's research demonstrates that tarantella performance, while different in each case, is an important part of at least three different saints' festivals in Calabria. In addition to the one in Polsi, Plastino describes one in Riace for the feast day of Saints Cosimo and Damiano, and another in Gioioso Ionica for the feast of Saint Rocco.[11] With a focus on changing gender norms in Calabria in the early 2000s, Plastino notes that the tarantella styles in Polsi align more closely to traditional gender norms of the past than those in Riace or Gioioso Ionica, but he does not propose an analysis as to why tarantella is performed at all at these festivals. I have not found an explanation as to why tarantella dancing has come to be associated with the pilgrimage to the sanctuary of the Madonna della Montagne in particular, except that it is the dance and music that is iconic with the region.

It is important to note that women have habitually danced two forms of tarantella during the pilgrimage to the shrine of La Madonna della Montagne: the communal, fluidly social dance in the *rota*, traditionally one of the few contexts where unrelated men and women were allowed to occupy the same public space and interact with one another; and the publically displayed yet private, embodied votive offerings in which women, having shed their familial and other social duties for the duration, dance their way along the pilgrimage route to the shrine of the Madonna. These two forms of tarantella are part of a web of dance phenomena found across the region for at least a millennium. In the region in southern Italy where Polsi is located, tarantella dance also has connections to tarantism, an illness theoretically caused by the bite of a kind of tarantula, the *Lycosa tarantula*, common in the Salento region, in particular the town of Taranto. That spider, aggressive and with a painful bite but not particularly venomous, was prevalent until the middle of the twentieth century, when pesticides decimated the species.[12]

Tarantism was most common in the sixteenth and seventeenth centuries, but it has continued into the twenty-first century.[13] Women who ostensibly had been bitten by tarantulas were struck with melancholia, malaise, and often erratic physical behavior. The symptoms of disease would reappear once or twice every year, often in the dry heat of midsummer. Most dramatically, the suffering women would drop to the ground and writhe around, shrieking and hollering, fearfully striking out at bold colors such as red, green, and white, hurling insults, feigning lewd gestures, unable to communicate with their family and friends. The tendency to be struck down by these traumatic bouts of maniacal behavior often lingered for days or weeks on end once the melancholic onset began. One apparently effective cure was for musicians to perform short excerpts of various folk song melodies—known as *tarantella pizzicata* after the name of the spider—until the patient stopped writhing and began to listen. Once her attention was caught, the musicians would continue the same melody that had caught her attention until the patient rose up from the floor to begin whirling around, stamping her feet, dancing as if, or actually, possessed and in trance. If the musicians stopped playing, the victim would drop to the ground in a catatonic state once again, and the exorcism had to start from the beginning. Great responsibility and considerable time constraints fell on the musician who agreed to tackle the task of finding the right tune and then healing the *tarantata*. When the venom of the spider had finally been expelled and the patient returned to herself through the cathartic effect of dancing wildly to the music, she would retire to her bed and sleep for several days, healed until the next bout struck.[14]

Tracing Tarantism to the Present

The history of the development of tarantism is murky. "A 1426 document written by the Venetian doctor Sante Ardoini, and printed in the *Sertum papale de venenis* series, is most commonly cited as the first literary evidence of tarantism," although there is another, more cryptic description in the same series from 1362 attributed to Guglielmo De Marra.[15] Ernesto De Martino's groundbreaking study of tarantism in 1961 defined the parameters within which all subsequent research on tarantism has been written.[16] After careful consideration of all written sources, De Martino suggests that the practice of tarantism developed between the ninth and fourteenth centuries, a time during which southern Italy was persistently at the crossroads between crusading armies from northern Europe and Muslim traders and warriors from the Ottoman Empire and points farther east. They were also repeatedly struck by many savage annihilating illnesses circulating through Europe and Asia during those centuries. De Martino suggests the rise of the tarantism cult was a result of the confluence of long-term destabilizing cultural aspects and the subsequent pressures to conform to the Latin Rite beginning in the fifteenth century, when the population was urged to abandon the pre-Christian, fertility, and other cultic practices that had persisted and coexisted, more or less peaceably, with the Greek Rite.[17]

Connections to the pre-Christian cults are circumstantial but compelling. The Apulian region was once part of Magna Graecia, an area in which the cult of Dionysus was important.[18] Some have suggested that the constant beating of tambourines in the pizzica rhythm has connections to Greek culture and myth.[19] Lee Robert Blackstone cites De Martino, Lewis, Sigerist, and the musician dancer Alessandra Belloni in connecting these types of dance to ancient Greece and Greek women's cults of Dionysus. Those women who followed Dionysus were known as *maenads*. When they heard the drums and tambourines playing the rhythms used to worship Dionysus, they were "'called away' from their domestic chores. . . . [They would] cry out and wildly dance in their passion for Dionysus."[20] This festival was not celebrated with expressions of the abandonment of sexual mores, nor was it associated with fertility. Rather, it was a festival of inversion of gender norms and cross-dressing identity. The women who ran away from their domestic duties at the sound of the drums and tambourines took the place of their social superiors—men—becoming hunters, rushing into the hills to catch small animals, ripping them apart and eating them raw.[21] Blackstone notes that this abandonment of the duties, hierarchy, and order of daily life to indulge in an ecstatic experience in which the self is temporarily lost and then regained is similar to the *tarantata* ecstatic experience.[22]

The last known remaining musician who was able to "cure" patients afflicted with tarantism was Luigi Stifani (1914–2001). He was a self-taught barber and musician who grew up in Salento playing music for another curer in the area. A sailor, he found himself in Greece in 1937 and witnessed a man repeatedly inching his way up a high rope only to throw himself down to the ground. Stifani understood that he was afflicted by a similar kind of illness as tarantism and taught the musicians who were accompanying the actions of the man to play a *pizzica-pizzica indiavolata* from Salento, a melody Stifani knew to be efficacious in similar situations. The man danced wildly to the rapid tempo for more than an hour and then fell down, cured. It was at this point that Stifani realized his calling.[23] This anecdote tells us that the phenomenon of tarantism, or similar afflictions, was reasonably widespread in southern Europe even as late as the middle of the twentieth century and that music is thought to be curative in at least two places.[24] Although southern-Italian men also were occasionally struck as in the previous anecdote (and in the case of "Matteo," discussed by Lüdtke), it is, nevertheless, predominantly women who endure and engage in an embodied way with tarantism.

Whether tarantism is a psychological illness, an imagined and constructed state, or something else completely is a debate that has been present since the first documentation of the phenomenon. The ailment captured the attention of many different writers and thinkers, from doctors to philosophers and other culture observers in Europe. In his *Magnes sive de arte magnetica* (Rome, 1641) the Jesuit priest Athanasius Kircher argued in favor of the affliction being related to magic and Renaissance interpretations of magnetism and for efficacy of music and colors therapy in curing the ailment.[25] Others, such as Giorgio Baglivi in 1704, advocated medical explications and cures, noting a causal relationship between spider bites and psychological disorders.[26] Beyond these analyses of tarantism as a physiological ailment, one sociological explanation for the phenomenon occurs reasonably often in nineteenth- and twentieth-century sources. The argument begins with the idea that because women live/were living in a state of exclusion and repression, in a society founded on the limitation of female freedom at all levels of social life, and with the fifteenth-century reduction of access to pre-Christian fertility celebrations that involved possession and trance dancing by women, women found themselves cut off from the one important, socially sanctioned, expressive moment in the yearly cycle when they could be released from society's everyday restrictions.[27] Porcino reminds her readers that tarantism is most often a mid-summer phenomenon, one that occurs when people are harvesting in the fields, disturbing areas where spiders might have set up their webs, but also the time when local pre-Christian fertility celebrations had traditionally been celebrated.[28] This argument binds the twentieth-century phenomenon of tarantism to gender, season, and ancient cultural traditions reaching back millennia.

Some local people interviewed for recent ethnographic studies think that the whole phenomenon has been overstated, pointing out that tarantism is most likely a ploy by the women to get attention, or money, or their way with their families who were thwarting their goals to marry one man or another.[29] In whatever way one might choose to read these explanations, it is clear that the phenomenon of women dancing in an extroverted, ecstatic manner in the summer in southern Italy has been ongoing, very likely since the pre-Christian period. Exploring the range of definitions and analyses over time reveals the phenomenon as malleable but persistently present. It is this malleability that allows for an articulation of the connections between the tarantellas danced on the pilgrimage to the Sanctuary of the Madonna della Montagne and those suffering with tarantism.

Saint Paul and Tarantism

Saint Paul is known as a protector against poisonous animals primarily because of his experiences in southern Italy and Malta. In the *Acts of the Apostles* 28: 3–5 Paul is shipwrecked and lands on Malta, off the southern coast of Italy. When he builds a fire one evening, a snake crawls out and bites him on the arm. Paul simply knocks the reptile off his arm and it falls into the fire. Amazed that Paul does not keel over and die in agony, his companions declare that he is a god. Significantly, Paul is also thought to have landed on the Otranto peninsula on the far eastern side of the "heel" of Italy. From there he journeyed to the town of Galatina to visit some Christians who were known to live there. "While there, he bestowed upon a local Christian, and his descendants, the power to heal those bitten by poisonous animals by making the sign of the cross over the wound and having the victim drink water from the well attached to the house now known as *Casa di San Paolo*."[30] This connection with protection from venomous animals makes St. Paul and the curative properties of the water in the well he blessed in Galatina obvious points of interest and engagement for *tarantate* and their families.[31]

In the eighteenth century a chapel to St. Paul was built at the Casa di San Paolo with its enclosed well on Via Garibaldi in Galatina, officially commemorating the visit of Paul in the first century CE. It is perhaps not a coincidence that this Chapel was built at the same time that the "Catholic Church began again to clamp down on dance rituals . . . with pagan roots in Southern Italy."[32] Although there are no documents that speak explicitly about the reasons for the development, after that time tarantate from around the region regularly made a yearly pilgrimage to Galatina to honor St. Paul and to sample ablutions from the therapeutic waters of the well to thank him for their relief from their yearly midsummer bouts with tarantism. Saint Paul's feast day is conveniently coordinated with harvest season and the timing of the fertility festivals prevalent in the pre-Christian period. This new pilgrimage was, Lüdtke and others suggest, a convenient coalescence, a mutual appropriation between Church goals and local practice. Although the well has long since been sealed for hygienic reasons, crowds are still gathering in Galatina on and around June 29 every year in the twenty-first century. The crowds are much smaller than they were in the middle years of the twentieth century. Stories are still told of tarantate who, overcome as they approached Galatina, began to dance wildly from the edge of town to the chapel, accompanied by the musicians who traveled with them. On the way, they were known to have assaulted various townspeople verbally or to have lashed out at individuals wearing bright colors and glinting silver or gold in the crowd that gathered to watch the proceedings.[33]

There is a delicious incongruity in the fact that women suffering a kind of disorderly possession can be cured only by ecstatic dance and a subsequent pilgrimage to a site dedicated to St. Paul. It is true that Paul is the saint who protects against venomous animals; hence, it makes sense that people suffering from the effects of a venomous bite would turn to him for solace. But it was also Paul who vehemently argued against the orgiastic, disorderly nature of some aspects of the worship, generated mostly by women, that had been ongoing in the Church at Corinth twenty centuries earlier,[34] not to mention the fact that Paul argued that women should be silent and modest in church.[35] The friction or even irony one might enjoy in this convergence is not necessarily significant for the tarantate or their families or possibly even for the officials from the Catholic Church who were inclined in Italy, as in other places around the world, to appropriate and reorient to the Church's own purposes local practices that might otherwise have served as alternative spiritual practices and moorings.[36] That said, it was only after centuries of having the local services in the Church of Saints Peter and Paul in Galatina disrupted by tarantate in the summer months—not to mention years of bickering, delay, and at least one court case—that it was finally declared that a chapel for St. Paul, different from the Church in Galatina and proximate to the well of water sought by the tarantate, could be built in the Casa di San Paolo. In the report of the archbishop Vincenzo Andrea Grande in 1837, the Catholic Church finally accepted that the tarantate were part of the traditional cult of St. Paul. The church insisted, however, that the healing was actually performed by God, through St. Paul, and the prayers of the faithful and the clergy.[37] In one move the Church both acknowledged the power and importance of the tradition to the local people and claimed that power for itself.[38] In this process the music that accompanies and aurally enables the cure is simultaneously constructed as ritually efficacious. It should be noted that "the figure of St. Paul is extremely ambivalent" in this context. As I. M. Lewis notes, St. Paul is also "credited with causing the spirit-spider affliction he cures. On the one hand, there is the benevolent figure of St Paul, protector and healer of those bitten by the spider; on the other, there is a punitive St Paul who sends the tarantula to bite sinners. There is further the hybrid figure of St Paul-the-tarantula . . . which appears in the course of the exorcistic rites where the possessed victim speaks both as the tarantula and as St Paul. This identification is furthered in the experience of those women bitten by the spider who may have visions and dreams of St Paul, summoning them to mystical marriage."[39] References to St. Paul "pricking" the tarantate or biting the tarantate "just under the hem of her night dress" or "under the fringe of her skirt" are made in songs collected by De Martino from Kircher's report and from an exorcism performed in 1931.[40]

Interpreting Tarantate

As the ethnographic accounts[41] demonstrate, tarantate occupy a complicated cultural location as women. They are well known in their communities, positively and negatively received, as is the case for celebrities in general.[42] An aura of suspense surrounds them due to their potential to be out of control and wild at unpredictable moments, especially as the days of St. Paul's feast approach. Hence, even when they are not suffering an onset of tarantism, they are a spectacle to be observed from a distance. While some people think the tarantate are making it all up to draw attention to themselves, others believe that their periodic possession comes from some kind of repressed sexual desire[43] or from the evil connections of spiders with Satan.[44] The bite of the tarantula is sometimes understood as a metaphor for sex, as if the tarantate are willing themselves to be bitten. Occasionally, the tarantate are connected with the biological fact that female tarantulas often eat their mates. The tarantate's having been "spider-bitten" conjures the idea that they too might devour their mates once they have copulated. Lüdtke points out that analogies of women to spiders are common in the region. One interviewee whom she quotes suggests that all women are like spiders, weaving their webs around men, entangling them, first mothers and then wives, devouring the men.[45] The layering and interweaving of these varied images and constructions over one another does not have the effect of obscuring any of them. Tempting, fear-inducing, untamable, ill, and in need of healing, suffering the pleasures and pain of ecstatic expression, mysteriously connected with the orgiastic elements of the ancient, pagan worship of Dionysus[46] as well as the healing powers of St. Paul and by extension the Church, tarantate simultaneously inhabit all of these cultural locations.

The tarantate embody/occupy an ambiguous position near one end on the continuum of possibilities for Christian femininity that ranges from whore to virgin/madonna.[47] Simultaneously confirming and challenging male authority and hierarchy in both their own communities and the Catholic Church, tarantate can be seen to represent the rupture and disorder caused by Eve. But their public catharsis, now constructed as an illness, is healed by the intervention of the Christian male "order" in the form of St. Paul who is, ironically, both their seducer and their exorcist. In this context, the tarantate represent an embodied form of the human race that also tends to veer away from right conduct and become "possessed" in different ways by un-Christian things. Tarantella music, nearly always played by male performers, is the medium that diagnoses and cures, one that restores order by creating the pathway through the disorder to the (more socially acceptable) peace of catharsis. Without the fast pulse and dotted rhythms, without the repetitive, angular melodies played on the accordion and violin accompanied by the relentless skipping pattern of the tambourine, the dancing cure would fail; the rehabilitation of the tarantate from Eve's chaotic and socially disruptive end of the continuum of Christian femininity and the restoration, however momentary, of the tarantata to a state of normalcy and productivity would be incomplete. Here, the music—possibly a remnant from the pagan past—performs its duty of guiding the possessed through catharsis and back to normalcy.

From another perspective, if the music and dance are not interpreted as a cure for an ill individual but rather as a means of community communication and confirmation, the power and efficacy of the performance is similar. The joining together of music and dance, performed by male and female participants in order to communicate with and provide a propitiatory offering during the summer, a moment of intense agricultural activity, to ensure the upcoming harvest and the benefit of the community makes a certain amount of sense in the context of the non-Christian world where the gods (as nature) are multiple, demanding, and unpredictable. From this perspective, the process of the harvest and the offering of music and danced possession performed by men and women together could represent the fertile efficacy of male and female conjoining, a fusion of maleness and femaleness on practical and aesthetic expressive levels replicating the unpredictable but generative process in nature. Beginning from this interpretation of the cultural practice, Gilbert Rouget suggests that the tarantism had to be reimagined as individual illness at some point because the Roman Church "could never for a moment have tolerated its existence as an overt possession cult."[48] In essence, the spider bite and the related "illness" provided cover for the continuation of a tenacious cultural practice: women who were possessed were not sinners but victims in need of cure, and the musicians were no longer pagan accomplices but healers working to bring solace and comfort to the individual and peace and order to society. From a gendered perspective, there are subtle shifts in constructions of control and power in the situation: from women as dancers in control of communicating with the gods to victims in need of cure, from men as accompanists actively engaged in communicating with the spirits to healers, restorers of calm, and a controlled community.

In a testament to their deep-rooted, persistent nature, the traditions of tarantism and tarantella in the region are experiencing a resurgence of community and national interest and participation. Nevertheless, contemporary practitioners of neo-tarantism scoff at the medical perspectives, both biological and psychological, described above and so important to Christian and later anthropological interpretations of tarantism. For these contemporary, urban, Italian girls and women, from many different socioeconomic levels, performing tarantella and tarantism accompanied by the driving, skipping beats of the tambourine and accordion—some reenacting possession, others exoticizing themselves for the pleasures of performing, and still others performing on stage for national folk festivals—is all part of an effort to recover or discover Salentino identity for themselves and the world.[49]

Disruptive Women: Mediating Gender Norms through Performance

Music fulfills similar functions for the women who dance their embodied offerings along the entire pilgrimage route to the shrine of La Madonna della Montagne. Male performers arrive with the women who plan to dance their way down the entire pilgrimage route. The tarantella melodies played on their accordions, violins, and bagpipes, and the relentless, infectious, dotted pounding of their tambourines create the soundscape for the dancers as they demonstrate their devotion to La Madonna in an effort to secure her beneficence. The sound of tarantella makes it possible for the dancers to have the physical energy and mental endurance to complete their vow, rendering efficacy to their offering. The sounds of other musicians, also playing tarantella but for dancers in rota, blend into, playfully confuse, and resonate with the melodies of the musicians accompanying the devotional dancers and people singing songs for the Madonna on their way down to the shrine. The dancing pilgrims' own movements are jostled, impeded, and urged forward by the crowds that throng the pathways and stationary rota filled with other dancers entertaining themselves. Cacophony, physical and aural, permeates the environment. The soundscape of the entire festival is composed of the thrum of the crowds, shouts, laughs and gasps, the dotted pulsations of tarantella, the shuffle of feet and the singing of pilgrimage songs (mostly by elder women), and the blessings of priests and other clergy. There is chaos and musical catharsis on the pilgrimage to the shrine of La Madonna della Montagne, but it is primarily communal. Not constructed as the curing of an ill and suffering woman or an individualized battle with good and evil, it is, rather, a communal expression at an appointed and appropriate moment in the year, the feast day of La Madonna della Montagne.[50]

When they vow to dance the pilgrimage to La Madonna della Montagne, the devotional dancers make a decision to deny themselves rest and comfort during their journey. They ignore their daily routines and duties in order to devote themselves to completing their vow. Their abstinence from physical ease links them to the many Christian women who have denied themselves aspects of everyday life in order to demonstrate their intensity of commitment to religion. The gendering of women who devote themselves in an uncompromising manner to living a Christian life is complicated as they were often, at least in the early years of Christianity and through the Medieval period, referred to, and referred to themselves as, "becoming male," having moved beyond the normative engagement of women with Christianity. Saint Gregory of Nyssa describes his sister, Saint Macrina the Younger (324–379), nun and educator of women and devoted Christian ascetic, as having surpassed the nature of woman, implying that she had become male. Perpetua, an early, third-century Carthaginian Christian, saw herself as invested with Christ's power and dreamed of herself as having a male body before she was martyred.[51]

There is no confusion about the gender of the devotional dancers in Polsi. They have not renounced life in the everyday world for Christianity and so do not teeter on the verge of "becoming male" in any interpretation, but for the days of their pilgrimage they are physically and emotionally single minded in their goal of communicating their intensity of commitment to La Madonna della Montagne. If the tarantate are located on Eve's end of the continuum of Christian femininity, the devotional dancers at the Polsi pilgrimage can be located closer to the end of the continuum associated with Mary, who, ascetic-like and virginal, magically pregnant, still decidedly female and subject to male control, devoted herself to birthing and raising Christianity's primary martyr. But like the spirits that occasionally inhabit the tarantate of Salento, the manifestations of the Madonna herself, at least in southern-Italian Catholicism, are not unfailingly kind, good, or predictable. *La Madonna non solo rassicura ma anche intimorisce*—the Madonna not only reassures but also intimidates.

In *Madonnas That Maim: Popular Catholicism in Italy Since the Fifteenth Century*, Michael Carroll describes the florescence of saints as local patrons and Marian cults in Italy since the late 1400s. While the Universal Catholic Church in Rome constructs itself as the intermediary between the mundane and the divine, local patron saints and Marian shrines disturb the singularity of that mediation since individuals and groups can strive for and may even attain direct access to the saints and Mary herself if they travel to the local chapels and shrines to make offerings. Carroll points out that the Church fathers, predominantly Italian themselves over the centuries, have come from the same cultural milieu and hence understand how to turn the practice to their own advantage to some degree. For instance, the Church insists that the saints have power only because God heals through them. They acknowledge the sites of apparitions of Mary only after the seer and the apparitions have stopped and the danger of the seer's presence usurping the role of mediator between the Divine and the mundane dissipates. Nevertheless, the saints' shrines and chapels to Mary and various local saints are the sites where many Italian Catholics seek intercession from the Divine. Supplicants must wrestle with the uncertainty as to whether a particular pilgrimage, offering, or procession will achieve the desired outcome. Stories of Madonnas who apparate and request something like the building of a church at a particular location only to exact their revenge in a bodily form against the person who does not carry out her orders abound. These maiming Madonnas, as Carroll calls them, add an unpredictability and a fear factor to the constructions of Mary as Divine Mother, provider of hope and succor to all. The tension that exists between the merciful and the vengeful in Marian representations is part of what drives the fervor of the participants in the pilgrimages and processions.

The idea of Mary as vengeful also disrupts the binary opposition between evil and good on a continuum of Christian femininity, at least in Southern Italy. Similar tensions exist in the ways in which the tarantate are observed and othered as they enter into their summer harvest trances and to a lesser extent the receptions of the single-minded dancers fulfilling their vows on the pilgrimage in Polsi—recall Alvaro's comments about the dismay of the peasants when confronted by the women pilgrims whose legs were stronger than their own as they danced their way down to the Madonna. These women are intensely engaged in dancing tarantella in a manner that excludes all other foci and that distances them from any other form of interaction, distancing them, for the moment, from their other roles as mothers, nurturers, family, neighbors, co-workers, and so on. The dedication or physical need to dance tarantella in order to return to or affirm their normal states is one key element that connects tarantate with the women who dance the pilgrimage to visit La Madonna.

Connecting Tarantate and Pilgrims through Tarantella

The fact that women possessed, trancing, and expressing their needs and intentions through dance was an important part of the pre-Christian and Hellenic fertility and other rituals prevalent in the regions twenty centuries ago is important background to tarantella in its multiple manifestations in the present and recent past. The concatenation of women, tarantella, intense emotion, pilgrimage, and the seeking of intercession from a Christian intermediary in both Polsi and Galatina suggest that analytical comparisons connecting the tarantella traditions discussed here are reasonable. While tarantella is not exclusively danced by women, it is primarily women who, occasionally in extraordinary ways, use tarantella to connect with their spiritual worlds. What do these women represent? In both Polsi and Galatina, these women are supplicants seeking solace in some way. Their needs are expressed through dance, either an embodied offering or a body danced to expel a "poison": in one, the agency is active; in the other, passive. In the third group, women who dance tarantella to entertain themselves and others and to pass time and add to the festivities while on the pilgrimage but not as a vow, the dancing is a culturally sanctioned, perhaps dangerous moment in which the rules of modesty and correct behavior might be strained slightly: women and girls dancing in the same circles as men and boys, appearing publically together in the same context. If the traditional male and female forms of tarantella dancing in the rota are designed so that the women's moves deflect the danced advances of male moves (an embodied articulation of cultural mores), flirtation and nearness are still embedded in the process, anticipated and enjoyed by both men and women. In all three, an aura of the possibility of immodesty or impropriety as well as extraordinariness hover over the female dancers even though the sensuality of these performers is not necessarily their primary performative intent but rather a seemingly inevitable byproduct that results whenever women express themselves physically in extraordinary contexts in public. They are all women who have stepped outside the bounds of usual ways of being, albeit in different ways but to similar music. As such, they are occupying multiple spaces, some of which are in conflict with one another and some of which challenge the parameters of appropriate behavior for women in their cultural context.

What does the musical accompaniment do in these three types of tarantella performance situation? As the music is most often performed by men, one might argue, simplistically, that the male music controls the female dancing, paralleling their relationships in everyday, patriarchal Catholic southern Italian society. The strongest case for this particular analytical position is found with the accompaniment for the tarantate where men control the medium that brings a cure. The dancer is rehabilitated to societal norms through "medicinal" male music. In the devotional dancing at the festival for La Madonna della Montagne, however, the dancer is only encouraged and urged on by the music in her journey to the shrine to fulfill the vow she has made to La Madonna. Her suffering and intensity is eased and supported by the music but not controlled by it, and she has made the decision to dance to the Madonna. For dancers in the rota, in the more traditional contexts of the past, the music would have provided the soundscape in which certain kinds of (usually prohibited) male-female interaction could take place. In the festival today, amid the increasing informality and mixture of contemporary urban culture, and where many participants are outsiders—even foreign tourists—carrying the differences of other worlds to the event, the dancing is no longer as constrained or regulated by the music. But women may still be heard to seek forgiveness from the Madonna, exclaiming amid other shouts and whoops in the dark, "Madonna, forgive us, because we are sinning."[52] A more nuanced perspective on the role of music in the performance of tarantella argues that in each manifestation the music enables and speeds the desired goal of the dancers. In these semi-religious contexts tarantella as a female expressive form allows the women who perform to explore the edges between condoned and condemned behavior in their society. Trancing, dancing in public, removing oneself from daily activity and familial responsibility to fulfill vows, subtly flirting with men—all of these activities cross socially proscribed boundaries, albeit with varying degrees of transgression. Performing tarantella while crossing those boundaries mediates the disruptions, creating a context in which women can do what they need to do and still maintain their positions in society. That the boundaries are crossed during the performance of tarantella, a culturally sanctioned context for breaching gender and other social boundaries, means that the dissolution of the boundaries by tarantate and pilgrims through their performances serves to affirm the very boundaries that have been traversed. The ambient haze of religiosity that hovers around tarantella dancing in the performance contexts discussed here amplifies both the transgressions and their nonpermanence.

Afterword

Mid-twentieth-century predictions that the importance of religion would continue to retreat due to the relentless push of rational secularism seem to have been wrong. In 2015 the journal *Gender and Society* published a special issue on religion, identifying a resurgence in religious participation by people in all socioeconomic levels, races, and ethnicities and an increase in the importance of religion in political and economic discourse in the United States and around the world. The editors of the special issue note an impoverished understanding of the intersections between religion and gender among sociologists and a marginalization of interdisciplinary scholarly discussions of gender and religion.[1] They comment that "gender is an especially salient feature of religion. In many parts of the world, and in many religious traditions, cultural and religious continuity hinges on gendered and sexual practises and regions."[2] With the current rise in religious fundamentalism, with world politics (and economies) embroiled in debate about women's bodies and their comportment in public, it is essential that sociologists, anthropologists, ethnomusicologists, and other scholars study the ways their own disciplinary topics intersect with religion and gender. Although rooted in an academic interest derived from my own fieldwork in a place that has absorbed and accommodated four major world religions, in working on this project I have become increasingly intent on finding ways to demonstrate analogous relationships between religions through my comparisons. That is, my goal has been to show some correspondence between things that are otherwise dissimilar in an effort to interrupt the idea that people practicing different religions cannot understand or value one another.

The chapters in this book document some of the ways in which women's performance practices engage and localize world religions and the ways in which those performances create opportunities for women's own agency. The book has been constructed in two sections. The first employs comparison across religions to explore the ways in which women use performance to mediate their anxieties and enthusiasms about what is arguably the most dramatic upheaval in women's lives—that is, marriage, their own and those of their children. Weddings are constructed as beneficial for individual and community but also involve the transgression of many societal norms and significant levels of uncertainty—both for women themselves and later for their children—about how the future will unfold for all involved. In short, they are uprooting and even frightening, but still exhilarating and happy affairs. Women have developed myriad practices to accompany the process of preparing and ushering their children into marriage bonds. Even as they push their children forward and the children themselves yearn for the next stage in life, all feel the tension and uncertainty. I have found that two genres—wedding lamentation and wedding mockery—provide telling examples for discussing the mediation of these emotions. These two unusual-seeming categories of expression can be found in women's performance traditions around the world and across different religions. Expressions of sadness and longing, impropriety and satire abound. Both can be understood to galvanize and inspire the participants while externalizing, making public and observable, the emotional experiences of those most involved.

I link these two comparative chapters with an exploration of the wedding abduction of Persephone. The mother's grief of Demeter is all consuming. She laments the departure of her daughter for many months. The communication that finally begins to heal her enervating malaise is a kind of women's mockery, humorous actions and words that ultimately galvanize Demeter to recover herself and take action to redress the abduction. While the Zeus-sanctioned wedding-abduction of Persephone by Hades is more dramatic and cataclysmic than an average wedding in any religion, it must be noted that one benefit of storytelling and its sister, performance, is to externalize, amplify, and subsequently relativize the emotional experiences of individuals in those who hear the story.

The chapters in the second part of the book explore the idea that in some instances women can use religiously sanctioned public performance to mitigate actions that might normally be considered inappropriate within their communities. While this is true to some extent for some of the examples from the lamentation and mockery chapter, the audience for most of those transgressions is the safe and private realm of other women. When a Muslim Berber teenager declines the husband her father has chosen for her in a song performed at another girl's wedding, or when a married Catholic Italian woman dances the tarantella for the duration of the pilgrimage to the Madonna della Montagne to fulfill a vow, each is performing actions in public that would normally be discouraged or condemned. In these contexts, however, the women performers take advantage of the liminality of ritual context and boldly contravene cultural norms for women in their communities. The performance context itself provides socially acceptable cover for women's agency in these ritual moments.

On Meta-Analysis and Comparative Ethnomusicology

I have described this book as a meta-ethnography. Meta-analysis studies are unusual in ethnomusicology, but they are an essential analytical tool in the sciences, particularly the life sciences, where they are used to combine the results of separate studies examining different aspects of one phenomenon. The goal is to see whether there is enough agreement between the studies to determine if the results, combined or otherwise, are significant. If the findings are determined to be scientifically significant, then researchers can hone their experimental approaches to accommodate that discovery, developing next steps with reasonable expectations as to the productivity and eventual success of their research.

Despite the old, "heroic" trope of the ethnomusicologist or anthropologist heading off into the "bush" to spend a year documenting an "undiscovered" people somewhere, there are now enough generations of scholarly work in many areas to allow for meta-ethnographic work to be engaged on particular local contexts. And, as demonstrated in chapters 2 and 4 in this book, it is also possible for a particular cultural theme or practice to be examined through cross-cultural, meta-ethnographic analysis as well. As in the sciences, meta-analysis of ethnographic work clears the view into the future somewhat, revealing possibilities for moving forward by identifying compelling similarities or differences that may have previously been unacknowledged. Meta-ethnography need not be an end, in and of itself. Rather, I suggest it is one analytical tool in a subdiscipline that we might call "comparative ethnomusicology," an approach that invites ethnomusicologists back into comparative work, offering them encouragement to think across disciplinary and cultural boundaries.[3] A comparative approach allows an analyst to explore the fault lines between difference and similarity, between the possibility of universals and cultural specifics, to gain a generalized and more abstract perspective without losing sight of the details of local cultural practice. Comparative ethnomusicology maintains a primary focus on ethnographic research but employs comparative techniques that allow the researcher to move fluidly between cultures and periods, taking advantage of previous ethnographic and historical research to amplify future analyses, ethnographic or otherwise—allowing history to resonate in the contemporary through an integrated approach.

Without invoking universals and in the spirit of a gentle call for increased academic inquiry across religious cultures and practices, the identification of analogous phenomena in themes and expressive methods articulated in my study reveals parallels in women's experiences across religions and cultures. If intersections like these are easily discovered, it is certain that other similarities are present and awaiting description. Reading deep into, but also across, the ethnographic detail of multiple studies, it is possible to see large-scale patterns emerging between non-related, musical performance cultures. As the chapters in this book demonstrate, through the study of performance in context, ethnomusicology can also help to counter the corrosive rhetoric of religious exceptionalism and stark difference by revealing the many ways in which religions are like one another.

Notes

Introduction

1. Recent research on music and religion is reflected by the following: Babiracki (2001); Beck (1993, 2006); Becker (2003); Bohlman, Blumhofer, and Chow (2006); Bohlman and Englhardt (2016); Cusic (2002); Shiloah (1992; 1995); Smith (2011); Spencer (1991); Sullivan (1997); Viladesau (2000); Wilson-Dickson (1996).

2. Studies representative of work on women, gender, and religion include: Ahmed (1992); Berger (1999; 2011); Frahm-Arp (2010); Fulkerson (1994); Kassam (2010); Pintchman (2007); Sharma (1987; 2000); Subbamma (1992).

3. Studies representative of recent work on women, music, and religion include: Abbas (2002); Harvey (2010); Koskoff (1993); Carol Muller (1999); Raheja and Gold (1994); Rasmussen (2010); Raudvere (2002); Sengers (2003). Some of the many edited collections on women and performance include: Bernstein (2004); Koskoff (1987); Magrini (2003); Marshall (1993); Moisala and Diamond (2000); Singh (2008). These volumes contain some selections on women as performers in religious contexts but generally do not attempt to theorize about women's engagements across religions.

4. Noblit and Hare (1988).

5. Comparison has a checkered history in the field of ethnomusicology, which I will address in more detail.

6. Patton (2000, 157).

7. The word "localizing" references Oliver Wolters's (1999) use of the term "localization" to describe the way in which communities in Southeast Asia appropriated and modified Indic ideas, languages, religions, and practices as they encountered and then gradually incorporated them into their own societies at many different levels.

Chapter 1. Women Performers and World Religions

1. See the following for examples: Cooey, Eakin, and McDaniel (1991); Sharma (1987); Joseph (1996); Wadud (2009); Fulkerson (1994); Daly (1985); Chakravarty (1998); Sugirtharajah (2002, 2003).

2. Here I am paraphrasing Leslie Cook (1999, 40), who makes similar statements referring specifically to Jewish women and their activities in the synagogue.

3. See comments on comparison and cultural relativism below.

4. Tiele (1876); Kuenen (1882); Chentepie de la Saussaye (1887); Müller (1898). Abraham Kuenen presented his work in English as part of the Hibbert Lecture Series in England. The series, founded by Unitarian Robert Hibbert, presents nonsectarian lectures on theological issues. In 1894 the lectureship assumed its association with a chair of ecclesiastical history at Manchester College (http://www.thehibberttrust.org.uk/lectures.htm). Friedrich Max Müller presented his work several times as a Gifford lecturer in Scotland (1888–1892). The Gifford Lectures were established in the will of Adam Lord Gifford to promote and diffuse the study of natural theology, or knowledge of God. The series is associated with several major Scottish universities; the lecture presentations rotate between them (http://www.giffordlectures.org).

5. Masuzawa (2005, 19).

6. Ibid., 6–21.

7. Ibid., 20.

8. Ibid., 20–21.

9. See discussion of ethnoreligions and universal religions below.

10. Masuzawa (2005, 13). It is likely that the term world religion was first used in 1893 at the Parliament of World Religions that took place in Chicago when that city hosted the World Columbian Exposition.

11. Gross (2015, 33). Note that one positive aspect about these categories is that they avoid the problematic identification of religions as Eastern or Western.

12. Yet another reason to avoid the term is the fact that in the nineteenth-century debate about the topic, and up until the end of the twentieth century, it is occasionally suggested that Christianity is the only "true" universal religion.

13. I note here that the distinction between music and world music maintains a problematic colonial separation between the "West and the rest" (Weiss 2014, 509). The term "world music" as generally used by ethnomusicologists includes musics from traditional, fusion, and contemporary genres of popular and classical musics from around the world, making the category unwieldy at best. Nevertheless, ethnomusicologists around the globe teach courses with the term "world music" in their titles, replete with topics ranging across the capacious musical offerings of the world, only sometimes with the exception of Western art music, a term which is itself a difficult category to define and defend. (For instance, is it Western art music or world music when a musician plays a Tchaikovsky violin concerto on an *erhu*?).

14. Noblit and Hare (1988).

15. The word *Hindu* is derived (via Persian) from *sindhu*, the Sanskrit word for the Indus River that runs between what are now India and Pakistan. Gavin Flood (2015) states, "It is

important to bear in mind that the formation of Hinduism, as the world religion we know today, has only occurred since the nineteenth century, when the word was used by Hindu reformers and western orientalists. However, its origins and the 'streams' which feed into it are very ancient extending back to the Indus valley civilization." Flood takes the view that Hinduism is partly a construction of the orientalists and partly a "development of Hindu self-understanding; a transformation in the modern world of themes already present" (8).

16. Masuzawa (2005, 3).

17. Wahhabism is a religious movement within Sunni Islam. It was developed by the eighteenth-century theologian Muhammad ibn Abd al-Wahhab (1703–1792), who was native to Najd, Saudi Arabia. He advocated purging Islam of all local impurities and innovations. Wahhabism is now the primary form of Islam practiced in Saudi Arabia.

18. Hindu nationalism refers to the interweaving of social and political thought based on the indigenous spiritual and cultural traditions of the land now called India. At the end of the eighteenth century the term *Hindu* referred more to the population of the land of India, based on the name of a primary river in the region Sind, than to any particular religious group or entity. Increasingly, over the last two hundred years, the word *Hindu* came to be primarily associated with followers of Hinduism. Leading up to the Independence of India, there was a debate among Indian nationalists (who wanted a secular India) and the Hindu nationalists (who wanted a Hindu India). The independence movement in India found power in the blurring of the definitions of the term, and the concept of Hindu nationalism was an effective agent in galvanizing the population of India to strive for independence. Once independence was gained, and although the nation is constitutionally secular, Hindu nationalism was taken up by many political parties and has often been employed in helping to articulate differences between followers of Hinduism and followers of the many other religions also practiced in India (Bhatt 2001, 77–112 in particular). See J. Orsi (2003) for discussion of Hindu nationalism as manifested in Trinidad in the second half of the twentieth century. Orsi notes that the Trinidadian movement aims to raise the marginal status of Indians in their own context in Trinidad by increasing their connections to Hindus and the idea of independent India. Prema Kurien (1998) notes a similar dual effect in analyzing the religious trends of Hindu Indians living in America who have adopted a newfound religiousness in the process of identifying themselves as American when they discover a need or experience community pressures to define themselves with an ethnic or religious identity.

19. Arising out of British and American Protestantism in the late nineteenth and early twentieth centuries—and constructed of many different ideological and political goals—the Christian fundamentalist movement sought, and continues to seek, to defend basic Protestant orthodoxy against political and cultural secularism, liberalism, and immorality. Woodberry and Smith (1998) document the history and development of the many, often unrelated, strands that make up the movement. It could be argued that the sixteenth-century Protestant Reformation itself was a fundamentalist movement.

20. Robert Hefner (1998, 92) notes that fundamentalist developments in Christianity, Islam, and Hinduism around the world underscore that the "real 'clash of civilizations' in our era is not between the West and some homogeneous 'other' but between rival carriers of tradition within the same nations and civilizations." Other studies of the complicated

emergence and interactions between fundamentalist movements around the world are increasingly prominent: using Indonesian case studies, Thomas Reuters (2012) finds revitalization, new-age spirituality, and fundamentalism in Christianity, Islam, and Hinduism. Nasser Mustapha (2004) describes fundamentalisms in Trinidad and Tobago and analyzes the effects of Indian Islam on them. Paul Gifford (1996) analyzes the rise of fundamentalism among African Pentecostal Christians throughout the continent.

21. See Nothaft (2011) for an overview of this much-debated topic and an explication of the two streams of thought on how Christmas came to be celebrated on December 25. There is no indication anywhere in the Bible that the birth of Jesus should be celebrated. Such observance was not practiced until some time in the fourth century CE. One might also note the elevation of Hanukkah—celebrated in December—to the status of a major, gift-giving holiday among Jews primarily in America, but not worldwide, as a latter-day example of the accommodation of the observance of one religion's high holy day to the more extravagantly practiced holiday of another. See Rose (1994) for details and discussion.

22. Barbara Andaya (2006) explores the ways in which women's positions in both royal and peasant, family and community structures changed as Southeast Asian communities gradually converted to Islam over the course of the second millennium.

23. See Olupona and Rey (2008) for discussion of Yoruba and Catholic elements in Santeria. Ruwanpura's (2006) research in Sri Lanka reveals that in Muslim, Hindu, and Buddhist villages alike, strong matrilineal community and family structures are prominent, suggesting that the construction of women and their role in organizing family patterning in Sri Lanka are more influenced by local culture than by any of the three world religions present, all of which are prominently patriarchal. It should be noted that female-centered structures of this sort do not necessarily result in increased power for women in the community in general. See Andaya (2006) and Weiss (2006, in particular chap. 2) for discussion of situations in which women can be empowered even though the existence of multiple and competing valuation systems limits the cultural power that may accrue to them as a result.

24. First published in 1909 (Picard), the book was translated into English and published in 1960 (University of Chicago).

25. van Gennep (1960, in particular 15–25).

26. Among others van Gennep (1960, 189–194) mentions Henri Hubert and Marcel Mauss's (1897/1964) work on sacrifice and Robert Hertz's (1907/1928) work on death and funerary rituals.

27. See Turner (1968; 1986).

28. See the collection of essays in St. John (2008), for instance.

29. Goody (1977), in particular 27, 29.

30. Bell (1992, 7).

31. Bell (1992, 221).

32. Tomoko Masuzawa discusses this perspective as a primary topic (2005, see chap. 2, 72–105).

33. Rooted in Herder's observations of cultural and linguistic diversity of European folk cultures and their ties to local and national identity, American linguistic anthropologists, such as Franz Boas and his student Melville Herskovits, observed that people

make judgments based on their interpretations of lived experiences and that language is essential to the construction of human experience even as it is itself constructed by experience. The implication of this observation is that because human culture is based in the experiences of people living it, the particular experiences of one linguistic group cannot be usefully compared with that of other groups because their categories will not necessarily map onto one another.

34. Dempsey (2011, 5).

35. See the edited volume by Patton and Ray (2000); Dempsey (2011); Lambek (2002); Paden (2001).

36. Wendy Doniger, "Post-Modern and—Colonial—Structural Comparisons (2000, 64–66).

37. Dempsey (2011, 8).

38. Patton (2000, 157).

39. Bruno Nettl (2010, 66) notes that the first usage is unclear, but cites Adler (1885, 14) as the likely first appearance in print.

40. Schneider (2006, 240).

41. Quoted in Schenider (2006, 248).

42. Ibid., 254.

43. Nettl (2010, 75).

44. Nettl (2006, 75–77).

45. Ethnographic material on the Greek Orthodox Dormition Feast pilgrimage in Jerusalem is drawn from a 2011 study by Nurit Stadler of Hebrew University in Jerusalem. Stadler's research generally investigates life and religious practice in the Jewish and Christian Orthodox communities in Jerusalem.

46. There are various belief traditions among Christian denominations, and therefore disagreement, about the concept of dormition, in particular whether "sleeping" in the texts means sleeping or dying (see 1 Corinthians 15:18 and 20 as well as 1 Thessalonians 4:14–15 for the relevant biblical texts). In general, the Orthodox traditions believe that Mary died a normal human death and was then taken to heaven. Catholic tradition understands that Mary merely slept, that she did not die and was taken to heaven while sleeping. Catholics call the feast the Assumption of Mary. Mary's Assumption, however, was not declared an infallible teaching of the Roman Catholic Church until Pope Pius XII issued his *Munificentissimus Deus* (November 1, 1950). Eastern Orthodoxy has not declared the Assumption dogma but celebrates the feast (Flinn 2007, 442–44). See Economides (2004) for detailed discussion of the differences between Catholic and Orthodox Churches and their celebrations of the various festivals that make up the Christian year.

47. Stadler (2011, 646).

48. Ibid., 646–47.

49. Ibid., 656.

50. From Stadler's text it is unclear if the Palestinians lining the road and singing in Arabic are Christian or not. Not every Christian Palestinian would necessarily walk the pilgrimage every year.

51. Stadler (2011, 653–57). In her discussion of the Dormition pilgrimage on Tinos Island, Håland (2012) describes the ritual chaos that is particularly apparent in that proces-

sion as well. She interprets the situation as a female world contra—and often in conflict with—a male official world represented by the church and the police.

52. Ibid., 660–62.

53. Håland (2012) discusses the productive chaos of the Dormition feast on the Greek island of Tinos, where pilgrims travel at least 800 meters on their hands and knees from the ferry wharf to the Panangia Evangelistria Church.

54. Stadler discusses only this particular form of resistance in her article (2011, 652–55). Stadler does not interview any of the women on the meaning of their songs or provide lyrics, and so it is not possible to speak directly about what the songs mean for the pilgrims, other than to point out that they are adamant about singing in their own languages. This suggests that they believe that their songs have a communicative potency that is greater than that afforded by the songs they might sing from the Greek language liturgy. Perhaps they feel they can be more persuasive if they are speaking in a language that is their own.

55. Christine de Pizan 1363–1430 CE was a Venetian poet whose *Book of the City of Ladies* (1405) explores and valorizes the contributions of women to society through history (Brown-Grant 1999). She was inspired to write the book as a response to her reading of the misogynist construction of women and their deleterious effects on men in Jean de Meun's *The Romance of the Rose*. De Pizan's last written work was a eulogy of Joan of Arc finished in 1429. Olympe de Gouges published *Declaration des droits de la femme et de la citoyenne* (Declaration of the Rights of Woman and of the Female Citizen) in 1791, and Mary Wollstonecraft published *Vindication of the Rights of Woman* in 1792 (Macey 2000, 122–123).

56. Gutierrez (1988), first published in 1971.

57. Here I am referencing the title of Ashcroft, Griffiths, and Tiffin (2002) in which novelists and other authors in postcolonial worlds "write back" to the empires that oppressed them.

58. Elizabeth Cady Stanton's *The Woman's Bible* (1895) was developed as she worked with Susan B. Anthony and others for women's suffrage in America in the late nineteenth century. Just as the publication was about to be adopted as part of the platform of the National American Women Suffrage Association in 1896, members of the association voted against it, arguing that the inclusion of the *Women's Bible* would distract attention from voting rights and perhaps derail the endeavor (Avery 1896, 91–97). The next time feminist engagements with Christianity rose to significant public attention was in the 1950s and 1960s, in the wake of liberation theology and burgeoning during the civil rights era when, as so often in world history, political and religious revolution moved in tandem.

59. See Weiss (2006, chap. 2) for an overview of patterns in efforts to include women in scholarly discourse in areas where they have formerly been ignored.

60. Fulkerson (1994, 4–5).

61. Henderson and Gilman (2004).

62. See Kwok (2002) for discussion of the gradual development of a growing awareness of cultural difference in the Western Christian feminist theology movement as well as commentary about kinds of women's movements in Christian theology around the world.

63. Kimberle Crenshaw (1991) coined the term "intersectionality." The idea behind the concept is that race, ethnicity, class, gender, and every other sociological position a person occupies simultaneously impact one another all the time, in so doing also helping to determine one another. Patricia Hill Collins enhanced the theoretical possibilities of the idea in her work over the course of the 1990s, arguing that cultural patterns of oppression are interrelated, mutually constituted and constituting by race, class, gender, and ethnicity. See Collins (2000) for a fully developed analysis using an intersectional approach in which gender, race, class, and ethnicity are examined together for their influence on the situating of black women in the United States.

64. Walby (2000, 190).

65. I am not arguing here that only women create local practice or that all local practice has been created by women. Rather, I am suggesting that it is productive to recognize the role of women when contemplating the development of local practices and their relationships to the various levels of universals with which they and their male co-culturalists engage.

66. Without women contesting the authority of the Greek Orthodox Patriarchy in Jerusalem, the vibrancy of the pilgrimage might soon diminish and the practice would perhaps whither.

67. These four locations represent the imagined centers of four different religions, Catholicism, Islam, Anglican Protestantism, and Hinduism, respectively. Mount Meru represents the center of the cosmological universe of the Puranic texts recognized by most branches of Hinduism. The decentralized nature of Hinduism prevents any one particular temple or site from being universally considered the most important or central. Of course, many sites have that status, depending on location and ethnolinguistic grouping.

Chapter 2. Wedding Lamentation

1. These scenes are drawn from the ethnographic work of Pnina Werbner (1986).

2. Henna is also applied to the groom but in a simpler design, such as a dot at the center of each palm.

3. Fatima Mernissi (1987, in particular, chap. 1–3, pp. 27–86) explores the Muslim concept of active female sexuality and its regulation in her examination of male-female dynamics in modern Muslim society.

4. Werbner (1986, 240–45).

5. Urban (1988, 386).

6. Ibid., 389–90.

7. Berthomé and Houseman (2010, 60).

8. The extensive literature on Greek Orthodox death lamentations includes critical works by Alexiou (1974), Danforth and Tsiaras (1982), Holst-Warhaft (1992), Panourgiá (1995), Suter (2008), and Wilce (2009). Several of these richly developed studies cross between ethnographic and literary analyses.

9. These descriptions of Potomian lamentation are based on Loring Danforth's (1982) work in Greece from the 1970s. James Wilce has documented changes in the reception of

lamentation over the last half-century. He notes an increase in the association of shame with public mourning (2009, 118–38) and positions lament as premodern or primitive in the context of modernity as it is understood in Greece.

10. My thanks to Loring Danforth for digitizing this unpublished recording and sending it to me.

11. Caravelli-Chaves (1980).

12. Holst-Warhaft (1992, 69–71). Also, Michael Herzfeld (1981) discusses the problems in assuming a connection between melodies that are used in both funerals and weddings, as well as in adopting their classification by rural Greek lament singers. Danforth's 1982 study demonstrates the direct usage of similar texts and melodies for lamentation at weddings and funerals.

13. When this same lament is sung in the context of a funeral, the partridge represents the deceased, who is about to be consumed by the earth (Danforth 1982, 114).

14. Ibid., 78–79.

15. Translated in ibid., 77.

16. Ibid., 77–78.

17. Ibid., 77.

18. Tolbert (1990, 80).

19. Raudalainen (2004).

20. The data for this case study is drawn from Liz Tolbert's (1990) fieldwork data, Helena Henderson's (1999) work on Finnish folklore, Matti Sarmela's (2010) comparative study of weddings in Finland and Thailand, and a silent film directed by A. O. Väisänen with a script by U. T. Sirelius dated from 1921.

21. Juha Pentikäinen provides a brief history of the "discovery" of the female and male singers of runes by Finnish folklorists over the course of the nineteenth and twentieth centuries in his *Kalevala Mythology* (1999, 97–130). He includes detailed ethnographic description of his own communications with three female rune singers who in the early part of the twentieth century learned to sing by listening to other singers and storytellers in their communities.

22. Sarmela (2006, 9).

23. Tolbert (1990, 80–81).

24. Henderson (1999, 154).

25. Whether this lament was indeed sung by the bride or by a professional lamenter is not indicated in the source.

26. These elements are audible on different selections from the CD titled *Itkuja: Laments from Karelia, Ingria, Finland*, produced by the Finnish Literature Society.

27. Väisänen (1921). These three segments have been edited out of the original film. Another, more heavily edited, version with Kantele—a plucked zither found in Finland, Karelia, and Estonia, accompaniment as the soundtrack—can be found at http://www.youtube.com/watch?v=254dsgA-PoY.

28. The dialogue is silent because the film has no audio track but there are occasional subtitles.

29. Perhaps it is some type of kantele, but its shape is more reminiscent of an Appalachian dulcimer.

30. This attitude is also suggested by the tussling and roughhousing of groups of boys and by their joyous chasing after the wedding entourage on its return to the groom's home.

31. Pentikäinen (1999, 46–47).

32. Shehan (1987); Sunde (2006); Mazo (1994); Tolbert (1990).

33. Alexiou (1974).

34. Ibid., 47–53.

35. Panourgia (1995, 163–67).

36. Alexiou (1974, 24–25).

37. Ibid., 49–50.

38. Caravelli-Chaves (1980, 143).

39. The gendering of foreigners, others, and outsiders, as female has a long tradition in the representation of intercultural relations in Indo-European history and beyond.

40. Holst-Warhaft (1992, 129, 133, 161).

41. Ibid., 169.

42. Weinbaum (2001, 22–28).

43. Alexiou (1974, 24–52).

44. Compiled from McGuckin (2011).

45. Ibid., 187.

46. Tolbert (1990, 80). The Ingrian Lutherans of Estonia used both funeral and wedding laments learned from their Orthodox Finnish neighbors well into the twentieth century (Pentikäinen 1999, 201). None of the lamentation traditions has, however, survived in a robust manner into the twenty-first century.

47. Lauri Honko postulates this idea with respect to the Russian Orthodox Church and the maintenance of the Karelian lamentation tradition (Honko 1974, 56). Lysaght (1997) provides extensive documentation of attempts by the Catholic Church to suppress Irish keening from the seventeenth to the twentieth centuries. Paul condemns cries and immoderate grief for the dead in his epistles to the Thessalonians (4:13): "But I would not have you to be ignorant, brethren, concerning them which are asleep, that year sorrow not, even as others have no hope." In his *Homilies on First Thessalonians* (347–407), John of Chrysostom spends many more words than Paul on this verse, arguing with his imagined female interlocutors and explaining why it is that women should not lament the loss of their husbands and sons, claiming that to lament any loss in life was to deny Jesus will rise again and to join those without hope and without faith (Homily 6: http://www.newadvent.org/fathers/230406.htm). I have not been able to identify a specific papal prohibition of lamentation. Teresa Berger (2011, 64) notes: "A canon of the Synod of Elvira held in Spain in A.D. 306 stipulates: 'Women are forbidden to spend the night in a cemetery since often under the pretext of prayer they secretly commit evil deeds.'" Through such evidence a picture emerges of a reasonably systematic and negative perspective on women's lamentation and death rituals.

48. Alexiou (1974, 23–51).

49. Holst-Warhaft (1992, 170–72).

50. Standhartinger (2010, 559–70). She also notes that remnants of mourning rituals from antiquity appear throughout the New Testament. She contests the common idea

that there are no mourning rituals for Jesus by finding hints of such rituals in the actions described.

51. I anticipate that similar claims could be made for other Christian traditions in different places with different practices.

52. Wilce (1999, 46–54).

53. These rituals commemorate the death of Husayn ibn Ali, grandson of Muhammad, at the hands of the army of Yazid I. This rendering of Husayn as a martyr is the catalytic event that caused the first major schism in Islam, generating the development of the Shia branch of Islam.

54. Khan, Chaudhry, and Badshah (2014). The authors are investigating rituals among Muslims who have only recently converted and who still have members of their families who are Hindus and who can remember when the area was predominantly Hindu. The article is written in a presentist manner with respect to the mourning rituals and songs. They recount the history of the development of Shia identity in the region but do not connect it to any aspects of culture that were previously present. Hence, there is no way to determine if the mourning songs they study have connections with older mourning traditions in the region. This author hopes someone will go and investigate this interesting question.

55. Wilce (1999, 50).

56. Wilce (1999, 50). In his study examining changing perspectives on public singing in Bangladesh, Greater Bengal, and South Asia, James Wilce notes that not only do men, especially younger ones, shun public weeping and lamentation shunned by men in general, but they also disparage "tuneful" prayer as performed by men even when the one who is praying is not intending to call attention to himself. Wilce concludes that men oppose tuneful expressions of emotion in reformist Muslim contexts because those utterances could be interpreted as a subversive or at least as publically expressed emotion. He notes a communal striving to "replace emotionality with disenchanted expressions of religious seriousness."

57. Tiwary (1978). I have been unable to locate any recordings of this form of Bihari weeping, and Tiwary provides no descriptions except "tuneful." Wilce finds parallels with these Bihari laments reported by Tiwary in his work in Bangladesh. Wilce (1998, 7–9).

58. Tiwary (1978, 25).

59. Ibid.

60. Ibid., 26. Reference also Stephen Feld's (1988) discussion of "lift-up-over sounding" among the Kaluli for another example of the communal assessment of the effectiveness of weeping.

61. Tiwary (1978, 25).

62. Ibid., 26.

63. Ibid.

64. Narayan (1986). Many of the *suhāg* texts are exceedingly sad, but they maintain a connection only with weddings. They do not intersect with a local lamentation tradition that is also performed by women at funerals. See also Raheja and Gold (1994, 136–46).

65. S. Banerjee (1989) makes the case for this through her whole article, but particularly in the conclusion (160–69). Nirmala Banerjee (1989) documents that the modernization

process in northern India was devastating for women's traditions of doing and making. While some, especially tribal women, were absorbed as cheap labor in the mills, most others were marginalized to work in agricultural jobs, activities in which women had not traditionally engaged. Their presence in community life was radically altered, and their songs of longing and lament took on new meaning (291–98).

66. S. Banerjee (1989, 133).

67. Ibid. The "bounder" who sold all of Uma's clothing and ornaments in this Bengali song is none other than Shiva, the god for whom Uma/Durga is a consort. This particular interpolation is found primarily among Bengali-speaking communities. Personal communication from Lisa Knight.

68. Ibid., 134. S. Banerjee notes the extensive legends and anecdotes that have sprung up around Krishna in Bengal over the centuries. These stories, are "at variance with the ancient Sanskrit texts (1989, 171n17).

69. See S. Banerjee (1989, 136–47) for a fulsome account of the many kinds of song traditions that utilize the tensions of the Radha-Krishna/consort-God relationship to explore women's perspectives on the human conditions of love, lust, adultery, widowhood, abandonment, and forgiveness.

70. The endings vary depending on who is recounting the tale and the geographic location of the variant. Sita can demonstrate her purity in the fire and then live happily ever after, or she may decline to deal with the restrictions of palace life and ask the earth, her mother, to swallow her up once she sees her two boys reunited with their father, Rama. Several other versions are also extant.

71. Sutherland (1989); Sugirtharajah (2002).

72. The essays in Harlan and Courtright (1995) explore the experiences of women in Hindu marriage not from the perspective of an idealized norm but from what they term the margins of the society: they consider, for example, not the daughter who gets married but the wife who is widowed or the wife who decides to become a *bhakti*, or celibate renouncer of all usual womanly duties. The editors argue that the central idealized and muted construction of Hindu women can be viewed from these peripheral positions.

73. Dev Sen (2002). I should note that speakers of Bengali live predominantly in the far eastern states of India and those of Marathi in Maharashtra state in the Western midland areas of India. Although the northeast corners of Bihar state border West Bengal state, neither West Bengal nor Maharashtra has exactly the same cultural traditions or languages as Bihar. Nevertheless, that Sen has been able to find Sita song traditions with strong similarities across languages and states suggests that the emotions and interpretive experiences described in the songs may be present to some degree throughout India among rural women.

74. Dev Sen (2002, lines 26–29).

75. Ibid., lines 50–55.

76. Ibid., lines 155–63.

77. Dev Sen (2000, 51) recounts her own discovery of Chandrabati's sixteenth-century text in Bengali and Molla's sixteenth-century text in Telugu, each recounting the *Ramayana* in which Sita's perspective is foregrounded.

78. See Paula Richman (1991) for a compilation of multiple *Ramayana* variations organized by theme and (2008) for an overview on contemporary poetic and literary interpretations of the tale.

79. De Martino (2000). To my knowledge there are no studies of any continuing wedding lament tradition that has been maintained in Northern Italy.

80. Keller (1994, 41–43).

81. Ibid., 43. Additionally, Tullia Magrini (1985) has documented Italian verse forms in Crete in which there is a particular form of text fragmentation where lines or even words are left incomplete, to be partially repeated and finished in the succeeding line. She points out that this form of poetic structuring is still in use in the Greek islands of the eastern Mediterranean (30–34, cited in Keller 1994, 43).

82. Keller (1994) points out that Permenides, Zeno, Empedocles, and Archimedes were all, geographically speaking, Italians, but culturally Greek (46).

83. Federico Follino, commissioned to record the occasion, described the events in his *Compendio delle sontuose feste fatte l'anno MDCVIII nell città di Mantova* (Mantua: Aurelia and Lodovico Osanna, 1608). He even included a full performance text of Monteverdi's opera *Arianna*, which contained the famous *Lamento d'Arianna* (cited in MacNeil 1999, 416).

84. The others were the *Ballo delle ingrate*, the *intermedi* performed between the acts of Battista Guarini's comedy, *L'idropica,* and a second ballo *Il Sacrifcio d'Ifigenia* (MacNeil 1999, 407).

85. See Cusick (1994) and Mazo (1994) for differing perspectives on the meaning of women's weeping in marriage contexts.

86. MacNeil (1999, 408–10).

87. Carter (1999, 395, 398–402).

88. Cusick (1999, 445–47).

89. Danforth (1982, 145).

90. Ibid., 59.

91. Rosand (1979).

92. Support for this latter interpretation might be found by asking why, if the falling tetrachord was already an important icon for lamentation, Monteverdi did not use it in his *Lamento d'Arianna* when he used it to a most affecting degree thirty years later, in 1638, for his *Lamento della ninfa*. My thanks to Gary Tomlinson for sparking this idea.

93. I am inspired here by Caravelli-Chaves (1980, 143–44).

Chapter 3. Demeter's Lamentation and Baubo's Mockery

1. This outline is drawn from the *Homeric Hymn to Demeter* (lines 1–202), translated by Gregory Nagy: http://www.uh.edu/~cldue/texts/demeter.html. The hymn, most likely dated to some time between the seventh and early sixth centuries BCE, may have been sung at festivals (O'Higgins 2001, 37; Foley 1994, 169–78). Sandin (2008) discusses alternative versions and interpretations of the chthonic nature of the Demeter/Persephone story.

2. *Kheuêis* (from line 202 in the *Homeric Hymn to Demeter*) suggests not just jesting and obscenity but also satirical inversions and a mild poking of fun at the listener. My thanks

to George Syrimis and Stephen Colvin for clarification on this point. Clay (2006, 234–35) interprets the word as invective and insult directed at someone.

3. In versions of the story found in Orphic literary fragments (ca. sixth century BCE) an old woman named Baubo is the one who makes Demeter laugh. After failing with jesting words and mockery, she raises her skirts, revealing what is normally hidden: either a face that is also a vulva, or a pregnant belly. Fertility is implied by either image, and female transgression of societal norms is suggested by both the images and the verbal insults and mockery. See O'Higgins (2001, 141) and Rosen (2007, 49) for recent discussions of this long-studied episode. O'Higgins (2001, 142) suggests that Iambe may well have been invented by the author of the hymn as a figure to serve as catalyst for Eleusinian mysteries who was more refined than the traditional but crude Baubo.

4. The number of seeds consumed by Persephone varies across the many versions of this story that have been recorded over the millennia. Usually described as either four or six seeds, the number may depend on the duration of the winter experienced in the location of the retelling of the myth.

5. *Homeric Hymn to Demeter*, lines 296–495, translated by Gregory Nagy: http://www.uh.edu/~cldue/texts/demeter.html.

6. Alexiou (1974); Danforth (1982); Holst-Warhaft (1992).

7. Foley (1985, 84–92); Lardinois (2001, 82–88); Danforth (1982, 71–115); Seaford (1987); Holst-Warhaft (1992, 98–103), Alexiou (1974, 120–22).

8. See Oakley and Sinos (1993) for suggestions, perhaps symbolic, of abduction of brides on ancient vases from Athens. In part based on the ethnographic material described by Alexiou and Dronke (1971) and Alexiou (1974), Ian Jenkins (1983) explores details of the depictions of marriage on vases and other forms of Athenian pottery. Using ideas from van Gennep's theory of ritual process, Jenkins suggests there are connections to be made among the visual representations of abductions of brides, the narrative of the abduction of Persephone, and the way in which we might imagine early Greek marriage rituals.

9. "Now I have set out. Now I am about to depart from my home and from my dear brothers and sisters. Everyone is driving me away; everyone is telling me to leave. Even my mother is driving me away. She doesn't want me. And my father too, he tells me to leave. I am leaving with tears and with a heavy heart" (Potomian wedding lament cited in Danforth [1982, 86–87]). Note that both her mother and father tell her to leave, demonstrating the role of women in constructing and enforcing the androcentric nature of society. Alexiou (1974) notes a similar helplessness on the part of mother and bride alike with respect to male authority in a wedding lament from Crete. The daughter cries for her mother to hide her, and the mother laments, "How can I hide you, dear one, now you belong to him: wear the stranger's cloths, wear the stranger's rings, for you belong to him and he will take you" (120–22).

10. There is debate about the function of the Thesmophoria. Some view it purely as a women's initiation rite (Prytz-Johansen 1975), others as an agricultural festival (O'Higgins 2001; Brumfield 1981), or as some combination of the two (Humphreys 1993). Clay (2006) rereads the *Homeric Hymn to Demeter*, questioning the common assumption of

direct connections between ceremonial acts of the Eleusinian cult and details articulated in the hymn.

11. Stallsmith (2008, 129–30).

12. Ibid., 122–25.

13. O'Higgins (2001, 160). See Blundell (1995) for discussion of early Greek constructions of female goddesses and humans and the omnipresence of nonmerged oppositional elements—fertile/infertile, old/young, active-destroyer/inactive-destroyed—in contexts other than the Thesmophoria, Eleusinian Mysteries, and other Demeter festivals.

14. Danforth (1982, 73).

15. See Holst-Warhaft (1992, 4) and also Alexiou (1974, 3–23) for a detailed discussion of the legislation.

16. Holst-Warhaft (1992). Nicole Loraux (2006) explores the shifting construction of death in Athenian democracy and the development of funeral oration.

17. O'Higgins does not elaborate the meaning of "worrisome natures," although the context suggests that women were not as strictly regulated by the order and hierarchies that controlled male-to-male communications.

18. O'Higgins (2001, 145–48).

19. Holst-Warhaft (1992) argues for this possibility in chapters 4 and 5, and her whole study locates the performance of lament in rural Greece in the 1980s in the context of the representations of lamentation in ancient Greek literature and law.

20. In using this term "decenter" I am referencing Derridean and poststructuralist theories but also the postcolonial feminism of the authors in collections such as Narayan and Harding (2000).

Chapter 4. Revelry and Resistance

1. For work on mockery and ingroup/outgroup ideology formation see the edited collection by Reyes and Lo (2009) and Elgee (2003).

2. Scott (1986) and (1990).

3. For example, the Spring of Nations, or the 1848 revolutions in Europe, was a wave of political upheaval that started in France and spread to more than fifty nations in Europe and Latin America. The revolutionary efforts were thwarted by reactionary forces around the world in less than a year (Rapport 2008). The Irish Rebellion of 1798 is a much-reported failed effort to overthrow British rule in Ireland (Whelan 1996). The Taiping Rebellion (1850–1864) was a failed civil war against the Manchu-led Qing Dynasty (Spence 1996).

4. See James Scott (1986; 1990). For instance, the acts of sabotage against the introduction of mechanical farm equipment in Malaysia in the mid-1970s as reported in Scott (1986) or the Occupy Wall Street movement in New York in 2011–12 (Byrne 2012).

5. Scott (1990).

6. Ibid., 70–107, 130–35.

7. Finding examples from literary descriptions as well as historical and contemporary contexts, Scott (1990) demonstrates in a fulsome manner the use of mockery as a form of resistance by dominated groups; see in particular chap. 6, pp. 136–82.

8. Bennett (1989, 262); Chauduri and Strobel (1992).

9. I have seen this word spelled/transliterated in the following ways in various places: *matkor*, *matikoor*, *matticore*, *matkorwa*, and *matikonwa*.

10. Ramnarine (1999, 12).

11. http://www.youtube.com/watch?v=B9r2I-3Dvog&feature=related. This video was shot in 2003. See: https://www.youtube.com/watch?v=7chlz_U8cik for footage of a Caribbean matikor evening in 2012. The event has been professionally filmed, and a montage of clips has been created and posted on YouTube, to allow others to see the event as well as to advertise the work of the photography studio.

12. Grierson (1926, 366) states that in Bihar, India, the same ceremony takes place on the same night in the groom's home as well, performed by his female relatives. Although it is only raw, unedited ethnographic film, shots of a young man being treated and cared for in the midst of a large crowd of women and girls who obviously know him suggests that these activities called *matkor* are very likely occurring in the groom's home: See http://www.youtube.com/watch?v=qA70LVg6nNg for a video labeled *Matkor Bihar*. Harry Ramnath (n.d., 97, quoted in Ramnarine 1999, 6) states that in Trinidad the mothers and other female family members of both the bride and the groom participate in the ritual that is held at the bride's home. Helen Myers recorded lachari songs performed at matikor or matikonwa at houses of both brides and grooms (Myers 1998, 151–72.) Some video footage of matikor dancing from Trinidad can be found in the videos at http://chutneyontheweb.blogspot.com/2009/10/history-of-chutney-music-in-trinidad_06.html.

13. *Kumkum* is made from powdered turmeric mixed with slaked lime, turning the mixture a rich red color, which is then pressed into the forehead in the shape of a small circle. *Kumkum* conveys a variety of social and religious meanings.

14. In the Espinet epigram the drums are played by women; in contemporary Trinidad they are often played by men who pretend they are not watching the events as they unfold (Ramnarine 1999, 7).

15. This description compiled from Ramnarine (1999, 4–9).

16. Manuel (1998, 22).

17. Ramnarine (1999, 28n10) notes this, quoting a personal communication from Peter Manuel. If the dancing for matikor is more overtly sexual than the descriptions and pictures of traditional folk dancing in Bihar and other areas in northern India, there are similarities with the dancing seen in the videos of contemporary Bihari weddings that are available online at http://www.youtube.com/watch?v=qA70LVg6nNg, in which women sing raucously and dance close to one another while laughing.

18. See "Maticoor Night: The Dulahin's Feminine Zone" at http://www.triniview.com/Hindu_Wedding/151206.html for extensive description of one particular wedding in Trinidad in December 2006. The article was written by staff writers for the online publication TriniView.com. See Myers (1998, 151–72) for description of another Hindu Trinidadian wedding. The application of ornamental henna designs on the body of the bride is a tradition that reaches across the Middle East, Northern Africa, South Asia, and down through Southeast Asia, quite separate from any specific religion but also used as

an important ritual activity by some women marrying primarily in Hindu and Islamic contexts.

19. This text is quoted in Myers (1998, 211). In an extraordinary compendium of musical and cultural data on the performance cultures of Hindu Trinidad, Myers has included translations and transcriptions of many byah ke git.

20. Williams and Windebank (1998).

21. Myers (1998, 155).

22. Translated and quoted in full in Myers (1998, 169–70).

23. Baksh-Soodeen (1991, 7) quoted in Ramnarine (1999, 12–13).

24. Bergman (2008, 7).

25. http://www.triniview.com/Hindu_Wedding/151206.html.

26. Manuel (1998, 25).

27. Manuel (1998, 22–24).

28. Bergman (2008).

29. Grierson (1926).

30. Grierson (1926, 362 [par. 1306]).

31. *Songs for the Bride: Wedding Rites of Rural India* was published posthumously in 1985, based on a manuscript Archer had prepared in the 1950s.

32. Archer (1985, xv–xvi).

33. Auspicious marriage song from Bihar. Quoted in Archer (1985, 103).

34. Henry (1988).

35. Raheja and Gold (1994).

36. Ibid., 31.

37. The Christian Mary-Eve dichotomy is one obvious comparison. See Tumanov (2011) for discussion of the development of this dichotomy during the early centuries of Christianity and the ways in which myth represents biology, in particular through psychological traits developed over millennia.

38. Raheja and Gold (1994, 31).

39. Ibid., 71.

40. Ibid., 45.

41. Ibid., 58.

42. Ibid., 58.

43. Ibid., 58–62.

44. Ibid., 61–62.

45. Ibid., 51–52.

46. Ibid., 69.

47. This tradition is reported in Shiloah (1992, 174) but is unattributed, and I cannot find another scholar who has studied it. Shiloah makes no mention of the nature of either the drink or the songs. I can easily imagine that the drinks are alcoholic and the songs are full of invective, given the nature of some of the other Sephardic women's song traditions described herewith.

48. Shiloah (1992, 175).

49. Ibid.

50. Weich-Shahak (1979, 82–85).

51. Sephardic Jews living in the Middle East often refer to the ritual bathhouse, known as *mikvah* in Hebrew, with the Arabic word *hammam* or *hamam*.

52. Weich-Shahak (1979, 83–85).

53. Ibid., 87.

54. Quoted in Weich-Shahak (1978, 98–99).

55. The persecution that has plagued Jewish communities throughout their history has positioned them outside the hegemon at many times and in many places. In-group modes of communication in which mockery and satire of the hegemonic culture is prominent function in the way Scott (1990) articulates, both distancing the hegemonic culture and confirming local Jewish identity. Ziv (1998) and Greenspoon (2011) explore Jewish humor traditions from around the world; in the Greenspoon volume there are several articles on Jewish women who are comediennes, but there is no scholarship on women's insult and mockery traditions in either of these collections.

56. Cohen (1987a, 57). Judith Cohen also identifies four approaches to humor: bawdy songs; merriment relating to life and calendrical cycle festivities; satire and parody; and the generally amusing or ridiculous (Cohen 1987b).

57. Cohen (1987b, 60).

58. The term used here is *frasquito*, which refers also to a hip flask and anything else that can stick out from below one's waist.

59. This song is mentioned in Cohen (1987a; 1987b). My thanks to Cristina Cruz-Uribe for translating this text.

60. None of the sources suggest that Sephardic Jewish women's wedding mockery traditions are still vibrant, only that some women still remember them. Without the ethnographic data, it is impossible to comment on the relationship of the song traditions to the practice of Judaism in the three locations discussed. That said, it is apparent that a feisty sensuality is valued in a bride. Perhaps these attributes are understood as ensuring success within the hierarchy of her new family.

61. Kligman (1984, 167).

62. Quoted in ibid., 170.

63. Ibid.

64. Ibid., 171.

65. Ibid., 170.

66. Kligman (1984) provides extensive description of prenuptial rituals including the shaking of hands by the bride and her mother-in-law to be through a woolen apron, symbolizing both submission on the part of the bride and also a willing of prosperity on the couple-to-be, for wool—through its connections to sheep—symbolizes wealth and well-being. Another ritual involves the making and "dancing" of the groom's flag on a long pole and the bride's crown by same-sex friends at their individual houses. The flag and the crown, displayed and frolicked/danced with by the friends of the couple, are obvious sexual symbols (171–75).

67. My thanks to Gabriela Ilnitchi Currie for her help with cultural details and translation of the strigatura from Romanian to English in a personal communication of May 12, 2011.

68. See the performance at http://www.youtube.com/watch?v=ooPV-oafMuc.

69. This text is translated by Gabriela Ilnitchi Currie, where audible, from the video at http://www.youtube.com/watch?v=ooPV-oafMuc. I have edited her translations slightly to make the English more comprehensible and accept responsibility for any misinterpretation these changes have caused.

70. Performances can go on for more than seven or eight minutes when a series of strigatura is sung by several different people.

71. Kligman (1984, 171–74).

72. Quoted in ibid., 179.

73. Ibid., 175–79.

74. Ibid., 168.

75. Rasmussen (1997, 2–4, quote at 4).

76. Rasmussen (1995, 5).

77. Rasmussen (1997; 1995, 4–7).

78. Rasmussen (1997, 7–8).

79. Nana's tebateq was recorded and translated by Rasmussen. I include here only the lines about which I comment. For all one hundred lines see Rasmussen (1997, 9–12).

80. Rasmussen (2003, 497).

81. Rasmussen (1997, 11).

82. Ibid., 17.

83. Ibid., 17.

84. Rasmussen (2003, 497).

85. This description is also true of British hen parties and American bachelorette parties, two prenuptial traditions not covered here in which mockery, ridicule, and sexual innuendo are primary elements. Eldridge and Roberts (2008) and Tye and Powers (1998) describe the rise of bachelorette parties as prenuptial events in the Anglo-phonic West (Canada, Britain, United States) in which the brides and their close friends celebrate a night of debauchery devoted to the bride's impending loss of sexual freedom. These parties may or may not replace the more traditional and sexually tame bridal shower. They can involve an exchange of sex toys, viewing of pornography, and trips to male strip clubs during which the bride may wear clothing on which candies have been stuck for the purpose of offering nibbling/sucking opportunities for anyone at the club who might be interested. These traditions have not yet evolved a strong musical expression. So, despite "performances" brimming with mockery and sexual send-up, they have not been included in this study.

86. van Gennep (1960) and Turner (1986).

87. Wolin and Bennett (1984, in particular p. 408); Bossard and Boll (1950).

Chapter 5. Girl's Poetry and Social Critique at Muslim Berber Weddings

1. Hoffman (2008) and Goodman (2005).

2. This ethnographic data is taken from Terri Brint Joseph's 2003 work with girls from several communities in Morocco and her 1987 work with Roger Joseph on poetry from the region. I use the term Berber throughout this chapter as that is the name given to the

Riffian group by the authors whose ethnographic work I am using. The various groups of indigenous Moroccan people also call themselves *Imazighen/amazigh* (singular) among several other terms.

3. In the epigraph/couplet that opens this chapter, washing a "fringed headscarf" refers to wedding finery and suggests getting rid of the proposed groom. Hanging that washed fringed headscarf on a "*fades* bush" lets everyone in the village know that the promise has been broken. "Take your sugar away" is a reference to the cone-shaped sugar offerings that a groom's family brings to a possible future wife's father when they come to ask for permission for the marriage. If the girl's father accepts, the cone is crushed and the men each use part of it in their hot drink, symbolizing harmony and sweetness in interfamilial relations and in the marriage itself (Joseph 2003, 242–43).

4. Joseph (2003, 238).

5. Joseph (2003, 238). Katherine Hoffman (2002) has done fieldwork with performers of similar kinds of wedding songs, among other genres, in the Berber community of Ida ou Zeddout Ishelhin in the Anti-Atlas Mountains. Her ethnographic data is comparable to Joseph's, although there is some variety in cultural details. Hoffman is looking at generational change in the song texts and constructions, and Joseph is presenting a gendered snapshot using the performance songs as a fulcrum.

6. Among others: William Starbuck Mayo (1850); Edward Westermarck (1914); Clifford Geertz (1968); Fatima Mernissi (1987), originally published in 1975; Roger Joseph and Terri Brint Joseph (1987).

7. Joseph (2003, 235).

8. Joseph (2003, 235–36).

9. Chanting techniques are varied and debated. Several schools of recitation are found around the Muslim world; seven of them, most associated with particular people and geographic locations, are considered reliable—Muhammad himself said that the Qur'an was revealed in seven styles—three more are perceived as permissible, and at least four, and perhaps more, are thought noncanonical. Each of these schools has a variety of styles such that there are at least eighty different varieties of chanting tradition. Much of the debate has to do with the ways in which the Arabic is pronounced and, hence, the alternative meanings that can be implied by the modulation of vowel and consonant combinations. See, for example, http://bewley.virtualave.net/qira.html. Most sources discussing this topic are, understandably, in Arabic, although there is a significant body of work on *qira'at* in Indonesian.

10. See Maria Ulfah's website, http://www.mariaulfah.com/index.html, and Rasmussen (2010).

11. In some South Asian immigrant communities in North America, women have also taken a more active role in recitation both at home and in some instances in the public arena of the mosque. Regula Burkhardt Qureshi has documented shifts in women's practice of qur'anic recitation and the singing of hymns in South Asian communities in Edmonton, Alberta, noting that while women have traditionally sung hymns in various informal, occasionally mix-gendered contexts, in immigrant communities recitation is a fundamental tool for community building in both public and private contexts. While the recitation of the whole Qur'an is customary at the time of a death in South Asian Islamic communities, in

Edmonton this tradition has become more public and community based in that men and women assemble together in the mosque for the recitation (Qureshi 1996, 55–58).

12. In developing this analysis I have relied on Ibsen-al Faruqi (1985), Lengel (2004), Qureshi (1996), Touma (1996), and Walther (1999).

13. Ibsen-al Faruqi (1985).

14. The same can be said to varying degrees about performers in general and female performers in particular in many societies, contemporary and past. This factor contributes to popular interest in performers who can go beyond the fame and appreciation generated by their artistic expression. With respect to women performers, it can be argued that variations across societies are of degree, not kind.

15. There is evidence of women wearing veils in the geographic area of the Middle East in middle-Hittite culture around the thirteenth century BCE. Whether veiling indicated modesty, ownership, marriage, or class and who was supposed/allowed to be veiled and when are all matters of debate. See Tsevat (1975) for a thorough argumentation of all possibilities.

16. Syed (2010).

17. See Badran and Cooke (2004) for more than seventy selections written by Muslim women wrestling with Islamic discourse and cultural patterns relating to women.

18. Brenner (1996); also see http://www.religiondispatches.org/archive/sexandgender/152/17_reasons_why_women_wear_headscarves.

19. See Zimmerman (2014) for discussion of young Arab women attending college in the United States and France and their contestations of Western feminisms, in particular their perspectives on the role of agency in the decision to veil themselves.

20. The five pillars of Islam outline the religious duties of a Muslim as they should be performed over the course of that individual's lifetime. Whatever the local manifestations of their ritual practices, Muslims all over the world endeavor to embrace the actions outlined as the five pillars. (Shi'a Muslims recognize eight pillars, but these overlap substantively with the Sunni five.) The five pillars are *Shahadah*, or the profession of the faith that there is only one God, Allah; *Salat*, or the practice of praying five times a day; *Zakaat*, or almsgiving, recognizing the needs of others and diminishing their suffering, usually by offering up to 2.5 percent of one's family income per year; *Sawm*, or the act of fasting during the month of Ramadan; *Hajj*, or the pilgrimage to Mecca that each Muslim must make before he or she dies, if one can afford it. Of these five, only the obligation to make the Hajj is missing from the list in this Surah.

21. Mernissi (1987, viii).

22. Ibid., 27–45.

23. Ibid., 34–35.

24. Ibid., 35.

25. Mernissi's comparative analysis ultimately focuses on Freud's construction of women and female sexuality as passive and seeking/needing subordination.

26. Mernissi (1987, 36).

27. The work was written during al-Ghazali's retreat from the academic and juridical worlds of Baghdad in the years after 1095 and was an attempt to bridge the ongoing

tension between an educated minority that advocated stricter orthodox practice and the majority of Muslims who combined their worship with local forms of Islamic-inspired mysticism.

28. Quoted from Mernissi (1987, 37–38).

29. Al-Ghazali suggests that the Prophet also advised foreplay and that men not throw themselves on their wives like beasts. There should be a messenger between man and woman—that is, kisses and words (Mernissi 1987, 40).

30. Mernissi (1987, 41–43) paraphrasing al-Ghazali.

31. There is much debate and polemic about how to interpret the prohibitions and admonitions described in the Qur'an. The Surah and verses from which those who argue for Qur'anic support for these prohibitions begin their justifications are the following: 24:31, veiling, although most agree that *hijab* refers more specifically to modesty for men and women in general; 2:229, divorce or renunciation of wives; 4:3, polygamy; 33:53, seclusion of women: in this case it is only Muhammad's wives who are mentioned; 23:5, 24:30–31, and 70:29, chastity, but in these instances once again it is both men and women who are instructed in various ways to lower their gazes, protect their private parts, keep chaste until marriage, and keep chaste while their spouse is absent.

32. Sabbah (1984, 118).

33. See Ghafournia (2017) for an analysis of Quran 4:34, including a critical assessment of the two primary streams of interpretation which she calls patriarchal and egalitarian.

34. For *Sahih International Translation*, see http://quran.com/4; for *Sublime Quran Translation* by Laleh Bakhtiar, see http://www.sublimequran.org/images/quran-p2.jpg (this translation and Surah 4:34 are discussed extensively in Bakhtiar [2011]).

35. Bakhtiar (2011, 435).

36. Ibid., 432, 437–38.

37. Marín (2003, 8–9). See also Mahmoud (2006) for alternative discussion of similar issues.

38. Mernissi (1986, 94). Mernissi's recounting of this story is based in histories written in Arabic—*Agani* XIV and *Kitab al Maradafat*.

39. The husband seems to have come through history without a specific name, unlike Sakina's woman friend.

40. Mernissi (1986, 95).

41. Mernissi (1987, 51–53).

42. Joseph (2003, 239).

43. Joseph (2003, 248–49).

44. Joseph's analysis touches on both interpretations.

45. Kapchan (1996, 193–94, who quotes Barbara Babcock, "Reflexivity: Definitions and Discriminations," *Semiotica* 30, no. 1–2 [1980]: 1–14).

46. Kapchan (1996, 161).

Chapter 6. Transgression and Tarantella among Catholic Women in Calabria

1. Papilia (2008).

2. Papilia (2008).

3. https://www.youtube.com/watch?v=hikEEs74rhA. This is the site for the first of the videos. Every year new footage of the popular festival is posted on YouTube or as Livestream, and some disappears. Also, there are numerous official reports from television and other network features about the event telling different sides of the story and describing many aspects of the event such as this one. https://www.youtube.com/watch?v=W13CNUY8h4A.

4. Plastino (2003, 148).

5. Quoted in ibid., 149–50.

6. For a YouTube clip of pilgrims on their way to the festival in Polsi, see http://www.youtube.com/watch?v=4XcBLeU1kzA&feature=related.

7. https://www.youtube.com/watch?v=WaQgIjlEBOA shows a good example of a rota and the crush of the crowd around the dancers and musicians during the night at the festival in 2014. https://www.youtube.com/watch?v=qMleh2d422k shows tarantella in the daytime with a wider circle. Note that women and men are dancing as couples and touching one another, something that is not common in earlier descriptions of tarantella.

8. Plastino (2003, 151–52).

9. See the edited volume Magrini 2003 for various essays in which authors contest these constructions of Mediterranean femininity, offering deeper, more complex interpretations of gender constructions and relations. Plastino (2003) effectively decenters the persistent construction of Calabrian women (like their counterparts in many Mediterranean societies) as shy and devoid of agency, controlled entirely by their male-dominated societies in which their movements (and their fertility before and after marriage) are carefully monitored and guarded. His analyses of dance at three different festivals reveals women contesting that construction and even dominating in performance contexts.

10. Plastino (2003, 148).

11. Plastino (2003).

12. There were in fact two similar spiders, one *Lycosa tarantula* and the other *Latrodectus tarantula*, commonly found in the region. The latter was smaller and not at all aggressive, but its venom was found to contain a substance that could produce psychoactive effects, including twitching and shaking of limbs, weakness, nausea, and muscular pain in its victims. That spider, however, was not the one that was understood to be the cause of tarantism in Apulia. Instead, it was the larger, more aggressive *Lycosa tarantula* whose bite was painful but relatively harmless, that was believed to be the cause of the tarantism. The *Lycosa tarantula* is found in other places in the world but it is not associated with any form of dance mania similar to tarantism—from Bartholomew (2000, 44), who was following Lewis (1991).

13. Lüdtke (2009); De Martino (2005, originally published in Italian in 1961); Blackstone (2009).

14. Description drawn from Lüdtke (2009, 31–49) and Porcino (2006, 434).

15. Lüdtke (2009, 57).

16. De Martino's study has been translated into English as *The Land of Remorse: A Study of Southern Italian Tarantism* (London: Free Association, 2005).

17. De Martino (2005, 212–36). Bartholomew (2000) details the rise of dance manias in Europe and explores their intersection with the myriad plagues and political

disasters that spread across Europe from the tenth century through the seventeenth century.

18. De Martino (2005, 190).

19. Blackstone (2009, 190–91).

20. Ibid., 190–91, quoting from Ehrenreich (2006, 37–38).

21. Ehrenreich (2006, 37–40). Euripides represents the productive and destructive elements of the worship of Dionysus while exploring the possibilities and effects of rage and irrationality in his play *The Bacchae*.

22. Blackstone (2009, 190–92). That tarantism has been reconstructed as an illness has to do with the post-enlightenment constructions of gender, Church politics from the sixteenth century and beyond, as well as the emergence of scientific method in the interpretation of human experience. See Blackstone (2009), Bartholomew (1994; 2002) for discussion of these trends with respect to tarantism in particular.

23. Porcino (2006, 435). Stifani was known personally by Porcino and Lüdtke, two prominent scholars working on the history of tarantism in Southern Italy in the first decade of the twenty-first century.

24. There have been efforts to link tarantism with other exciting ailments that involved uncontrolled movements such as St. Vitus's and St. John's dance prevalent in the thirteenth and fourteenth centuries in Germany and the Lowlands. These recountings make no mention of spiders or insect bites and, although there is music involved, there is no direct connection between music and healing Lüdtke (2009, 58); Bartholomew (2000); De Martino (2005, 215–18).

25. De Martino (2005, 95–97) and Porcino (2006, 433).

26. De Martino (2005, 226–29) and Lüdtke (2009, 3, 61, 171). See also Baglivi (1714).

27. Porcino (2006, 438).

28. Ibid., 438.

29. Lüdtke (2009, 93–96).

30. Gentilcore (2000, 267).

31. *Tarantata* is a person who is afflicted by tarantism; *tarantate* is the plural form.

32. Lüdtke (2009, 32). See also Blackstone (2009, 192).

33. Lüdtke (2009, 34–36).

34. 1 *Corinthians* 1:11–14.

35. 1 *Corinthians* 1:14. For an excellent overview of the polemics and varied interpretations that these four verses from 1 *Corinthians* have generated, not to mention some astute analysis, see Jorunn Økland's *Women in Their Place: Paul and the Corinthian Discourse of Gender and Sanctuary Space* (Clark, 2004).

36. See Albrecht 2007 for an ethnographic study of a similar process in a Roman Catholic ritual in northern Chile.

37. Porcino (2006, 436). See Blackstone (2009, 191–92) and De Martino (2005, 66–80) for extensive detail on all the stages of the developments of spaces for the tarantate to worship Saint Paul in Galatina.

38. See Carroll (1992) for a discussion of these kinds of what he terms Italian traditions of "popular Catholicism," by which he means local traditions with which the church has connected itself, not necessarily through acknowledgment by the universal church but,

at the very least, because the local clergy silently condone the traditions by participating, perhaps by following along with the procession, blessing the participants, or allowing the celebrants to use the sanctuary. Carroll's study is of this phenomenon in Italy but it goes on in many places around the world in areas where the Catholic Church is prominent.

39. Lewis (1991, 516).

40. Ibid. and De Martino (2005, 100), respectively.

41. Lüdtke (2009); De Martino (2005); Porcino (2006).

42. Both Lüdtke (2009) and Blackstone (2009) explore the idea of the tarantate as modern-day celebrities.

43. Blackstone (2009, 190).

44. Lüdtke (2009, 55–57).

45. Lüdtke (2009, 202).

46. Blackstone (2009, 190) and Lüdtke (2009, 56).

47. See for Tishkoff (2006) and Tumanov (2011) for recent extensive discussion about the virgin/whore or Madonna/whore binary in the constructions of gender in Abrahamic, particularly Catholic, religions.

48. Rouget (1985, 162). This interpretation has been reconfirmed by, among others, Lewis (1991), Bartholomew (1994; 2000), and Blackstone (2009).

49. Karen Lüdtke (2009, 159–87).

50. Although there is nothing in the literature about them, it is possible that the men who perform the music for these devotional dancers may also have understood their performance as an offering to the Madonna. Men who are not musicians are certainly involved in the pilgrimage and can be seen in the available video footage struggling to reach the processing statue as it is carried through the town of Polsi.

51. Miles (1989, 55–56). Margaret Miles devotes a whole chapter to exploring the regendering of women as male when they adopted an ascetic lifestyle (1989, 53–77).

52. Plastino (2003, 153).

Afterword

1. Avishai, Jafar, and Rinaldo (2015, 5).

2. Ibid., 7.

3. Although I imagined this term myself, subsequent searching discovered that it has been used at least two times in previous publications, once by Katie Trumpener (2000) in an article on Béla Bartók's folk-music-collecting activities and once by David Locke (2014) in a published debate of comparative work and music analysis. Neither scholar is using the term to describe precisely what I am suggesting here, but both are doing kinds of analysis that I am advocating might fit under the umbrella term comparative ethnomusicology as I have described it.

Bibliography

Abbas, Shemeem. 2002. *The Female Voice in Sufi Ritual: Devotional Practices of Pakistan and India*. Austin: University of Texas Press.

Adler, Guido. 1885. "Umfang, Methode und Ziel der Musikwissenschaft." *Vierteljahrschrift für Musikwissenschaft* 1: 5–20.

Ahmed, Leila. 1992. *Women and Gender in Islam*. New Haven, Conn.: Yale University Press.

Alexiou, Margaret. 1974. *The Ritual Lament in Greek Tradition*. Cambridge: Cambridge University Press.

Alexiou, Margaret, and Peter Dronke. 1971. "The Lament of Jephta's Daughter: Themes, Traditions, Originality." *Studi Medievali* 12, no. 2: 819–63.

Andaya, Barbara W. 2006. *Flaming Womb: Repositioning Women in Early Modern Southeast Asia*. Honolulu: University of Hawai'i Press.

Archer, William G. 1985. *Songs for the Bride: Wedding Rites of Rural India*. Edited by Barbara Stoler Miller and Mildred Archer. New York: Columbia University Press.

Ashcroft, Bill, Gareth Griffiths, and Helen Tiffin. 2002. *Empire Writes Back: Theory and Practice in Post-colonial Literatures*. London: Routledge.

Aslan, Reza. 2014. "Bill Maher Isn't the Only One Who Misunderstands Religion." *New York Times*, October 8, 2014. http://www.nytimes.com/2014/10/09/opinion/bill-maher-isnt-the-only-one-who-misunderstands-religion.html?_r=0.

Avery, Rachel Foster. 1896. "Proceedings of the Twenty-Eighth Annual Convention of the National American Woman Suffrage Association, 23–28 January 1896." Edited by Rachel Foster Avery. Washington, DC: Ferris.

Avishai, Orit, Afshan Jafar, and Rachel Rinaldo. 2015. "A Gender Lens on Religion." *Gender and Society* 29, no. 1: 5–25.

Babiracki, Carol. 2001. "Religion, Musically Speaking." *Spotlight on Teaching, Religious Studies News* 16, no. 2: 5–8.

Badran, Margot, and Miriam Cooke, eds. 2004. *Opening the Gates: An Anthology of Arab Feminist Writing*. 2nd ed. Bloomington: Indiana University Press.

Baglivi, Giorgio. 1714 (1704). "De anatome morsu et effectibu tarantulae." *Opera Omnia medico-practica et anatomica*. Lugduni (Leiden): Sumptibus Anisson and J. Posuel.

Bakhtiar, Laleh. 2011. "*The Sublime Quran*: The Misinterpretation of Chapter 4 Verse 34." *European Journal of Women's Studies* 18: 431–39.

Baksh-Soodeen, Rawwida. 1991. "Power, Gender, and Chutney." *Trinidad and Tobago Review* 13: 194–98.

Banerjee, Nirmala. 1989. "Working Women in Colonial Bengal: Modernization and Marginalization. In *Recasting Women: Essays in Indian Colonial History*," edited by Sangari Kumkum and Sudesh Vaid, 269–301. New Brunswick, N.J.: Rutgers University Press.

Banerjee, Sumanta. 1989. "Marginalization of Women's Popular Culture in Nineteenth Century Bengal." In *Recasting Women: Essays in Indian Colonial History*," edited by Sangari Kumkum and Sudesh Vaid, 127–79. New Brunswick, N.J.: Rutgers University Press.

Bartholomew, Robert. 1994. "Tarantism, Dancing Mania, and Demonopathy: The Anthropolitical Aspects of "Mass Psychogenic Illness." *Psychological Medicine* 24: 281–306.

——. 2000. Rethinking the Dancing Mania. *Skeptical Inquirer* July/August: 42–47.

Beck, Guy. 1993. *Sonic Theology: Hinduism and Sacred Sound*. Columbia: University of South Carolina Press.

——, ed. 2006. *Sacred Sound: Experiencing Music in World Religions*. Ontario, Calif.: Wilfred Laurier University Press.

Becker, Judith. 2003. *Gamelan Stories: Tantrism, Islam, and Aesthetics in Central Java.* Southeast Asian Studies Monographs. Tempe: Arizona State University Program for Southeast Asian Studies.

Bell, Catherine. 1992. *Ritual Theory, Ritual Practice*. New York: Oxford University Press.

Belloni, Alessandra. 2000. Liner Notes. *Tarantata: Dance of the Ancient Spider*. Sounds True STA MM00117D.

Bennett, Judith. 1989. "Feminism and History." *Gender and History* 1, no. 3: 251–72.

Berger, Teresa. 1999. *Women's Ways of Worship: Gender Analysis and Liturgical History*. Collegeville, Minn.: Liturgical.

——. 2011. *Gender Differences and the Making of Liturgical History: Lifting a Veil on Liturgy's Past*. Aldershot, UK: Ashgate.

Bergman, Sara. 2008. "Matikor, Chutney, Odissi, and Bollywood: Gender Negotiations in Indo-Trinidadian Dance." *Caribbean Review of Gender Studies: A Journal of Caribbean Perspectives on Gender and Feminism* 2: 1–28.

Bernstein, Jane, ed. 2004. *Women's Voices across Musical Worlds*. Boston, Mass.: Northeastern University Press.

Berthomé, Francois, and Michael Houseman. 2010. "Ritual and Emotions: Moving Relations, Patterned Effusions." *Religion and Society: Advances in Research* 1: 57–75.

Bhatt, Chetan. 2001. *Hindu Nationalism: Origins, Ideologies, and Modern Myths*. Oxford: Berg.

Blackstone, Lee Robert. 2009. "The Spider Is Alive: Reassessing Becker's Theory of Artistic Conventions through Southern Italian Music." *Symbolic Interaction* 32, no. 3: 184–206.

Blundell, Sue. 1995. *Women in Ancient Greece*. Cambridge, Mass.: Harvard University Press.

Bohlman, Philip, Edith Blumhofer, and Maria Chow, eds. 2006. *Music in American Religious Experience*. New York: Oxford University Press.

Bohlman, Philip, and Jeffers Englhardt, eds. 2016. *Resounding Transcendence: Transition in Music, Ritual, and Religion*. Oxford: Oxford University Press.

Bossard, James, and Eleanor Boll. 1950. *Ritual in Family Living*. Philadelphia: University of Pennsylvania Press.

Brakel, Clara. 1997. "'Sandhang-pangan' for the Goddess: Offerings to Sang Hyang Bathari Durga and Nyai Lara Kidul." *Asian Folklore Studies* 56, no. 2: 253–83.

Brenner, Suzanne. 1996. "Reconstructing Self and Society: Javanese Muslim Women and the 'Veil'." *American Ethnologist* 23, no. 4: 673–97.

Brown, C. MacKenzie. 1990. *The Triumph of the Goddess: The Canonical Models and Theological Visions of the Devi Bhagavata Purana*. Albany: State University of New York Press.

Brown-Grant, Rosalind. 1999. *Christine De Pizan and the Moral Defence of Women: Reading beyond Gender*. Cambridge: Cambridge University Press.

Brumfield, Allaire. 1981. *The Attic Festivals of Demeter and Their Relation to the Agricultural Year*. New York: Arno.

Byrne, Janet, ed. 2012. *The Occupy Handbook*. New York and Boston: Back Bay / Little, Brown.

Caravelli-Chaves, Anna. 1980. "Bridge between Worlds: The Greek Women's Lament as Communicative Event." *Journal of American Folklore* 93, no. 1: 129–57.

Carroll, Michael P. 1992. *Madonnas that Maim: Popular Catholicism in Italy Since the Fifteenth Century*. Baltimore, Md.: Johns Hopkins University Press.

Carter, Timothy. 1999. "Lamenting Ariadne?" *Early Music* 27, no. 3: 395–405.

Chakravarty, Uma. 1998. *Rewriting History: The Life and Times of Pandita Ramabai*. New Delhi: Kali for Women.

Chantepie de la Saussaye, P. D. 1887–1889. *Lehrbuch der Religionsgeschichte*. Freiburg: Mohr (Siebeck).

Chaudhuri, Nupur, and Margaret Strobel, eds. 1992. *Western Women and Imperialism: Complicity and Resistance*. Bloomington: Indiana University Press.

Clay, Jenny Strauss. 2006. *The Politics of Olympus: Form and Meaning in the Major Homeric Hymns*. Bristol: Bristol Classical. (Originally published in 1989 by Princeton University Press.)

Coburn, Thomas. 1991. *Encountering the Goddess: A Translation of the* Devī-Māhātmya *and a Study of Its Interpretation*. Albany: State University of New York Press.

Cohen, Judith. 1987a. "The Lighter Side of Judeo-Spanish Traditional Musica: Some Canadian Examples." *Canadian Journal for Traditional Music*. http://cjtm.icaap.org/content/15/v15art4.html.

——. 1987b. "*Ya Salio De La Mar*: Judeo-Spanish Wedding Songs among Moroccan Jews in Canada." In *Women and Music in Cross-Cultural Perspective*, edited by Ellen Koskoff, 55–67. Westport, Conn.: Greenwood.

Collins, Patricia Hill. 2000. "Gender, Black Feminism and Black Political Economy." *Annals of the American Academy of Political and Social Science* 568, no. 1: 41–53.

Cooey, Paula, William Eakin, and Jay McDaniel, eds. 1991. *After Patriarchy: Feminist Transformations of the World Religions*. Maryknoll, N.Y.: Orbis.

Cook, Leslie A. 1999. "Body Language: Women's Rituals of Purification in the Bible and Misnah." In *Women and Water: Menstruation in Jewish Life and Law*, edited by Rahel R. Wasserfall, 40–59. Hanover, N.H.: Brandeis University Press—University Press of New England.

Crenshaw, Kimberle. 1991. "Mapping the Margins: Intersectionality, Identity Politics, and Violence against Women of Color." *Stanford Law Review* 43, no. 6: 1241–99.

Cusic, Don. 2002. *The Sound of Light: A History of Gospel and Christian Music*. Milwaukee, Wis.: Hal Leonard.

Cusick, Suzanne. 1994. "Feminist Theory, Music Theory, and the Mind/Body Problem." *Perspectives of New Music* 32, no. 1: 8–27.

——. 1999. "Re-Voicing Arianna (and Laments): Two Women Respond." *Early Music* 27, no. 3: 436–49.

Daly, Mary. 1985 (1968). *The Church and the Second Sex*. Boston: Beacon.

Danforth, Loring. 1982. *The Death Rituals of Rural Greece*. Photography by Alexander Tsiaras. Princeton, N.J.: Princeton University Press.

De Martino, Ernesto. 2000. *Morte e Pianto: Dal Lamento Funebre Antico Al Pianto Di Maria; Introduction by Clara Gallini*. Torino: Bollate Boringhieri.

——. 2005 (1961). *The Land of Remorse: A Study of Southern Italian Tarantism*. Translated by D. L. Zinn. London: Free Association.

Dempsey, Corinne. 2011. *Bringing the Sacred Down to Earth: Adventures in Comparative Religion*. New York: Oxford University Press.

Dev Sen, Nabaneeta. 2000. "Flowering of the Poison Tree: The *Ramayana* in the Words of Women." *Little Magazine* 1, no. 5: 14–25.

——. 2002. "Sita's Garden of Epic Longing." *OutlookIndia.com*. October 28. http://www.outlookindia.com/article.aspx?217691.

Doniger, Wendy. 2000. "Post-modern and -colonial -structural Comparisons." In *A Magic Still Dwells: Comparative Religion in the Postmodern Age*, edited by Kimberley Patton and Benjamin Ray, 63–74. Berkeley: University of California Press.

Eagleton, Terry. 1996. *Illusions of Postmodernism*. Malden, Mass.: Blackwell. Kindle edition.

Economides, Irene. 2004 (1986). *Differences between Orthodox Church and Roman Catholicism*. 16th ed. Athens: Editions Nektarios D. Panagopoulos.

Ehrenreich, Barbara. 2006. *Dancing in the Streets: A History of Collective Joy*. New York: Metropolitan / Holt.

Eldridge, Adam, and Marion Roberts. 2008. "Hen Parties: Bonding or Brawling?" *Drugs: Education, Prevention, and Policy* 15, no. 5: 323–28.

Elgee, N. J. 2003. "Laughing at Death." *Psychoanalytic Review* 90: 475–97.

Eliade, Mircea. 1959. *Patterns in Comparative Religion*. Translated by Rosemay Sheed. New York: Sheed and Ward.

Espinet, Ramabai. 2003. *The Swinging Bridge*. Toronto: Harper.

Falcón, Sylvanna and Jennifer Nash. 2015. "Shifting Analytics and Linking Theories: A Conversation about the 'Meaning-Making' of Intersectionality and Transnational Feminism." *Women's Studies International Forum* 50: 1–10.

Feld, Steven. 1988. "Aesthetics as Iconicity of Style; or 'Lift-Up-Over Sounding': Getting into the Kaluli Groove." *Yearbook for Traditional Music* 20: 74–113.

Flinn, Frank. 2007. *Encyclopedia of Catholicism.* New York: Facts on File.

Flood, Gavin. 2015 (1996). *An Introduction to Hinduism*. Cambridge: Cambridge University Press.

Foley, H. P. 1994. *The Homeric Hymn to Demeter*. Princeton, N.J.: Princeton University Press.

Frahm-Arp, Maria. 2010. *Professional Women in South African Pentecostal Charismatic Churches.* Leiden: Brill.

Fulkerson, Mary McClintock. 1994. *Changing the Subject: Women's Discourses and Feminist Theology*. Minneapolis: Fortress.

Geertz, Clifford. 1968. *Islam Observed: Religious Development in Morocco and Indonesia.* New Haven, Conn.: Yale University Press.

Gentilcore, David. 2000. "Ritualized Illness and Music Therapy: Views of Tarantism in the Kingdom of Naples." In *Music and Medicine: The History of Music Therapy Since Antiquity,* edited by Peregine Horden, 255–72. Aldershot: Ashgate.

Ghafournia, Nafiseh. 2017. "Towards a New Interpretation of Quran 4; 34." *Journal of Women of the Middle East and the Islamic World* 2017:1–14.

Gifford, Paul. 1996. "Christian Fundamentalism, State, and Politics in Black Africa." *Questioning the Secular State: The Worldwide Resurgence of Religion in Politics,* edited by David Westerlund, 198–215. London: Hurst.

Goodman, Jane E. 2005. *Berber Culture on the World Stage: From Village to Video*. Bloomington: University of Indiana Press.

Goody, Jack. 1977. "Against Ritual: Loosely Structured Thoughts on a Loosely Defined Topic." In *Secular Ritual,* edited by Sally Moore and Barbara Myerhoff, 25–35. Assen: Van Gorcum.

Greenspoon, Leonard, ed. 2011. *Jews and Humor.* Lafayette, Ind.: Creighton University Press.

Grierson, George. 1926. *Bihar Peasant Life: Being a Discursive Catalogue*. 2nd ed. Patna: Superintendent, Government Printing, Bihar and Orissa.

Gross, Rita. 2015. "Models of Religious Belonging." In *Religious Conversion: Religion Scholars Thinking Together,* edited by Shanta Premawardhana, 32–44. Oxford: Wiley-Blackwell. Published under the license of the World Council of Churches.

Gutierrez, Gustavo. 1988 (1971). *A Theology of Liberation: History, Politics, and Salvation.* Translated and edited by Caridad Inda and John Eagleson. Maryknoll, N.Y.: Orbis.

Håland, Evy Johanne. 2012. "The Dormition of the Virgin Mary on the Island of Tinos: A Performance of Gendered Values in Greece." *Journal of Religious History* 36, no. 1: 89–117. http://onlinelibrary.wiley.com/doi/10.1111/j.14679809.2011.01157.x/full.

Harlan, Lindsey, and Paul Courtwright, eds. 1995. *From the Margins of Hindu Marriage: Essays on Gender, Religion, and Culture*. New York: Oxford University Press.

Harvey, Susan. 2010. *Song and Memory: Biblical Women in Syriac Tradition.* Milwaukee: Marquette University Press.

Hefner, Robert. 1998. "Multiple Modernities: Christianity, Islam, and Hinduism in a Globalizing Age." *Annual Review of Anthropology* 27: 83–104.

Henderson, Clara, and Lisa Gilman. 2004. "Women as Religious and Political Praise Singers within African Institutions: The Case of the CCAP Blantyre Synod and Political Parties in Malawi." *Women and Music: A Journal of Gender and Culture* 8: 22–40.

Henderson, Helena. 1999. "An Anthology of Finnish Folklore." Viewed as unidentified pdf.

Henry, Edward. 1988. *Chant the Names of God: Musical Culture in Bhojpuri-Speaking India*. San Diego: San Diego State University Press.

Hertz, Robert. 1928 (1907). *Melanges de sociologie religieuse et folklore*. Paris: Alcan.

Herzfeld, Michael. 1981. "Performative Categories and Symbols of Passage in Rural Greece." *Journal of American Folklore* 94, no. 371: 44–57.

Hoffman, Katherine E. 2002. "Generational Change in Berber Women's Song of the Anti-Atlas Mountains, Morocco." *Ethnomusicology* 46, no. 3: 510–40.

———. 2008. *We Share Walls: Language Land, and Gender in Berber Morocco*. Malden, Mass: Blackwell.

Holst-Warhaft, Gail. 1992. *Dangerous Voices: Women's Laments and Greek Literature*. London: Routledge.

Homeric Hymn to Demeter. 2012. Translated by Gregory Nagy. http://www.uh.edu/~cldue/texts/demeter.html.

Honko, Lauri. 1974. "Balto-Finnic Lament Poetry." *Studia Fennica* 17: 9–61.

Hubert, Henri, and Marcel Mauss. 1964. *Sacrifice, Its Nature and Function*. Translated by W. E. Halls. Chicago: University of Chicago Press. (Originally published as *Essai sur la nature et le function du sacrifice*, 1897.)

Humphreys, Sarah. 1993. *The Family, Women, and Death: Comparative Studies*, 2nd ed. Ann Arbor: University of Michigan Press.

Ibsen-al Faruqi, Lois. 1985. "Music, Musicians, and Muslim Law." *Asian Music* 17: 3–36.

Itkuja: Laments from Karelia, Ingria, Finland. n.d. Finnish Literature Society with support from the Finnish Performing Music Promotion Center.

Jagadisarananda, Swami. 1953. *Devi Mahatmyam (Glory of the Divine Mother): 700 Mantras on Sri Durga*. Mylapore: Sri RamaKrishna Math. English translation of the text.

Jenkins, Ian. 1983. "Is There Life after Marriage? A Study of the Abduction Motif in Vase Paintings of the Athenian Wedding Ceremony." *Bulletin of the Institute of Classical Studies* 30, no. 1: 137–145.

Jordaan, Roy. 1984. "The Mystery of Nyai Lara Kidul, Goddess of the Southern Ocean." *Archipel* 28: 99–116.

Joseph, Roger, and Terri Brint Joseph. 1987. *The Rose and the Thorn: Semiotic Structures in Morocco*. Tucson: University of Arizona Press.

Joseph, Terri Brint. 2003. "Poetry as a Strategy of Power: The Case of Riffian Berber Women." In *Music and Gender: Perspectives from the Mediterranean*, edited by Tullia Magrini, 233–50. Chicago: University of Chicago Press. Originally published in *Signs* 5, no. 3 in 1980.

Joseph, Suad. 1996. "Patriarchy and Development in the Arab World." *Gender and Development* 4, no. 2: 14–19.

Kapchan, Deborah. 1996. *Gender on the Market: Moroccan Women and the Revoicing of Tradition*. Philadelphia: University of Pennsylvania Press.

Kassam, Zayn, ed. 2010. *Women and Islam*. Santa Barbara, Calif.: Praeger.

Kassam-Hann, Zayn. 2002. "Transcendence and the Body: Fatimah as a Paradigmatic Model." *Feminist Theology* 10: 77–93.

Keller, Marcello. 1994. "Reflections of Continental and Mediterranean Traditions in Italian Folk Music." In *Music Cultures in Contact: Convergences and Collisions*, edited by Margaret Kartomi and Stephen Blum, 40–47. Sydney: Currency.

Khan, Sarfraz, Waheed Iqbal Chaudhry, and Ikram Badshah. 2014. "Ethnographic Study of Muharram Rituals in a Punjabi Village in Pakistan." *Journal of Asian Civilizations* 37, no. 2: 123–138.

Kircher, Athanasius. 1641. *Magnes sive, De arte magnetica opus tripartum*. Rome: Ludovici Grignani (typographer)/Hermanni Scheus (underwriter).

Kligman, Gail. 1984. "The Rites of Women: Oral Poetry, Ideology, and the Socialization of Peasant Women in Contemporary Romania." *Journal of the American Folklore* 97, no. 384: 167–188.

Koskoff, Ellen, ed. 1987. *Women and Music in Cross-Cultural Perspective*. Westport, Conn.: Greenwood.

———. 1993. "Miriam Sings Her Song: The Self and the Other in Anthropological Discourse." In *Musicology and Difference: Gender and Sexuality in Music Scholarship*, edited by Ruth Solie, 149–63. Berkeley: University of California Press.

Kuenen, Abraham. 1882. *National Religions and Universal Religions. Lectures Delivered at Oxford and in London, in April and May, 1882*. London: Williams and Norgate.

Kurien, Prema. 1998. "Becoming American by Becoming Hindu: Indian Americans Take Their Place at the Multicultural Table." In *Gatherings in Diaspora: Religious Communities and the New Immigration*, edited by Stephen Warner and Judith Wittner, 37–69. Philadelphia: Temple University Press.

Kwok, Pui-lan. 2002. "Feminist Theology as Intercultural Discourse." In *The Cambridge Companion to Feminist Theology*, edited by Susan Parsons, 23–39. Cambridge: Cambridge University Press.

Lambek, Michael. 2002. "A General Introduction." In *A Reader in the Anthropology of Religion*, edited by Michael Lambek 1–18. Malden, Mass.: Blackwell.

Lardinois, André, and Laura McClure, eds. 2001. *Making Silence Speak: Women's Voices in Greek Literature and Society*. Princeton, N.J.: Princeton University Press.

Lengel, Laura. 2004. "Performing In/Outside of Islam: Music and Gendered Cultural Politics in the Middle East and North Africa." *Text and Performance Quarterly* 24: 212–32.

Lewis, I. M. 1991. "The Spider and the Pangolin." *Man* 26, no. 3: 513–25.

Locke, David. 2014. "Let It Be Called "Comparative Ethnomusicology." *Analytical Approaches to World Music* 3, no. 2. http://aawmjournal.com/articles/2014b/Locke_AAWM_Vol_3_2.pdf.

Loraux, Nicole. 2006. *The Invention of Athens: The Funeral Oration in the Classical City*. Cambridge, Mass.: MIT Press.

Lüdtke, Karen. 2009. *Dances with Spiders: Crisis, Celebrity, and Celebration in Southern Italy*. New York: Berghahn.

Lysaght, Patricia. 1997. "Caoineadh os Cionn Coirp: The Lament for the Dead in Ireland." *Folklore* 108: 65–82.

Macey, David. 2000. *The Penguin Dictionary of Critical Theory*. London: Penguin.

MacNeil, Anne. 1999. "Weeping at the Water's Edge." *Early Music* 27, no. 3: 406–17.

Magrini, Tullia. 1985. *Forme Della Musica Vocale e Strumentale a Creta*. Milan: Ricordi.

———. 2003. *Music and Gender: Perspectives from the Mediterranean*. Chicago: University of Chicago Press.

Mahmoud, Mohamed. 2006. "To Beat or Not to Beat: On the Exegetical Dilemmas over Qur'an, 4:34." *Journal of the American Oriental Society* 126, no. 4: 537–50.

Manuel, Peter. 1998. "Chutney and Indo-Trinidadian Cultural Identity." *Popular Music* 17, no. 1: 21–43.

Marín, Manuela. 2003. "Disciplining Wives: A Historical of Qur'an 4:34." *Studia Islamica* 97: 5–40.

Marshall, Kimberly, ed. 1993. *Rediscovering the Muses: Women's Musical Traditions*. Boston, Mass.: Northeastern University Press.

Masuzawa, Tomoko. 2005. *The Invention of World Religions; or, How European Universalism Was Preserved in the Language of Pluralism*. Chicago: University of Chicago Press.

Mayo, William Starbuck. 1850. *Berber or the Mountaineer of the Atlas: A Tale of Morocco*. New York: Putnam.

Mazo, Margarita. 1990. "Stravinsky's *Le Noces* and Russian Village Wedding Ritual." *Journal of the American Musicological Society* 43, no. 1: 99–142.

———. 1994. "Wedding Laments in North Russian Villages." In *Music Cultures in Contact: Convergences and Collisions*, edited by Margaret Kartomi and Stephen Blum, 21–39. Sydney: Currency.

McDaniel, June. 2004. *Offering Flowers, Feeding Skulls: Popular Goddess Worship in West Bengal*. Oxford: Oxford University Press.

McGuckin, John Anthony. 2011. *The Orthodox Church: An Introduction to its History, Doctrine, and Spiritual Culture*. Chichester, UK: Wiley-Blackwell.

Mernissi, Fatima. 1986. "Femininity as Subversion: Reflections on the Muslim Concept of Nushuz." In *Speaking of Faith: Cross-Cultural Perspectives on Women, Religion and Social Change*, edited by Diana L. Eck and Devaki Jain, 88–100. London: Women's Press.

———. 1987. *Beyond the Veil: Male-Female Dynamics in Modern Muslim Society*. Rev. ed. Bloomington: Indiana University Press.

Mohanty, Chandra Talpade. 1988. "Under Western Eyes: Feminist Scholarship and Colonial Discourses." *Feminist Review* 30: 61–88.

———. 2003. "'Under Western Eyes' Revisited: Feminist Solidarity through Anticapitalist Struggles." *Signs: Journal of Women in Culture and Society* 28, no. 2: 499–535.

Moisala, Pirkko, and Beverley Diamond, eds. 2000. *Music and Gender*. Urbana: University of Illinois Press.

Muller, Carol Ann. 1999. *Rituals of Fertility and the Sacrifice of Desire: Nazarite Women's Performance in South Africa*. Chicago: University of Chicago Press.

Müller, Friedrich Max. 1882. *Introduction to the Science of Religion*. London: Longmans, Green.

———. 1898. *Natural Religion: The Gifford Lectures Delivered before the University of Glasgow in 1888*. London: Longmans, Green.

Mustapha, Nasser. 2004. "The Influence of Indian Islam on Fundamentalist Trends in Trinidad and Tobago." In *The Indian Diaspora: Dynamics of Migration*, edited by N. Jayaram, 127–46. Thousand Oaks, Calif.: Sage.

Myers, Helen. 1998. *Music of Hindu Trinidad: Songs from the India Diaspora*. Chicago: University of Chicago.

Narayan, Kirin. 1986. "Birds on a Branch: Girlfriends and Wedding Songs in Kangra." *Ethos* 14, no. 1: 47–75.

———. 1997. "Singing from Separation: Women's Voices in and about Kangra Folksongs." *Oral Tradition* 12, no. 1: 23–53.

Narayan, Uma, and Sonia Harding, eds. 2000. *Decentering the Center: Philosophy for a Multicultural, Postcolonial, and Feminist World.* Bloomington: Indiana University Press.

Nettl, Bruno. 2010. *Nettl's Elephant: On the History of Ethnomusicology*. Urbana: University of Illinois Press.

Noblit, George W., and R. Dwight Hare. 1988. *Meta-ethnography: Synthesizing Qualitative Studies*. Newbury Park, Calif.: Sage.

Nothaft, Carl Philipp Emanuel. 2011. "From Sukkot to Saturnalia: The Attack on Christmas in Sixteenth-Century Chronological Scholarship." *Journal of the History of Ideas* 72, no. 4: 503–22.

O'Higgins, D. M. 2001. "Women's Cultic Joking and Mockery: Some Perspectives." In *Making Silence Speak: Women's Voices in Greek Literature and Society*, edited by André Lardinois and Laura McClure, 137–60. Princeton, N.J.: Princeton University Press.

Oakley, John, and Rebecca Sinos. 1993. *The Wedding in Ancient Athens*. Madison: University of Wisconsin Press.

Økland, Jorunn. 2004. *Women in the Place: Paul and Corinthian Discourse of Gender and Sanctuary Space*. London: Clark.

Olupona, Jacob, and Terry Rey, eds. 2008. *Òrìṣà Devotion as World Religion: The Globalization of Yorùbá Religious Culture*. Madison: University of Wisconsin Press.

Orsi, Janelle. 2003. "Globalized and Localized Hindu Nationalist Ideologies: The Social Function of Hindu Nationalism in Trinidad." Paper presented at the annual meeting of the American Sociological Association, Atlanta, August 16, 2003.

Orsi, Robert. 2003. "Is the Study of Lived Religion Irrelevant to the World We Live In?" Special Presidential Plenary Address, Society for the Scientific Study of Religion, Salt Lake City, November 2, 2002. *Journal for the Scientific Study of Religion* 42, no. 2: 169–74.

Paden, William. 2001. "Universals Revisited: Human Behaviors and Cultural Variations." *Numen* 48, no. 3: 277–89.

Pal, Pratapaditya. 1967. "Vaisnava Art from Nepal in the Museum." *Boston Museum Bulletin* 65, no. 340: 40–60.

Panourgiá, Neni. 1995. *Fragments of Death, Fables of Identity: An Athenian Anthropography*. Madison: University of Wisconsin Press.

Papalia, Gerardo. 2008. "Migrating Madonnas: The Madonna della Montagna di Polsi in Calabria and in Australia." *FULGOR: Flinders University Languages Group Online Review* 3, no. 3: 57–71.

Patton, Kimberly. 2000. "Juggling Torches: Why We Still Need Comparative Religion." In Patton and Ray, *A Magic Still Dwells*, 153–71.

Patton, Kimberly, and Benjamin Ray, eds. 2000. *A Magic Still Dwells: Comparative Religion in the Postmodern Age*. Berkeley: University of California Press.

Pentikäinen, Juha Y. 1999 (1987). *Kalevala Mythology*. Expanded ed. Translated by Ritva Poom. Bloomington: Indiana University Press.

Pintchman, Tracy, ed. 2007. *Women's Lives, Women's Rituals in the Hindu Tradition*. New York: Oxford University Press.

Plastino, Goffredo. 2003. "Come into Play: Dance, Music, and Gender in Three Calabrian Festivals." In *Music and Gender: Perspectives from the Mediterranean*, edited by Tullia Magrini, 147–67. Chicago: University of Chicago Press.

Poerbatjaraka, R. M. Ng. 1926. "De Calon-Arang." *Bijdragen tot de Taal-, Land-, en Volkenkunde van Nederlandsch-Indië* 82: 110–80.

Pollock, Sheldon. 2006. *The Language of the Gods in the World of Men: Sanskrit, Culture, and Power in Premodern India*. Berkeley: University of California Press.

Pope Pius XII. 1950. *Munificentissimus Deus: Defining the Dogma of the Assumption November 1, 1950*. Apostolic Constitution of Pope Pius XII. http://www.vatican.va/holy_father/pius_xii/apost_constitutions/documents/hf_p-xii_apc_19501101_munificentissimus-deus_en.html.

Porcino, Marta. 2006. "Women in the Folk Traditions of the Salento: Tanrantismo." *Mother Language Over the History*. http://www.womanway.eu/studies/files/social2_it_en.pdf.

Prytz-Johansen, J. 1975. "The Thesmophoria as a Women's Festival." *Temenos* 11: 78–87.

Qureshi, Regula Burkhardt. 1996. "Transcending Space: Recitation and Community among South Asian Muslims in Canada." In *Making Muslim Space in North America and Europe*, edited by Barbara Daly Metcalf, 46–64. Berkeley: University of California Press.

Raheja, Gloria Goodwin. 1995. "'Crying When She's Born, and Crying When She Goes Away': Marriage and the Idiom of the Gift in Pahansu Song Performance." In *From the Margins of Hindu Marriage: Essays on Gender, Religion, and Culture*, edited by Lindsey Harlan and Paul Courtright, 19–59. New York and Oxford: Oxford University Press.

Raheja, Gloria Goodwin, and Ann Gold. 1994. *Listen to the Heron's Words: Reimagining Gender and Kinship in North India*. Berkeley: University of California Press.

Ramanujan, A. K. 1989. "Talking to God in the Mother Tongue." *Manushi* 50–51–52 (January–June): 9–14.

Ramnarine, Tina. 1999. "Historical Representations, Performance Spaces, and Kinship Themes in Indian-Caribbean Popular Song Texts." *Asian Music* 30, no. 1: 1–33.

Rapport, Mike. 2008. *1848: Year of Revolution*. Philadelphia: Basic.

Rasmussen, Anne K. 2010. *Women, the Recited Qur'an, and Islamic Music in Indonesia*. Berkeley: University of California Press.

Rasmussen, Susan J. 1995. "Zarraf, a Tuareg Women's Wedding Dance." *Ethnology* 34, no. 1: 1–16.

———. 1997. "Between Ritual, Theater, and Play: Blacksmith Praise at Tuareg Marriage." *Journal of American Folklore* 110, no. 435: 3–27.

———. 2003. "Gendered Discourses and Mediated Modernities: Urban and Rural Performances of Tuareg Smith Women." *Journal of Anthropological Research* 59, no. 4: 487–509.

Raudalainen, Taisto. 2004. "The Traits of Cultural Contacts between Orthodox and Lutheran Commemoration Practices among Ingrian Finnish Women." *Folklore* 28: 57–90. http://www.folklore.ee/Folklore/vol28/traits.pdf.

Raudvere, Catharina. 2002. *The Book and the Roses: Sufi Women, Visibility and Zikir in Contemporary Istanbul*. Istanbul: Swedish Research Institute.

Reuters, Thomas. 2012. "Religion in the Age of Globalization: Emerging Trends, Indonesian Examples." In *Flows of Faith: Religious Reach and Community in Asia and the Pacific*, edited by Lenore Manderson, Mandy Smith, and Matt Tomlinson, 13–33. Melbourne: Springer Science and Business.

Reyes, Angela, and Adrienne Lo, eds. 2009. *Beyond Yellow English: Toward a Linguistic Anthropology of Asian Pacific America*. Oxford: Oxford University Press.

Richman, Paula, ed. 1991. *Many Ramayanas: The Diversity of a Narrative Tradition in South Asia*. Berkeley: University of California Press.

——, ed. 2008. *Ramayana Stories in Modern South India: An Anthology*. Bloomington: Indiana University Press.

Rosand, Ellen. 1979. "The Descending Tetrachord: An Emblem of Lament." *Musical Quarterly* 65, no. 3: 346–359.

Rose, Elizabeth. 1994. "From Sponge Cake to 'Hamentashen': Jewish Identity in Jewish Settlement House, 1885–1952." *Journal of American Ethnic History* 13, no. 3: 2–23.

Rosen, Ralph. 2007. *Making Mockery: The Poetics of Ancient Satire*. Oxford: Oxford University Press.

Rouget, Gilbert. 1985. *Music and Trance: A Theory of the Relations Between Music and Possession*. Translated by Brunhilde Biebuyck and Gilbert Rouget. Chicago: University of Chicago Press.

Ruwanpura, Kanchana. 2006. *Matrilineal Communities, Patriarchal Realities: A Feminist Nirvana Uncovered*. Ann Arbor: University of Michigan Press.

Sabbah, Fatna. 1984. *Women in the Muslim Unconscious*. New York: Pergamon.

Santiko, Hariani. 1997. "The Goddess Durga in the East-Javanese Period." *Asian Folklore Studies* 56, no. 2: 209–26.

Sarmela, Matti. 2010. "Wedding Categories: Kinship and Village Weddings in Finland and Thailand." http://www.kotikone.fi/matti.sarmela/wedding.pdf.

Schneider, Albrecht. 2006. "Comparative and Systematic Musicology in Relation to Ethnomusicology: A Historical and Methodological Survey." *Ethnomusicology* 50, no. 2: 236–58.

Scott, James C. 1986. "Everyday Forms of Peasant Resistance." *Journal of Peasant Studies* 13, no. 2: 5–35.

——. 1990. *Domination and the Arts of Resistance: Hidden Transcripts*. New Haven, Conn.: Yale University Press.

Seaford, Richard. 1987. "The Tragic Wedding." *Journal of Hellenic Studies* 57: 106–30.

Sengers, Gerda. 2003. *Women and Demons: Cult Healing in Islamic Egypt*. Leiden: Brill.

Sharma, Arvind, ed. 1987. *Women in World Religions*. Albany: State University of New York Press.

Shehan, Patricia. 1987. "Balkan Women as Preservers of Traditional Music and Culture." In *Women and Music in Cross-Cultural Perspective*, edited by Ellen Koskoff, 45–53. Westport, Conn.: Greenwood.

Shiloah, Amnon. 1992. *Jewish Musical Traditions*. Detroit, Mich.: Wayne State University Press.

——. 1995. *Music in the World of Islam: A Socio-Cultural Study*. Aldershot, UK: Scholar.

Singh, Avadhesh, ed. 2008. *The Voice of Women: Gargi to Gangasati*. New Delhi: D. K. Printworld.

Smith, John. 2011. *Music in Ancient Judaism and Early Christianity*. Aldershot, UK: Ashgate.

Spence, Jonathan. 1996. *God's Chinese Son: The Taiping Heavenly Kingdom of Hong Xiuquan*. New York: Norton.

Spencer, Jon Michael. 1991. *Theological Music: Introduction to Theomusicology*. Westport, Conn.: Greenwood.

St. John, Graham, ed. 2008. *Victor Turner and Contemporary Cultural Performance*. New York: Berghahn.

Stadler, Nurit. 2011. "Between Scripture and Performance: Cohesion and Dissent at the Feast of Mary's Dormition in Jerusalem." *Religion* 41, no. 4: 645–64.

Stallsmith, Allaire. 2008. "The Name of Demeter Thesmophoros." *Greek, Roman, and Byzantine Studies* 48: 115–31.

Standhartinger, Angela. 2010. "'What Women Were Accustomed to Do for the Dead Beloved by Them' (*Gospel of Peter* 12.50): Traces of Laments and Mourning Rituals in Early Easter, Passion, and Lord's Supper Traditions." *Journal of Biblical Literature* 129, no. 3: 559–74.

Stanton, Elizabeth C. 1972 (1895). *The Woman's Bible*. New York: Arno.

Subbamma, Malladi. 1992. *Hinduism and Women*. Delhi: Ajanta.

Sugirtharajah, Sharada. 2002. "Hinduism and Feminism: Some Concerns." *Journal of Feminist Studies in Religion* 18, no. 2: 97–104.

——. 2003. *Imagining Hinduism: A Postcolonial Perspective*. London: Routledge.

Sullivan, Lawrence. 1997. "Enchanting Powers: An Introduction." In *Enchanting Powers: Music in the World's Religions*, edited by Lawrence Sullivan, 1–28. Cambridge, Mass.: Center for the Study of World Religions, Harvard University.

Šunde, Smiljana. 2006. "Funeral and Mourning Customs in Podgora." *Croatian Medical Journal* 47, no. 5: 681–84.

Suter, Ann, ed. 2008. *Lament: Studies in the Ancient Mediterranean and Beyond*. Oxford: Oxford University Press.

Sutherland, Sally. 1989. "Sita and Draupadi: Aggressive Behavior and Female Role-Models in the Sanskrit Epics." *Journal of the American Oriental Society* 109, no. 1: 63–79.

Syed, Jawad. 2010. "An Historical Perspective on Islamic Modesty and its Implications for Female Employment." *Equality, Diversity, and Inclusion: An International Journal* 29, no. 2: 150–66.

Tiele, C. P. 1876. *Geschiedenis van dan godsdienst, tot aan de heerschappij der wereldgodsdiensten*. Amsterdam: Kampen and Zoon. Published in English as *Outlines of the History of Religion to the Spread of the Universal Religions*. London: Trübner, 1877.

Tishkoff, Doris. 2006. *Madonna/Whore: The Myth of the Two Marys*. Bloomington, Ind.: AuthorHouse.

Tiwary, Kapil Muni. 1978. "Tuneful Weeping: A Mode of Communication." *Frontiers: A Journal of Women Studies* 3, no. 3: 24–27.

Tolbert, Elizabeth. 1990. "Women Cry with Words: Symbolization of Affect in the Karelian Lament." *Yearbook for Traditional Music* 22: 80–105.

Touma, Habib. 1996. *The Music of the Arabs*. Translated by Laurie Schwartz. Portland, Ore.: Amadeus.

Trumpener, Katie. 2000. Béla Bartók and the Rise of Comparative Ethnomusicology: Nationalism, Race Purity, and the Legacy of the Austro-Hungarian Empire." In *Music and the Racial Imagination*, edited by Ronald Radano and Philip V. Bohlman, 403–34. Chicago: University of Chicago Press.

Tsevat, Matitiahu. 1975. "The Husband Lifts a Veil: Hittite Laws, Sections 197–98." *Journal of Cuneiform Studies* 27, no. 4: 235–40.

Tumanov, Vladimir. 2011. "Mary versus Eve: Paternal Uncertainty and the Christian View of Women." *Neophilologus: An International Journal of Modern and Mediaeval Language and Literature* 95, no. 4: 507–21.

Turner, Victor. 1968. *Drums of Affliction: A Study of Religious Processes among the Ndembu of Zambia*. Oxford: Clarendon.

——. 1986. *The Anthropology of Performance*. New York: PAJ.

Tye, Diane, and Ann Marie Powers. 1998. "Gender Resistance and Play: Bachelorette Parties in Atlantic Canada." *Women's Studies International Forum* 21, no. 5: 551–61.

Urban, Greg. 1988. "Ritual Wailing in Amerindian Brazil." *American Anthropologist* 90: 385–400.

Väisänen, A. O. 1921. [Silent film.] Script by U. T. Sirelius. See especially http://www.youtube.com/watch?v=nnoxYC5n4yo&feature=related; http://www.youtube.com/watch?v=_Zhbi6HhE3M&feature=related; and http://www.youtube.com/watch?v=FMqgP8AU7yY&feature=related. See also http://www.youtube.com/watch?v=254dsgA-PoY.

van Gennep, Arnold. 1960. *The Rites of Passage*. Translated by Monika B. Vizedom and Gabrielle L. Caffee. Chicago: University of Chicago Press. First published in French in 1909 by Picard, Paris.

Viladesau, Richard. 2000. *Theology and the Arts: Encountering God through Music, Art, and Rhetoric*. New York: Paulist.

Wadud, Amina. 2009. "Islam beyond Patriarchy through Gender Inclusive Qur'anic Analysis." In *Wanted: Equality and Justice in the Muslim Family*, edited by Zainah Anwar. http://www.musawah.org.

Walby, Sylvia. 2000. "Beyond the Politics of Location: The Power of Argument in a Global Era." *Feminist Theory* 1, no. 2: 189–206.

Walther, Wiebke. 1999. *Women in Islam: From Medieval to Modern Times*. Translated by C. S. V. Salt. Princeton, N.J.: Wiener.

Weich-Shahak, Susana. 1979. "The Wedding Songs of the Bulgarian-Sephardi Jews: A Preliminary Study." *Orbis Musicae* 7: 81–107.

Weinbaum, Batya. 2001. "Lament Ritual Transformed into Literature: Positing Women's Prayer as a Cornerstone in Western Classical Literature." *Journal of American Folklore* 114, no. 451: 20–39.

Weiss, Sarah. 2006. *Listening to an Earlier Java: Aesthetics, Gender, and the Music of Wayang in Central Java.* Leiden: KITLV.

——. 2014. "Listening to the World but Hearing Ourselves: Hybridity and Perceptions of Authenticity in World Music." *Ethnomusicology* 58, no. 3: 506–25.

Werbner, Pnina. 1986. "The Virgin and the Clown Ritual Elaboration in Pakistani Migrants' Weddings." *Man* 21, no. 2: 227–50.

Wessing, Robert. 1997. "Nyai Roro Kidul in Puger: Local Applications of a Myth." *Archipel* 53: 97–120.

Westermarck, Edward. 1914. *Marriage Ceremonies in Morocco*. London: MacMillan.

Whelan, Kevin. 1996. *The Tree of Liberty: Radicals, Catholicism, and the Construction of Irish Identity, 1760–1830.* Cork, Ire.: Cork University Press.

Wilce, James. 1998. "The Pragmatics of 'Madness': Performance Analysis of a Bangladeshi Woman's 'Aberrant' Lament." *Culture Medicine and Psychiatry* 22: 1–54.

——. 1999. "Transforming Laments: Performativity and Rationalization as Linguistic Ideologies." In *Languages of Sentiment: Cultural Constructions of Emotional Substrates* edited by Gary Palmer and Debra Occhi, 39–64. Amsterdam: Benjamin's.

——. 2009. *Crying Shame: Metaculture, Modernity and the Exaggerated Death of Lament*. Oxford: Wiley-Blackwell.

Williams, Colin, and Jan Windebank. 1998. *Informal Employment in Advanced Economies: Implications for Work and Welfare*. London: Routledge.

Wilson-Dickson, Andrew. 1996. *The Story of Christian Music: From Gregorian Chant to Black Gospel: An Authoritative Illustrated Guide to all the Major Traditions of Music for Worship*. Minneapolis: Fortress.

Wolin, Steven, and Linda Bennett. 1984. "Family Rituals." *Family Proceedings* 23: 401–20.

Wolters, Oliver W. 1999. *History, Culture, and Region in Southeast Asian Perspectives*. Rev. ed. Ithaca, N.Y.: Southeast Asia Program, Cornell University.

Woodberry, Robert, and Christian Smith. 1998. "Fundamentalism et al.: Conservative Protestants in America." *Annual Review of Sociology* 24: 25–56.

Zimmerman, Danielle D. 2014. "Young Arab Muslim Women's Agency Challenging Western Feminism." *Affilia: Journal of Women and Social Work* 30, no. 2: 145–57.

Ziv, Avner, ed. 1998 (1986). *Jewish Humor*. Tel Aviv: Papyrus / Tel Aviv University.

Index

SARAH WEISS is a senior research scientist at the Institute for Ethnomusicology at the University of Music and Performing Arts in Graz (Kunst Universität Graz). She is the author of *Listening to an Earlier Java: Aesthetics, Gender, and the Music of Wayang in Central Java*.

NEW PERSPECTIVES ON GENDER IN MUSIC

In Her Own Words: Conversations with Composers in the United States *Jennifer Kelly*

Roll Over Tchaikovsky! Russian Popular Music and Post-Soviet Homosexuality *Stephen Amico*

A Feminist Ethnomusicology: Writings on Music and Gender *Ellen Koskoff*

Stunning Males and Powerful Females: Gender and Tradition in East Javanese Dance *Christina Sunardi*

Women Musicians of Uzbekistan: From Courtyard to Conservatory *Tanya Merchant*

Ritual Soundings: Women Performers and World Religions *Sarah Weiss*

The University of Illinois Press
is a founding member of the
Association of American University Presses.

University of Illinois Press
1325 South Oak Street
Champaign, IL 61820-6903
www.press.uillinois.edu